#FiftyDays

2020

FIFTY DAYS OF LOCKDOWN

BY MARK IND

Very Best Wishes

Mark

x

First Published 2020

FIRST EDITION

AUTHOR

MARK IND

Social Media @markI_N_D

PUBLISHER

Desire Dream Vision Ltd

Desire Dream Vision Ltd Registration No: 10676192

ISBN: 978-1-83853-988-7

A catalogue copy of this book is available in the British Library

PUBLISHED BY

DESIRE DREAM VISION LTD

DEDICATION

This book serves as a memory to those many people whose lives were impacted and cut short by Covid-19, that unpleasant and deadly strain of coronavirus, and especially to those in our celebrated NHS and care homes who perished whilst trying to save lives on the frontline – I salute them all and continue to feel a great deal of compassion for the families and friends that they left behind.

From a personal perspective the book is dedicated to the everlasting memory of Amelia Su Goodrum, taken so cruelly and prematurely from my nephew Craig and his wife, Sener, and their respective loving families just prior to Lockdown.

Finally I must thank all the amazing medical staff, surgeons, cardiologists and consultants at Southampton General Hospital whether in wards E1, E2, PICU (Paediatric Intensive Care Unit) or CICU (Cardiac Intensive Care Unit) for what they have done to help our son, Alex, through many challenging times; they are all truly awesome.

To continue to support the great work that Wessex Heartbeat do with the cardiac units at the hospital a contribution will be made to the charity for every book sold.

ABOUT THE AUTHOR - MARK IND

I never set out to be an author but the unparalleled period of Lockdown gave me the opportunity to keep a daily journal, not only of the chronicles of the Covid-19 pandemic but also of my daily activities and those of my close family. Having reflected on the large amount of data that I had compiled and not being in full-time employment, I thought that writing a book would be great fun and also incredibly fulfilling – this was a 'labour of love' to get me out of bed in the morning!

I had an amazing upbringing, with my two sisters and brother, from my incredible parents and was lucky enough to spend five years being educated at Tonbridge School in Kent. During my second year at school I was inspired by a careers talk to continue my studies after school life in hospitality and pursue a career in hotels. I therefore spent three years studying for a Higher National Diploma (HND) in Hotel Management, followed by a Graduate Management Trainee scheme with Norfolk Capital Hotels.

On completion of the Graduate scheme, in what was then the Caversham Hotel in Reading, I attained my first management position and a year later I met my future wife, Susie, who was a management peer in the same hotel. Two years later we married in Bournemouth and settled in Chandler's Ford in Hampshire, after which Susie gave birth to our two lovely children, Holly and Alex.

It was always my ambition to become a General Manager of a hotel by the age of thirty. This was achieved by becoming the General Manager of Elmers Court Hotel and Timeshare Resort in Lymington, where I stayed for just over two years. In the hotel world they used to say that your first General Manager role either 'makes or breaks you' because it is that big next step up in the career ladder. Although it was tough and I had some very challenging situations to deal with, it certainly stood me in good stead for the future.

I took on my next role as the General Manager of Audleys Wood just outside Basingstoke, a four star country house hotel with a very buoyant wedding trade. It was here that I had to deal with three deaths in the workforce including the infamous 'body in a suitcase' incident, in which one Sri Lankan employee murdered his compatriot and roommate, and put him in a suitcase, leaving him at Basingstoke railway station in December 2001. That was certainly an eventful two and a half years!

There followed just over 15 years as a Holiday Inn General Manager. Firstly nearly five years in Southampton with the annual Boat Show and everything maritime, during which time I also had to oversee a serious fire at the Holiday Inn Fareham. Next there were four years in Farnborough with the biennial Air Show and everything aviation. I was then offered the same role at Reading South for just over two years, where in 2013 I was fortunate enough to earn the accolade of 'General Manager of the Year' for the UK and Ireland, with the then management company and brand owner, IHG. This, in turn, then set me up for a move to London for four and a half years to take over at the Holiday Inn, London Mayfair. Throughout my career, especially during my time running Holiday Inns, I have been blessed to work with many amazing people, without whom I would not have achieved what I have.

When the Holiday Inn Mayfair closed for an extensive two-year refurbishment, I took redundancy and started what I thought would be a two or three month break. Covid-19 had other thoughts and I embraced the chance to try something new in Lockdown, writing a book.

A large part of our lives as a family has been dedicated to the challenges with congenital heart disease that our son, Alex, has encountered from birth. Whilst this has been at times incredibly stressful for us all, no more so than Alex himself, it has also given us the opportunity to raise thousands of pounds for Wessex Heartbeat, a charity that is based at Southampton General Hospital where Alex has undergone so much life-saving treatment, and that will benefit from the sales of this book.

As well as being a true lover of life, 'bon viveur' and a passionate family man, I love all sports and especially watching football and playing golf and cricket. I am also the proud Chairman of Oakmount cricket club which we formed from nothing five years ago and which so many people have so much fun with. I await with anticipation the next chapter of what has been an amazing life so far.

"October 3rd, 1992, the day I married Susan Jane Elliott in Bournemouth, pictured here with her nephew and niece, Craig and Lisa Goodrum"

COVID-19

The first cases of a new strain of coronavirus called Covid-19 were reported to the World Health Organisation (WHO) from Wuhan in China in December 2019. After this virus swept ruthlessly across the nations of the world it became a public health emergency of international concern, and during the early part of 2020, a global pandemic was declared. This was the start of something so serious that had not been seen since the Second World War and which was expected to have the most devastating effect on worldwide health and the economy. It is likely that the impact will be felt for many years to come.

By 12th May 2020, the point at which restrictions started to be eased after the 'Fifty Days of Lockdown' and the period covered in this book, the true and startling extent of Covid-19, this fast-moving and invisible killer, was realised in four key countries:

UNITED KINGDOM

Cases: 226,463 (1st case on 1st February) **/ Deaths:** 32,692 (1st death on 5th March)

UNITED STATES OF AMERICA

Cases: 1,395,026 (1st case 20th January) **/ Deaths:** 82,555 (1st death on 14th February)

ITALY

Cases: 221,216 (1st case on 31st January) **/ Deaths:** 30,911 (1st death on 1st February)

SPAIN

Cases: 269,520 (1st case on 31st January) **/ Deaths:** 26,920 (1st death on 3rd March)

(Source for all deaths and cases statistics: Worldometers)

CONTENTS

Foreword

'You must stay at home', Boris Johnson implored us on Monday 23rd March, 2020, as the reported death toll from Covid-19 in the UK rose to 335 and cases increased to 6,650. This 'moment of national emergency' meant one thing and one thing only, Lockdown!

Covid-19, a new strain of Coronavirus which swept ruthlessly across the world from its supposed source in China, brought about a most extraordinary sequence of events that may well have changed the landscape in the UK forever. With it also came physical pain, mental anguish, suffering and tragedy which many will have to live with for many years to come.

What I hope to share with you in the ensuing pages, is a sometimes light-hearted yet candid and sometimes deeply personal account of what I perceived not 'Lockdown' as such, but more of 'Shutdown' - an impingement on our right to live and enjoy life to its fullest, without all of the people around us that we normally enjoy it with.

After a detailed summary of the many events and occurrences leading up to Boris's sombre announcement I cover each day of the 50 with personal anecdotes and chronological virus dialogue, culminating in Boris starting to ease us back to doing some of the things that we might regard as mildly normal. I also refer to each of my 50 'Daily Tips in Lockdown', which I shared with family, friends and colleagues on social media on a daily basis. I hope that some of what you will read will evoke several memories, hopefully some good ones.

I am delighted to say that, at the time of writing, neither I nor any member of the family (Susie, my wife, Holly, my daughter and Alex, my son – and the new addition to the family, Tizzy the Border terrier) has knowingly contracted the virus.

Being confined at home in leafy Chandler's Ford (near Southampton) never at any time felt like we were denied our freedom, such as you would be banged up at Her Majesty's pleasure!

It was not like we were being incarcerated in Lockdown, rather we were improvising in and adjusting to being a household shut off to the outside world. Through a mixture of routine, fun and innovation, we found a way of riding out the so-called storm, and actually for the most part, really enjoyed ourselves.

As a family we are also blessed with a significant amount of perspective. This time last year our then 20-year-old son Alex had just undergone his fourth bout of major open-heart surgery, following a very serious onset of sepsis that nearly cost him his life. To make matters worse, he also suffered a mini stroke that hampered his recovery. Owing to this we do not take anything for granted and know how to live life to the full as far as possible, even in Lockdown. In fact, Alex undertook and achieved an incredible and heart-warming personal challenge which is covered in the book. Hopefully it will serve as a source of inspiration and a symbol of hope to many in what was a very difficult and unprecedented time.

For complete clarity, the words of this book represent my thoughts and perspective on what has been, and probably will be, one of the most challenging situations that many of us will have to deal with in this century. I do appreciate that many people's experiences will have been entirely different to mine; in some cases, and for many reasons with which I have the deepest sympathy, these will have been particularly unpleasant and distinctly unmemorable.

At the time of writing Britain is still very much being influenced by the movements of the virus and it is fascinating to compare what was predicted with what actually happened both from a medical and political perspective. I hope that the book may act as an important record of history for generations to come. What is for sure is that the arrival of Covid-19 may have altered aspects of our lives and the way in which we live them, forever.

2020 - Pre-Covid-19

January: Ecstasy to agony

It is 5pm, Friday 3rd January 2020, and time to go home, but this was no ordinary departure. I was battling my way through the packed highways of Piccadilly and Knightsbridge in my laden Audi A3 as New Year shoppers kept the ranks of London black cabs royally occupied. This was as opposed to my usual train journey from Waterloo station to the South Coast which would normally take a lot less time.

This journey home marked the sad end to my four and a half year sojourn as General Manager of the four star Holiday Inn, Mayfair on Berkeley Street, in the heart of London W1 directly opposite the famous Ritz Hotel. 'My' hotel had closed, finally, for its two-year transformation to a five star establishment which presented my amazing team and me with the opportunity to move on to pastures new with a pound or two in our pockets.

For me, there was the initial excitement of a weekend free of any professional responsibility and thought of waking up on Monday 6th January, the day many of the nation were returning to work after their festive breaks, and not having to jump on the 7.05am service from Shawford station to do my mundane commute up to London. Instead, days and weeks of freedom lay ahead to do those things I enjoy doing most for two to three months, most notably to improve the golf handicap, and then to return refreshed, hopefully to undertake a new role.

"Breakfast at the Ivy"

"A short early January break in Bath with Susie"

The first couple of weeks were both relaxing and enjoyable, with amongst other things, breakfast out becoming a regular and thoroughly enjoyable pastime (my particular favourite was eggs benedict with smoked salmon at the Ivy in Winchester), several rounds of golf in surprisingly mild and unseasonal weather, and the odd delightfully long lunch. It also included a reminiscent trip to Bath with my wife, Susie, a place dear to our hearts, where we had spent some of our honeymoon 27 years previously, and a couple of visits to see Holly appearing as the fairy in Rapunzel, the pantomime, at the local theatre..........oh yes I did!

"Holly as the fairy in Rapunzel"

Then, completely out of the blue, tragedy suddenly struck at its most cruel extreme. Early evening on Saturday 18th January, I received a message on the family 'WhatsApp' chat. My nephew, Craig and his wife, Sener had lost their beloved baby girl and first child, Amelia, after barely 10 hours of life. I can remember the dreadful cold feeling that rushed from the top to the bottom of my body when I read Craig's desperately sad message to my son, Alex. It was just so devastating and heart-breaking news, when everything had seemed so fine leading up to the birth. Clearly something had gone terribly wrong for her to perish after such a healthy pregnancy.

We rushed down Poole Hospital to be with the family and that journey was a sombre and reflective one. On reaching the Maternity Unit, we were greeted by a wave of grief as the shock of what had happened started to sink in. The poignancy of holding little Amelia in my arms, so perfectly formed, will forever remain a memory for as long as I live.

Several days of mourning ensued, supporting Craig and Sener, his sister and brother-in-law (Lisa and Kian) and parents (Joy and Mark), not to mention my 90-year-old father-in-law, Jim. Of course Susie, Holly and Alex were all absolutely devastated too. I guess a tragic occurrence such as this makes us reflect on how precious life really is and how important our relationships with each other are. I also came to appreciate how grief, especially when it is so unexpected, can affect your loved ones in so many different ways.

As we continued to mourn Amelia's passing over several weeks, I tried to establish some daily routines based loosely around something I learned a few years back from a book called, 'Seven Habits of Highly Effective People', by Stephen Covey. He expounded the theory on the 'Four Dimensions of Renewal', which emphasised the importance of having something physical, something mental, something spiritual and something social or emotional, in your daily routines. This was especially important now as a coping mechanism for the grief and also to ensure there was a sense of purpose to replace that which my professional life had given me.

There were a couple of events of note, that occurred during this time: most significantly, Alex started a phased return to Winchester University, where he was studying physiotherapy, as he finally recovered from the long-term effects of his illness last Summer (this is covered in an ensuing chapter); a trip to Anfield to see my beloved Southampton Football Club (the 'Saints') completely outplay the

Premier League Champions-elect Liverpool, only to succumb to a 4-0 second-half drubbing, impacted by the odd dodgy VAR decision; and notably, the advent of the new addition to the family, our little Border terrier puppy, Tizzy.

"Baby Tizzy in her new home"

Now, I was never a dog or even a pet lover growing up, particularly when I was quite badly scratched as a small child by our cat, Nimrod. Susie's situation was different however, as she was nurtured in the company of various loving canine pets by her parents, from an early age. During visits to Bournemouth to see their grandparents' dog this inspired our children to want to have a dog for themselves. I was subsequently 'bullied' into submission to accept that we were going to purchase our own dog.

Sully, a Border terrier puppy, duly came onto the scene back in 2003 and after bringing so much joy to the family, we sadly lost him after 14 years of life at the end of November last year. I never realised up until that point how devastating losing a pet could be not having experienced this before. The sense of loss when Susie and I returned home from the vets was unlike anything I had ever felt and Holly and Alex were utterly inconsolable. It was only then that I appreciated how much I had become attached to Sully, almost like a second son.

The house felt empty without Sully so rather than waiting a few months, we decided to source another Border terrier, to continue Sully's legacy. We came across a lovely family in Swindon, who had bred a litter of five puppies and we were lucky enough to secure one of them, a little 'girl' that we called Tizzy who we picked up on Friday 24th January.

The timing of course, was perfect with my enforced layoff so golf went on the back burner from the end of January as I committed myself wholeheartedly to nurturing Tizzy whilst Susie embarked on her new job. I will say at this point that caring for a six-week old puppy, born ironically on the day that we lost Sully, is all-consuming. With what lay ahead, in terms of Covid-19, it was certainly one of our better family decisions even though we did not know it at the time. I think it also helped us deal with the desperately sad loss of Amelia.

Meanwhile, the day after we finally bade farewell to the EU on Friday 31st January the first rumblings of UK Covid-19 cases were heard in a York hotel. Face masks were already selling fast in pharmacists and on Amazon as fears were growing of a British coronavirus outbreak. Across Europe Italy had declared a six-month state of emergency after two Chinese tourists tested positive for Covid-19. The Italian Prime Minister, Giuseppe Conte, announced funding to fight the virus's spread and flights to and from China were halted. Little did we really know at that stage, what was up ahead of us!

February: Tizzy and something called 'Covid-19'

Little Tizzy bounced around the home and the garden as she made her mark on the household, oblivious to the world she had been born into. My days became even more colourful, lurching from dog walks to poo-clearing to cleaning pee-soaked carpets but those early days with Tizzy were truly delightful; maybe I had been able to cement that bond with her earlier than I did with Sully.

"Cute little Tizzy growing up"

"Tizzy banished to the bin"

Covid-19 was still in its infancy in the UK although reports of a virus super-spreader on the South Coast began to surface. A Brighton businessman had recently returned from a conference in Singapore where he had contracted the virus. Before falling ill with mild symptoms the unidentified man had spent a Saturday evening on 1st February in a pub in Brighton. By tracing those who came in to contact with the infected man, 11 cases were identified on 11th February, enabling officials to prevent an onward spread – so you see, 'Track and Trace' came and went and finally came back again but only when it was probably too late!

Throughout the pandemic Italy were my yardstick as to the progress of the virus, being supposedly two weeks ahead of us and, on Friday 21st February, they experienced their first official death from Covid-19, the day that scientists in the

UK allegedly only deemed coronavirus to be a 'moderate risk' to the British people. Like several people I know I started monitoring and recording the daily increase in the number of cases of Covid-19 and related deaths across several countries; I guess it was my way of trying to get my head around what was happening, a sort of coping mechanism.

By now though, I felt that I had 'recharged the batteries' enough to start tentative enquiries about a new job. Despite some noise from the government about Covid-19's 'serious and imminent' threat life in the UK seemed to be continuing as normal. The feeling across the nation that it was 'never going to happen to us' was never so much in evidence. It certainly never crossed my mind that the rapid onset of the virus in the UK towards the end of March would actually compromise my return to the business world and a proper midweek structure.

Just as the first day of February had produced a resounding away 4-0 defeat for the Saints at Liverpool, the last day, a 29th – this year being a Leap Year – saw us take on a nervous West Ham, away at the London Stadium and suffer a similar outcome, an inept 3-1 defeat. West ham, threatened by relegation, were simply tactically more astute, technically more gifted and mentally more up for the fight.

"Craig on the train to London for Saints vs West Ham"

Despite the talk of a pandemic slowly ramping up London still had its usual hustle and bustle. Saints woeful display aside, it was so nice spending a pleasant yet reflective day with my nephew, Craig. This was really the first time since Amelia's passing that he opened up about his feelings and the chronology leading up to her death. Kian, his brother-in-law (husband to Craig's sister, Lisa) was also with us and naturally laden with grief, as well as my cousin, Pippa and her son, Adam. A competitive game of Jenga in the Brewhouse in Canary Wharf was a great antidote to some of the sadness of the day.

That Saturday was also the pre-cursor for the desperately sad and melancholy event that followed on Monday 2nd March, baby Amelia's funeral. Losing your child at any time is just one of the worst things that can happen to a couple and their families; but for it to be after a healthy pregnancy and where there was so much excitement, happiness and anticipation for their first child, the feeling of their sorrow, was unimaginable.

Week commencing 2nd March: Heartbreak: Rest in Peace Baby Amelia x

Family and friends packed into Bournemouth Crematorium for a most beautiful yet tear-jerking service and burial, which struck right to the core of one's heart. Seeing Craig and Sener's inconsolable outpourings of grief, not to mention those of the close family, was just heart-wrenching.

My daughter, Holly, who herself has had to endure untold mental suffering over the past 20 years, seeing her younger brother go through so much, did the most amazing reading – how she kept it together without crumbling was testament to her strength of character. A heartfelt mention also for Lisa, Craig's sister, so desperately saddened that she was denied the opportunity to fulfil her role as Amelia's loving Aunt, who produced the most wonderful poem that was recited by the Priest during the funeral. Occasions such as these, rare as they are, really do put our lives into perspective.

One of the more 'positive' aspects to Amelia's funeral was that we were able to remember her short life with everybody who wanted to be there able to attend, both for the service and a lovely wake afterwards. Later in the month, of course, deaths from Covid-19 started to proliferate meaning that those who so sadly perished were denied the proper and rightful send-off with only a handful of close family permitted to attend funerals and burials. The images on the news of the 14 year old boy from London, who died of rare disease linked to Covid-19, who was buried without any of his loved ones in attendance will live long, poignantly in the memory.

By Tuesday 3rd March, Covid-19 cases in the UK had increased to 51 but as yet no deaths; in Italy, however, there had already been over 50 Covid-19-related deaths with their cases increasing by the day. UK Prime Minister, Boris Johnson, who was predisposed with and now basking in the glory of 'Getting Brexit Done' was, at this stage, still seemingly oblivious to the serious threat of Covid-19.

Despite talks of 'coronavirus battle plans', Boris did not really want to entertain thoughts of any form of Lockdown in an attempt to avoid economic disruption. In fact being a libertarian this was probably not in his nature. Instead he preached, '.......but we can all do our bit to fight the virus – by washing our hands with soap and water for the length of time it takes to sing Happy Birthday, twice'!

One of Boris's most memorable yet controversial actions pre-Covid-19 was his almost naïve claim at a press conference on 3rd March, that he had shaken hands continuously with patients at a hospital who had contracted Covid-19. This happened to be on the same day that apparently SAGE (Scientific Advisory Group for Emergencies) were strongly recommending to those at Number 10 that the British public should be warned about shaking hands and it being a very probable vector for spreading the virus.

At the time, scientists believed that they had a handle on the spread of the virus, but as it increased its virulence it would become more difficult to control reaching a peak six weeks later; the outbreak would then be expected to last for several months. Although speculative, they also believed that approximately 80 per cent of people in the UK would be infected, with 4 per cent needing hospital treatment, which might lead thousands of extra deaths. As cases mounted the majority of patients would have mild symptoms and would be told to isolate at home, with remedies such as paracetamol used to treat the symptoms. As we look back now knowing what has happened, it is fascinating that the assessment made then appeared to be quite an accurate one, although it was highly unlikely that 80 per cent of the population had been infected.

On Wednesday 4th March, the highest daily rise in cases (36 - from 51 to 87) in the UK was recorded. Going forward tests for the virus, which became so key to controlling it, were only going to be offered if your case was deemed very risky by a local health team or hospital. Most of the new cases were linked to travel to and from Italy, but there were concerns about some cases detected in intensive care units in the UK in people with no recent travel history. With no obvious or consistent source of infection health chiefs were scrambling to find out how widely the disease was being passed on.

Professor Chris Whitty, the Chief Medical Officer who became so synonymous with this pandemic, started to talk about a ban on handshakes to stop the spread of the virus, something for many that was so important to their day-to-day interactions with friends and colleagues; heaven forbid, if they now also stop us hugging and kissing each other!

Meanwhile, back in Southampton, the airport was thrown into chaos with the collapse of the budget airline Flybe. Europe's biggest regional airline had actually nearly gone bust in January. Airlines around the world had suffered their worst month in almost a decade in February because of the global impact of Covid-19 and a fall in Flybe's passenger numbers pushed the airline over the edge. Their aircraft were impounded, flights were cancelled and travellers were stranded at airports all around mainland Europe. The skies above our house have never been so empty and peaceful with Flybe's collapse, though it is desperately sad that such a great little airport that served and supported so many of our local community may never be the same again.

Thursday 5th March was significant for several very different reasons: first and foremost, I had a job interview just over a couple of months after I had finished in London, which was great timing having had some really pleasant time off; secondly, and in order to attend the interview, I had to put my dog-sitting duties to one side and take the giant 'leap of faith', leaving Tizzy on her for the very first time – when I returned home two and a half hours later there was toilet roll strewn all around the house and little pools of pee on most of the carpets! One could argue that this was not too bad for a three month old little puppy but it did take some clearing up; thirdly, and most significantly, the UK experienced its first death from Covid-19, a 75-year-old British woman, who died at the Royal Berkshire Hospital in Reading - she had not travelled abroad or been in contact with a known case raising fears over the scale of undiagnosed cases in Britain with the virus being passed on undetected.

Cases of the virus had doubled to 116 in two days and supermarkets were suddenly inundated with demand for everyday staples notably toilet roll, as the first signs of panic buying set in and the police were bracing themselves for looting and theft! Face masks and hand sanitiser were also very much on the wanted list, particularly with Boris's national hand washing plea.

Over in Italy, cases and deaths had risen to 3,858 and 148 respectively only two weeks after their first death, with Northern Italy and Lombardy region being most infected. Suddenly millions of people were cancelling their foreign trips all around the world, with as many as ten million who had planned to go to Italy; the virus was finally starting to sweep around the globe, but still the UK appeared to be 'open' as normal.

Week commencing 9th March: A last normal week?

The second week of March has always been synonymous with a trip to the first day of the Cheltenham Festival, National Hunt racing at its best. For 12 years consecutively, my brother-in-law, Mark, would drive us to the Cotswolds to meet up with his brother, Paul, and three or four of his friends from the Derby and Stoke areas. It was always a fantastic day full of laughter and conviviality and much back-slapping and banter about the North / South divide.

I remember at my very first Cheltenham, in 2007 securing my legendary status by calling out 16-1 shot Sublimity, to win the feature race, the Champion Hurdle, by a solid three lengths; this earned us a very nice dinner out in Cheltenham town that evening, and in fact we had some tremendous meals out over the years. In 2019, however, I had to miss out due to work commitments and unfortunately in 2020 none of us were able to attend, which may have proved to be a blessing in disguise.

"Nephew Craig and Sener Goodrums and niece Lisa and Kian Sabet in Dublin pre-Lockdown"

The government insisted that there was 'no rationale for banning sport – yet', despite the growing threat of Covid-19 to the UK. As a result the four day Cheltenham Festival was permitted to start as planned on Tuesday 10th March and there was not really any thought that the Six Nations Rugby and the next round of Premier League games would not take place the following weekend. Contingency plans in the UK were still being discussed as sporting events that attracted large crowds were already being postponed or played behind closed doors in other parts of Europe.

So a reported 250,000 people descended upon the spa town of Cheltenham over the course of the week for what proved in time to be a very controversial race meeting. Allegations abounded subsequently that allowing the meeting to take place in such numbers was a major vector of the virus. Course officials, however, were convinced that the extra hand sanitiser stands would be enough to keep the virus at bay.

Ironically Italy's 60 million population had just been placed into national quarantine, their version of Lockdown, as Italy was fast becoming the epicentre for the virus in Europe. Despite my concerns and reservations about the racing going ahead, I had an enjoyable week watching the racing from comfort of my living room.

It was not the only large sporting contest that was played out that week; a crucial Champions League round of 16 matches between Liverpool and Atletico Madrid took place on Wednesday 11th March in a full house at Anfield, with over 3,000 supporters travelling from Spain. Inbound Spanish visitors and returning Brits were later proved to be a main cause of Covid-19 coming into the UK, in fact more so than those who had returned from Italy. With a large increase in the infection rate in Liverpool a couple of weeks later, the match that Liverpool actually miraculously lost to be dumped out of the competition, was very much blamed for the outbreak.

Who knows how many less cases of Covid-19 or deaths might have been prevented had large sporting gatherings ceased on Friday 6th March or when action was taken to stop events around Europe. The very next week, however, the decision was finally made with a blanket ban on all top flight football and a last minute postponement of the Six Nations Rugby match between Scotland and Wales.

This was also the week in which Rishi Sunak, the Chancellor of the Exchequer, announced on Wednesday 11th March, his post-Brexit budget, amidst a background of economic slowdown similar to the recession in March 1992. He unveiled a jaw-dropping £175 billion plan for public spending not seen since the days when Norman Lamont was Chancellor in the 1990's, and which would end austerity as we had known it in previous years. Money was to be set aside for upgrading of roads, improving flood defences, new housing and hospitals and investment in schools, amongst other things. At the same time, Mr Sunak also pledged what seems now to be a paltry £12 billion as means of fighting Covid-19, an amount that was to be increased a few weeks later by a significant amount as many people's livelihoods were suddenly put at risk. This was a clear indication that the government had underestimated the potential severity of Covid-19.

On the job front things were starting to look a bit more promising as I attended a second interview in London, also on Wednesday 11th March, to run a large branded high profile four star hotel back in the capital. The interview seemed to go pretty well and afterwards I headed off back in the direction of Waterloo station, stopping off for a quick pint with my brother Hugh for what was to be, although I did not know at the time, my last meaningful act in the capital for a while.

What did strike me during that day was how packed the City and in particular the London Underground still were and how carefree and unconcerned Londoners were of the virus. I barely saw a face mask being worn let alone any conscious effort by anyone to avoid bodily contact whilst packing into the tubes – and the pubs seemed no different.

Wednesday 11th March will also be indelibly printed in the history annals as the day on which a deeply concerned Tedros Adhanom, head of the World Health Organisation (WHO), announced that Covid-19 would now be characterised as a pandemic due to the alarming spread of the virus throughout many countries. On 4th January the WHO had first reported on social media that there was a cluster of pneumonia-like infections, thought to be the first cases of Covid-19, in Wuhan in the Hubei Province of China; from that point the virus started to spread across the world like wildfire.

As the week drew to an end pandemic panic was really starting to rise with concerns around potentially overstretched intensive care units in hospitals. There were also reports of supermarkets now running dry of children's medicines, pasta and tinned vegetables and Brits stranded abroad or on virus-stricken cruise ships.

On Thursday 12th March stocks and shares fell, resulting in the worst day for markets since the Black Monday crash of 1987. The outbreak had also knocked the pound down to its lowest level against the US dollar in five months. To make matters even worse, President Donald Trump imposed a blanket ban on all air travel between Europe and the US, which was a stark sign that there was a serious threat to the financial health of the airline industry, the very essence of global interconnection and a warning of what was to come.

When Boris spoke to the nation from Downing Street for the third time in ten days, flanked by his senior medical and scientific advisers Chris Witty and Sir Patrick Vallance, declaring that 'Many more families are going to lose loved ones', the nation's attention was suddenly drawn to a stark reality that we were about to be gripped by the worst pandemic in modern times and the first since 1918. He claimed also that Covid-19 was going to change the way in which those in Britain lived their lives.

No-one knows for certain where the 'Spanish' flu of 1918 came from, how many it actually did kill and why it apparently ended so quickly. The flu spread as a direct consequence of very poor levels of hygiene, malnourishment and wartime troop movements towards the end of the First World War, but it was allegedly not actually Spanish. It was thought that roughly 500 million people, and then a quarter of the global population, contracted the flu with the number of deaths broadly ranging from 17 million to 100 million! The flu outbreak, which was itself manifested by bouts of pneumonia, supposedly disappeared as suddenly as it had arisen with a rapid mutation to a less serious strain which can sometimes happen with pandemics.

Several weeks previously, we had purchased tickets for the Saints' away Premier League game against Norwich scheduled for Saturday 14th March, with a weekend planned in the delightful Suffolk countryside with one of Susie's best friends Debbie and her husband, Guy, a most hospitable couple. Alex and his girlfriend, Charlotte, herself an ardent Saints supporter were to join us also. The trip went ahead but the football did not!

"Alex and Charlotte en route to Ferryboat Inn near Felixstowe"

Once we had battled our way around the M25 in the usual chaotic Friday evening traffic and headed north-east on the A12, it was only a matter of time before we reached the flat terrain of Suffolk. We were headed towards Ipswich, to small, quiet and quaint hamlet called Henley – not to be confused with the Henley better known the rah-rah of the Henley rowing regatta, which usually takes place on the Thames in Berkshire, every July. This was something I used to attend regularly in my twenties.

"Susie and Tizzy in the Ferryboat Inn near Felixstowe during the Ipswich weekend"

Debbie and Guy, and Bella the Jack Russell, greeted us with refreshing and large gin & tonics, which signalled the start of a wonderful weekend, in a part of the country that had yet to experience any cases of Covid-19 whatsoever. The highlight was a trip to the outskirts of Felixstowe for a magnificent yet bracing walk on the Saturday with the dogs and along the seafront, accompanied by a lovely lunch at a beautiful little coastal pub.

What was striking about the pub, apart from its very appealing menu and pleasant maritime surroundings, was how aware all the staff were of the importance, even then, of hand sanitising and heightened levels of hygiene in light the impending threat of the virus; this was despite the fact that they had no reported cases as yet. We drove back to the South Coast on the Sunday afternoon feeling refreshed and invigorated for whatever challenges lay ahead of us.

By the evening of Sunday 15th March, cases of Covid-19 in the UK had increased to 1,372 with 35 deaths now reported. By way of comparison in Italy, cases had augmented to 24,747 and 1,809 deaths. Whereas much of Europe had imposed tighter restrictions on mass gatherings, travel, sporting events, activity in schools and areas of hospitality, the UK still only had partial restrictions in place. There were reports that 170 million people were already in Lockdown in France, Spain and Italy, under strict orders not to leave the confines of their own homes as cases of Covid-19 were rising at a rate of knots.

Countdown to Covid-19

Monday 16th March: There may be trouble ahead

I was becoming increasingly aware of the heightened levels of activity in our supermarkets in the UK so I decided to take a trip to our local Waitrose in Chandler's Ford early on the morning of Monday March 16th to stock up on some essential items. The store habitually opened at 8.00am daily so I joined the queue at around 7.30am, when it was ten people deep; within 20 minutes the queue was snaking round the corner onto the main road and you could sense the feeling of anxiety, especially amongst the older generation. As I readied myself for the rush at 8.00am, the store manager appeared in state of mild panic stating that the deliveries had only just arrived and therefore they were not in a position to open until at least 9.00am – of course, after that the level of panic rose even higher.

"Hand sanitiser, an essential item during Covid and beyond"

I did actually get into the store at just after 9.00am in the end and I make no apologies for stocking up on a few more toilet rolls, tins of tomato soup and bottles of liquid soap, than I would normally have done, but certainly not as many as some did. Supermarket insanity became one of the big stories associated with the virus that affected so many people; this in turn drove on-line sales through the roof and also the corner shop was re-born!

By now it was evident that the population was starting to think and act differently, although the country was still in essence 'open for business'. Those with virus symptoms were being asked to self-isolate for 7 days and anyone they had come into contact with, for 14 days (7 days for any symptoms potentially to arise and 7 days to recover from them).

The main symptoms of this so-called mild illness being highlighted at that stage were, a new and persistent cough and a feverishly high temperature in excess of 38 degrees. A severe headache, shortness of breath and abdominal pains were also muted as Covid-19 symptoms; a loss of taste and smell was later added to the list of symptoms following reports from patients, although this was only recognised by the medics and scientists during mid-May.

Different sectors of our state had started properly gearing up for a serious crisis: the police were given powers to ensure that those who had been asked to self-isolate remained in their homes, and they were readying themselves for riots and civil unrest in light panic-buying caused by food and fuel shortages; the National Health Service (NHS), that became such a revered body throughout the crisis, were reviewing their intensive care capacities, stocks of ventilators and availability of Personal Protective Equipment (PPE), whilst at the same time vast amounts of planned care were being cancelled, and retired medics and final-year medical students were being sounded out to beef up staffing resources; the British Army were preparing themselves to provide any amount of logistical support to drive food, fuel and supplies all around the country, as well as to aid the police in preserving peace amongst communities; air travel was at a near standstill with many restrictions now in place and airlines were furiously cancelling many flights worldwide – ferry, train and public transport services were all being scaled back in some way, shape or form; schools were still open for the time being with the government under increasing pressure to close them, but universities had started to suspend face-to-face learning; and more and more of the nation's workers were being encouraged to work from the confines of their homes, with video conferencing and most notably Zoom, becoming commonplace as part of habitual working practices. Everywhere around us things associated with our basic freedoms and normal ways of living were slowly but surely shutting down.

Herd immunity came to be another of the many phrases synonymous with Covid-19 and it had very quickly become the subject of intense debate amongst politicians and scientists. Sir Patrick Vallance, the Chief Scientific Adviser to the UK, had talked about broadening the peak of the virus, which was thought at this stage to be a mild illness, by enabling many more people in the population to contract it. The idea was not to suppress the virus completely but rather for as many people as possible to build up some kind of mass immunity against the virus once they had recovered from the infection. This would, however, bring to the question the NHS's ability to handle many extra cases, particularly if the virus was more serious than had been originally thought, requiring a greater level of hospitalisations. The Commons health select committee, ironically chaired by former Health Secretary, Jeremy Hunt, described this apparent strategy as 'surprising and concerning' and that 'the cost in terms of lives lost would be catastrophic irrespective of the long-term merits of herd immunity'.

The government, in the form of Matt Hancock, the incumbent Health Secretary and a figure that would come to divide opinion on his whole handling of the crisis, refuted any claims relating to herd immunity, claiming it '...is not our policy.........Our goal is to protect life and our policy is to fight the virus and protect the vulnerable and the NHS'.

Boris Johnson's sombre press conference on the evening of Monday 16th March brought about some of the most stark restrictions and curbs on daily life that were going to be imposed on the British public in peacetime Britain. The virus was clearly spreading faster than ministers had been anticipating and some of the news footage coming out of Italy led them and indeed many of us to believe that the NHS could be put under some severe pressure, something the government was so keen to avoid. This was also a realisation that the virus could no longer be described as a mild illness – it was deadly and it might affect anyone, and a swift change in strategy was required that hopefully would save many thousands of lives.

For now Boris urged us to avoid pubs, bars and restaurants, not to attend cinemas and theatres, to work from home if we could, and to stop non-essential travel - but schools were still to remain open. He also advised, controversially, for the nine million over-70s and those with significant health conditions, to self-isolate for the ensuing three months. Many in these groups were already living in isolation and the thought of being denied contact with their loved ones was pretty tough to take. Hugging loved ones and shaking hands with friends and colleagues had already become taboo, but now family get-togethers were about to be outlawed.

What seemed to me was most notable about Boris's announcement was the fact that he was urging us rather than telling us to make sacrifices to our daily lives; impositions such as these are not things Boris likes to place upon anyone as they are not in keeping with his libertarian nature and values. In a crisis, however, leaders sometimes do need to be strong in delivering certain difficult messages in a much more direct and uncompromising manner to leave the audience in no doubt as to what the objective is. A week later, the message was indeed to be very different.

Although many will say that mistakes and errors of judgement were made by the government throughout the crisis, particularly in their perceived slow responses and delayed actions, it is debatable whether any government would have struggled to respond much more effectively to such a fast-moving and aggressive situation. There was always the ultimate dilemma between protecting the health of elderly and the vulnerable versus compromising the future prosperity, particularly of the younger generations.

These so-called impositions still left the proverbial 'door ajar' for many to flout the rules and cause owners and managers, especially in the hospitality industry, to be confused as to whether they should actually close their doors or not – so during that week many carried on as normal almost viewing it as a week of 'last-hoorahs' before stricter denials of freedom may come further down the line. This was not quite yet full Lockdown, but more and more things were certainly continuing to shut down.

The UK seemed to be moving mercilessly towards a long period of recession and certainly this was a 'baptism of fire' for Andrew Bailey, the new governor of the Bank of England, someone who was only days into his new job. Against a backdrop of concern amongst business leaders and a call for emergency support to be made available for companies affected by Covid-19, Mr Bailey promised 'prompt action' to protect the economy and our future prosperity. Mr Bailey and Chancellor of the Exchequer, Rishi Sunak, would fast become extremely key players throughout the course of and in the aftermath of the crisis.

Covid-19-related deaths in the UK had now risen to 55 with 1,543 cases; in Italy, the death rate had risen to 2,158 with an increase of over 6,000 cases, to 27.980. And it was these daily updates on the numbers of deaths and cases that would become crucial to the public's awareness as to how the virus was spreading, not just around the UK but also around the world.

Tuesday 17th March: Rishi to the rescue

In light of the looming financial crisis, Rishi Sunak announced his coronavirus 'rescue package' with a pledge of £330 billion worth of loan guarantees for industry. This represented 15 per cent of the country's entire economic output, and quite a sizeable increase on the £12 billion that had been originally put aside in his budget speech the previous week; now it was about doing 'whatever it takes' – Mr Sunak's slightly over-promissory catchphrase - to counter the impact of the virus.

"Susie doing her Worldometer graphs"

The support covered mortgage 'holidays' for homeowners for up to three months, small business loans to help small and medium-sized businesses through the forthcoming lean periods, business rates holidays for those with commercial properties, big business loans in conjunction with the Bank of England, and finally grants for the smallest companies. Many thought this was an impressive set of actions although the thing about loans is that they need to be paid back at some point. There were also still major concerns around over a million expected job losses, especially within the airline and hospitality industries, within the coming months, and there did not appear to be support for these type of businesses at this stage.

On this day also, I understood that I was to be offered the role that I had been interviewed for the previous Wednesday, subject to agreeing terms and conditions. The only slight problem was that there was every indication that hotels all around the country were reviewing their feasibility to stay open and that the loosely proposed commencement date of Monday 20th April was going to be a non-starter, which although frustrating was somewhat inevitable.

That frustration was quickly replaced by concern, with cases and deaths in the UK rising to 1,950 and 71 respectively, and in Italy to an alarming 31,506 and 2,503 respectively. Central Europe in particular, seemed to be taking a pounding as cases and deaths were also increasing at a rate of knots in Spain and France. If Italy, with its ageing population and some very densely populated areas, was a template for what might happen in the UK in weeks to come, then the situation could become extremely grave, fighting this invisible killer.

Anxiety levels in households, including ours, started to grow as we were watching and hearing harrowing tales on our televisions and radios of those who were fighting and, at worst, perishing from Covid-19 in the UK. To counter the anxiety coping mechanisms were sought, whether that was watching minute-by minute updates on Sky News, or monitoring the increase in cases and deaths on 'Worldometers.com'. Susie, my wife, even produced graphs with daily updates of these increases comparing the UK with other countries in Europe – it was quite a work of art but with things changing so quickly on a daily basis vast amounts of paper and sellotape were required!

As London and other cities continued to empty, local supermarkets had really become frenzied centres of activity with fears of rationing for shoppers seeming a real possibility. Schools were still officially open but with staff shortages and more and more parents choosing not to send their children to school, there were inevitably some partial, if not full school closures. The warning against non-essential travel, with many airlines cutting up to 90 per cent of their flights, meant that Dominic Raab, the Foreign Secretary, was going to have the enormous challenge of repatriating thousands of Britons, who feared being stranded abroad for 'weeks if not months'.

Wednesday 18th March: Schools out for the foreseeable!

"Little Tizzy growing a bit bigger"

In one of the most historical occurrences in modern times, the long-awaited closure of schools was ordered affecting most children throughout Britain 'until further notice' from Friday 20th March – and what a time for it to happen with 4.5 million pupils' education thrown into chaos and confusion with the expected cancellation of GCSE's, A-Levels and AS-Level exams. It must have been incredibly frustrating for so many to have sat mock exams earlier in the year, then to be motivated to exceed grade predictions only to see nearly two or three years of hard graft go to waste, and not really knowing how grades were to be awarded. This was of course in addition to so many university under-graduates whose schedules and pre-finals studies had to change so drastically from face-to-face tutoring to interactive and on-line methods. Head teachers were left confused by the lack of detail regarding the implications of the closures as well how long they would actually be expected to be closed for.

Schools would remain 'open' to children of those who were regarded as 'key workers', another of the infamous terms associated with Covid-19. Professions such NHS and care workers, police and other emergency services, delivery drivers and supermarket staff, gas, water and electric operators, were all among those that were deemed essential to keep the country operational throughout the crisis. Although the usual teaching would not take place, at least the key workers had somewhere in which their children could feel safe, be kept busy and be fed and watered on a daily basis.

One of the slightly more amusing images of this particular Wednesday, was of Boris Johnson holding court during Prime Minister's Questions (PMQs) in a sparsely frequented House of Commons. There would normally be nearly 400 Members of Parliament (MPs) firing questions at the country's leader but due to the new rules around 'social distancing', another of the terms that became so associated with Covid-19, there were barely 80 MPs allowed in the Chamber, with a near six foot gap between them. There was none of the usual background hubbub or thankfully, the slightly discourteous barracking.

Social distancing was regarded as one of the key actions that we should all undertake to reduce the spread of the virus, particularly where people may be coughing and sneezing. We were encouraged as part of Boris's announcement the previous Monday and based on the advice of the scientists, to remain at least two metres apart from each other, especially when in confined areas or spaces. The imposition of a two metre rule rather than a one or one and a half metre rule, as had been imposed in other parts of Europe, would become a subject for great debate. It would take some getting used to, as human beings are such social animals – we were only just getting used to the ban on shaking hands and hugging each other!

For me, it was now a week since I had gone up to London to attend my second interview in Marylebone. I was acutely conscious that if I had contracted Covid-19 that Wednesday, in a part of the country that had now accounted for a third of the cases of the virus in the UK, I would have started to display symptoms in those ensuing seven days.

Now whether it was just anxiety or paranoia, I did experience a few days when my throat was sore and my quality of sleep was that much worse than I would have had normally, although I don't think I have ever been the greatest sleeper. Now these were not registered Covid-19 symptoms but I was certainly much more mindful of what I needed to do to avoid contracting the virus and protecting my immune system. I was also washing my hands now what seemed about 20 times a day evidenced by how dry my hands had become and how much hand cream I had been using!

Global financial markets continued to slump as many prized assets, notably in the oil and precious metal industries, were sold off at well below their value. Prices of crude oil fell to their lowest since 2003 as supply started seriously to outstrip demand. I saw this as the petrol prices in my local Shell garage decreased considerably. In fact, I remember at one point it was under £1.00 for a litre of unleaded petrol – it is a just shame I was not actually going anywhere so I could not take advantage of the low prices at the pump!

The pound also fell to its lowest level against the dollar for at least 30 years, another sign that we were heading for one of the deepest global recessions in living memory, although Andrew Bailey, Head of the Bank of England, re-iterated his support for business in providing continuous loans. A devastating 25 million job losses were now being predicted with the worst case fears of a full recovery not much before 2022.

Deaths and cases in the UK had now risen to 104 and 2626, the biggest daily rise in cases that had been recorded thus far, of nearly 700. A poignant reminder, if it was needed, that the virus was taking a feverish and deadly grip, was the construction of a temporary morgue outside the coroner's court in Westminster, with a capacity for 215 people. Plans were also afoot for similar mortuaries across other London Boroughs. Daily updates of the events in Italy were a stark reminder as to what might be ahead us; there the daily death toll rose by 475 to 2,978 and cases to 35,715.

Thursday 19th March: Preparing for Lockdown

"Pre-Lockdown fridge checks"

We are so lucky in this country to have had the same reigning monarch for such an amazing length of time. Queen Elizabeth II has ruled now for 67 years and has had to contend with many different challenges during this time including her sister's affair, the tragic death of her son's estranged former wife and several wars on foreign soils.

Now 94 years of age and still going strong, she had to withstand the impact of a global pandemic and on Thursday 19th March she left Buckingham Palace to self-isolate with her 98 year old husband, Prince Philip, the Duke of Edinburgh. Throughout her reign, she has been a constant source of strength to the nation and her words of encouragement for Britons in a statement prior to leaving the Palace: 'to come together to work as one' to defeat the virus, provided a much-needed rallying call in a 'period of great concern and uncertainty'; we would of course hear from her again as the crisis deepened, this time in person.

In the Ind household, it was now time to take stock, literally. As the supermarket queues grew longer and longer, amid concerns around the availability of certain foodstuff, I decided that it might a good idea to check what we were hoarding in our two freezers, one of which was in the garage and the other in the kitchen. It is quite often the case that we build up a 'mass' of items in our freezers that over a period of time we forget about; my freezer check did not disappoint! Rump steaks, salmon fillets and even duck breasts were amongst numerous gastronomic delights that I discovered, meaning the shopping list did not need to be quite as big. Eating well both in quantity and quality would become quite a theme as the days and weeks progressed.

Deaths and cases in the UK had now risen to 144 and 3,269 respectively, with Italy's rising steeply again to 3,405 and 41,035 respectively. In fact such was the mortality rate being now higher than China's at 3,248 that the Italian army were drafted in to assist with the removal of corpses from overwhelmed crematoria. Many in Italy were also very concerned at footage still coming from some parts of the UK, where pubs and bars were still being overly frequented. Lockdown in Italy had come into force nationwide on 9th March, but with the situation fast deteriorating police were now patrolling the streets in an ever more draconian fashion – would we suffer the same or a worse fate bearing in mind we were supposedly only 12 days behind Italy?

Friday 20th March: On the brink of Lockdown!

What a bitter / sweet day this proved to be for so many in the UK: on the one hand the Chancellor of the Exchequer, Rishi Sunak, announced his much-admired 'Furlough' (a temporary leave of employees due to the worsening of the economic conditions of an employer or in society as a whole) scheme to support the many thousands of workers who faced being laid-off for an unknown length of time; on the other hand, Prime Minister Boris Johnson finally and dramatically took away some of our nation's greatest liberties, an evening in a pub, café, bar or restaurant, so as to try to prevent the spread of the disease through what we all love doing, socialising.

"Holly in party mood, something that would become a thing of the past"

Trips to theatres, cinemas, nightclubs, gyms and even places of worship were also suspended until further notice, and in my profession, hotels would only likely be open for the foreseeable future for reasons of necessity, such as to accommodate key workers and for housing the homeless and needy. Boris even implored us not to visit our Mothers and / or Grandmothers for the forthcoming Mothering Sunday, which was a desperately sad consequence for many.

The Treasury's furlough scheme would ensure that workers, whose employers applied for the scheme, were paid 80 per cent of their income up £2,500 per month, and would potentially save many thousands of jobs. The concern was always that if the economy did not 'bounce back' immediately after the pandemic, that it could just be a means of a 'stay of execution' and a precursor to a raft of

"Holly's last night out pre-Lockdown"

job losses further down the line. That said, no other government in any other country in Europe was able at this stage to provide such a generous scheme to its workers and it was widely welcomed by both the Trade Union Congress (TUC) and the opposition Labour party alike – this was praise indeed!

The closing of the pubs and clubs, albeit necessary and inevitable, was likely to cause most consternation amongst the younger adult generations. Many millennials like Holly (those born between 1981 and 1996 or age between 23 and 38 in 2019) otherwise known as Generation Y, have grown up motivated by learning in group activities and as such are hugely 'social animals' who look out for each other. Along with their apparent confidence, ambition and high-achievement mentality is a desire to live and breathe different experiences over gaining material wealth, underpinned by the persistent need to socialise. For Holly, my 25 year old daughter, to be denied the ability to party at 'Pop World' with all her friends in Southampton on Friday and Saturday nights was almost as if life as she knew it was about to come to an abrupt halt!

'**STAY AT HOME**', '**PROTECT THE NHS**' and '**SAVE LIVES**' were the slogans on the lecterns that were to become all-too-familiar as we settled down to our late afternoon (circa 5.00pm) cuppa in front the government's daily Covid-19 briefings on Sky News. As the crisis intensified or key updates needed to be communicated, Boris Johnson would be flanked by his medical and scientific 'lieutenants', Dr Chris Witty and Sir Patrick Vallance.

Boris would very often refer to importance of the scientists' advice when making the key decisions and I must say both Dr Witty and Sir Patrick always spoke in a very reasoned and authoritative manner that gave one a certain level of reassurance. Their respective deputies, most notably Dr Jenny Harries and Professor Jonathan Van Tam, often took the stand most capably in their absence; I am not sure the same can always be said of Boris's various cohorts when dealing with the more mundane but very necessary issues, some of whom performed inconsistently, often displaying their obvious inexperience in dealing with the press – who I will deal with at a later stage!

"Alex not too happy about football being suspended"

So how were we going to fight this apparent deadly virus when there was nothing to prevent or cure it? The world had experienced two previous coronavirus outbreaks: in November 2002, cases of SARS (severe acute respiratory syndrome) was first reported in China's Guangdong province and in September 2012, MERS (Middle East respiratory syndrome) was first reported in Saudi Arabia. Both were thought to originate from bats. Cases were not nearly as widespread as Covid-19 (Coronavirus 2019 or SARS-CoV-2) and their death rates were generally very low. Neither virus was serious enough to cause a pandemic but the symptoms of fever, cough and shortness of breath were very similar to Covid-19. In an attempt to prevent future cases of both SARS and MERS, scientists all around the world worked to produce a vaccines, and to this day no vaccine for either virus has ever been found. It is thought that these viruses never mutated into anything more serious and fundamentally disappeared into the ether, never to be seen since.

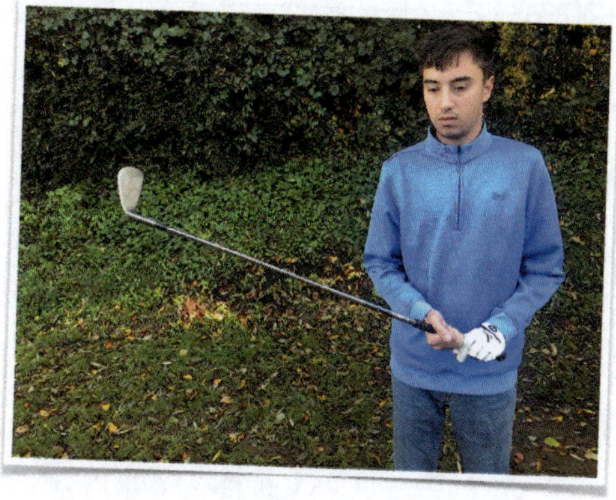

"Not only was football suspended but golf also; Alex very unhappy!"

We are blessed in this country with some of the world's best research centres and scientists, none more so than at Oxford University and Imperial College in London. Because of the work they had already done on vaccines and a basis for the prevention of SARS and MERS, a base formula for a vaccine had been produced. Amazingly human and animal trials were set to start at Porton Down, the infamous science park in Wiltshire, as soon as the week commencing Monday 23rd March. Trials can, of course, go on for months if not years, and volunteers were to come from different backgrounds and ages so as to test their effect in producing an immune response. Search for a vaccine was now very serious work in progress, not just in Oxford and London, but all around the world.

As for treatments to cure the virus, this was proving to be even more complicated. The advice at this stage was to take paracetamol, to try to bring down the fever and high temperature. One simply had to endure the cough and, later on, the shortness of breath, and hope that they did not become serious enough to necessitate hospital admission. One drug we were encouraged not to use was Ibuprofen, an anti-inflammatory that, although not proven and based on the advice of a French medic, can exacerbate the illness and dampen the immune response.

One of the main things that the government were trying so hard to avoid was the complete overwhelming of the UK's 1,257 NHS trust-managed hospitals and 'PROTECT THE NHS'. Grim images of many desperately sick individuals being left untreated in hospital corridors in Italy were a severe warning to the UK as to what might happen in a state of unpreparedness. The problem was, there were already reports of some London hospitals already running low on the availability of critical care beds. When a patient's breathing and general condition becomes so poor due to the virus's tight hold there is then the need for a ventilator to aid breathing, something that can only be administered when the patient is put to sleep in either critical care or intensive care units (ICU).

With serious cases increasing daily, bed space was reportedly running out, so hospitals were now required to focus all their attention on treating Covid-19 and re-arranging their departments so as to ensure they were fully ready for what was about to come. Letters were also being sent out to over 600,000 retired medics in the hope that they would return temporarily to help fight the impact of the pandemic – and then there was the personal protective equipment (PPE), so key to the frontline NHS workers, who were at such serious risk of catching this incredibly infectious disease if they were not properly safeguarded.

At this point in the evolution of the virus, the NHS were widely reporting that they had enough ventilators and disposable PPE (namely surgical gloves, face masks and visors, and protective aprons); but was there enough stock for all 1,257 hospitals and other establishments such as care homes, particularly if the virus was spreading as fast as it was in Italy? This would later become one of the government's greatest challenges and in fact something that they, and especially Matt Hancock the Health Secretary, were seriously taken to task over.

Meanwhile as teachers and pupils alike were coming to terms with the imminent closure of schools, it was announced that those taking exams would be graded by their teachers based on mixture of mock results, predictions and other assessed work that might be deemed helpful to produce a final grade. Whether this was fair or not was certainly open to question, but for those who really did think the process was now wholly unfair they would be given the chance to take their exams in September and, in the case of A-levels, entry to universities would have to be deferred for a year.

Many shelves were now so poorly stocked with basic items that the supermarket brands started to impose restrictions on how many of certain items we could purchase at any one time. Some were even introducing elderly and NHS hours to ensure that many vulnerable over-70s and those who were trying to look after us were not left short. Also there was a sudden demand for significant numbers of temporary staff to try to prevent the shelves from emptying so quickly – as fast as they were being stocked, they were being left vacant; it was just as challenging for on-line shopping where it was even impossible to get a delivery slot for three or four weeks hence!

With Boris Johnson's announcement on Friday 20th March, there was a growing feeling amongst many that a full Lockdown was only days away, but what exactly would a full Lockdown look like? In Europe's high profile countries such as Spain, Italy and France, police were now patrolling the streets challenging citizens as to why they were away from their homes and road blocks were in place to stop motorists from making unnecessary journeys to different regions, thus spreading the virus.

Boris regularly talked about how SAGE (The Scientific Advisory Group for Emergencies) were central to offering the advice to the government, for it then to take the most appropriate decision. It was because of SAGE's concerns over an impending human catastrophe with a mass loss of life that the decisions to close schools and halt socialising were made. Quite simply, if a vaccine or sustainable treatment could not be found, more restrictions to our civil liberties may have to be considered. By taking such drastic action there would be a distinct possibility that other serious issues such as poor mental health, domestic abuse, suicide and mass unemployment may abound. The very difficult challenge was to balance the health of the nation in this unprecedented crisis with the economy and the expected implications to people's lives.

Boris may have yearned for so long to become Prime Minister but would he at any stage have imagined how incredibly tough the first 100 days of his premiership would have been and some of the critical decisions that he would have to make? His ability to reassure those around him and his charismatic approach were clearly leadership strengths but would perceived procrastination and delays in making some of these key decisions, now become great weaknesses and sources of criticism?

Italy's 627 deaths were the highest recorded for any one day in the country during the pandemic and total deaths were now at 4,032, now by far the highest number in any country globally. Cases of the virus had now grown to 47,021, nearly half (22,264) of which were in Lombardy in the north of the country and there were fears that its capital, Milan, was about to be overwhelmed with new cases. The UK's death rate grew by 33 to 177, with cases increasing by a daily high of 714 to 3,983. Meanwhile, in China, traffic jams could now be seen on many of the roads leading in and out of Beijing, indicating that the virus may have started to disappear in the country where it was allegedly first conceived at the beginning of the year.

Saturday 21st March: A last family hoorah in Bournemouth

"A last hoorah in Bournemouth with Prosecc for sister-in-law Joy's birthday"

For those of us lucky enough not to have had to endure the fear and upset of the Second World War, the weekend comprising Saturday 21st and Sunday 22nd March must have been as close as we were ever going to get to experiencing what it was like in the 'Phoney War'. There was always an inevitability that Britain was going to be attacked from the air by Hitler, but between September 1939 and September 1940, and although we and our allies were officially at war with Germany, the skies remained quiet with not a hint of an air raid; this at least gave the country a bit more time to plan for what was ahead; the first stage of this period was known as the 'Phoney War'. Our inevitability was the imminence of 'full' Lockdown, but no-one quite yet knew when it was going to happen and to what extent our lives might be restricted. What we did know was that we were fighting an invisible and potentially deadly enemy, but how prepared were we for the battle ahead?

It was Joy, my sister-in-law's, birthday on the Saturday and the family debated whether we should jump in a car and venture down to Bournemouth to meet on the beach. It would also be an opportunity for us check on the welfare of Craig and Sener, also Bournemouth inhabitants, after the tragic loss of their daughter Amelia nine weeks earlier. Knowing that it might be the last time we could see our 'Bournemouth family' we had no hesitation in making the journey.

We were acutely aware of how the virus was spreading, hence the decision to meet in what we believed was a safe environment, in the open, breezy and coastal air of Dorset. We cracked open a couple of bottles of Prosecco that were consumed rustically in plastic cups, to toast Joy's birthday and of course, Amelia's memory. It was both so wrong and strangely surreal that we should be remembering someone so close that we never got the opportunity to get to know and properly bond with. Before we returned to Chandler's Ford we wolfed down pizza and bade farewell to Joy and Mark, Craig and Sener and Lisa (Craig's sister) for what we thought might be the last time for a while and we satisfied ourselves that we had done the right thing.

Saturday's UK death total was now at 233, 16 days after the first death, and had grown by the highest for any one day by 56. Cases alarmingly increased by a 1,098 to 5,081, evidence that the virus was spreading around the country at an astonishing rate. Italy had another record highest daily death amount at 793, now 29 days after their first death, and a total of 4,825 across the whole country. Cases had risen dramatically again in one day by 6,557, to a total of 53,578.

Sunday 22nd March: Meet the families on Mother's Day

Mothering Sunday, Sunday March 22nd, was a strangely quiet day. My mother and father, Elizabeth and Jack, live in Tonbridge, their second spell in this busy Kent commuter-belt town. I spent the first 13 years of my life living in Tonbridge, in fact we – my parents, sisters, Rebecca and Katharine and brother Hugh - lived right in the heart of Tonbridge School, one of the leading private schools in the country. My father was Housemaster of the largest boarding house, School House, and we were very privileged to be able to use the school's many facilities in the school holidays.

"Father-in-law Jim"

At 14 years of age, my father became Headmaster of Dover College, a co-educational private school on the Kent coast, so I spent the remaining four years of my school life as a boarder as Tonbridge, where I secured 10 O-Levels and 3 A-Levels; this was more than enough to enable to go to Torquay to study Hotel Management, the start of my life in hospitality.

My parents were always so supportive of my siblings and me and provided us with such a happy home, imbuing us with the right values and principles to take into our future lives. Mothering Sunday is always a day in which I reflect on my amazing upbringing, and my mother and father are just two of kindest, selfless and loving individuals you could ever wish to meet, who have always put the needs of others before theirs. Life has slowed down somewhat for them recently, particularly for my father, but they remain in good mental and physical health and I obviously 'phoned my mother to wish her a Happy Mother's Day.

"Mother-in-law Annette with niece Lisa"

On the other side of the family, we very sadly lost my mother-in-law, Annette Elliott in October 2015. She had suffered initially from myeloma, a form of blood cancer, and after what we thought were signs of recovery, she died suddenly of an aneurism, leaving behind her devoted husband of 57 years, Jim. Annette and Jim, like my parents, were such a kind and generous couple, who welcomed me wholeheartedly into their family in Bournemouth, when I met, courted and married their daughter, Susie, my wife of nearly 28 years – and counting! We were married in St Augustine's church, Bournemouth, as were Susie's sister and brother-in-law, Joy and Mark, and it was the venue for Annette's funeral; Annette was the matriarch for our many Bournemouth Christmases and is to this day missed by everyone, especially her grandchildren Craig, Lisa, Holly and Alex.

With all sporting events now on hold, Sunday did not seem quite the same. We would usually take in a couple of live football matches and maybe a bit of Six Nations rugby during the afternoon, and PGA golf from the US in the evening. It was probably just as well as we spent Mothering Sunday treating Susie and walking little Tizzy locally.

I did bump into one of our neighbours, Alison Rickman, early on the Sunday afternoon. Alison is an NHS worker and microbiologist at Southampton General Hospital, who was becoming more involved in testing for Covid-19. But it was her heart-warming story of her trip to Tesco's at Bursledon, near Southampton, that really touched me – Tesco's had just introduced their NHS shopping hour and not only did her and her husband, Andy, get to the front of the queue, but she also received a lovely bouquet of flowers and many words of gratitude for all her hard work. In my opinion, the management and employees of our supermarkets all around country deserved themselves all the praise in the world for the extra efforts they had to make in incredibly difficult and sometimes very volatile circumstances.

Many tourist attractions in different parts of the country were experiencing their busiest day of the year, and it was as if many in the population were aware of what was about to happen. Despite advice for people to stay at home, the Yorkshire Dales, Lake District, Snowdonia National Park, Bournemouth and West Wittering beaches were amongst many destinations that reported unusually high densities of the British public who were not keeping two metres apart. This was described by the government and medical experts as 'dangerous' and 'irresponsible' in light of the worsening of this national crisis and may well have been what finally pushed Boris over the edge!

In other developments: some councils had announced park and playground closures; volunteers were being sought to help care for the 1.5 million elderly and vulnerable individuals who had been asked to stay at home for 12 weeks; hospitals were continuing to re-organise wards so as to accommodate more Covid-19 patients, with many children's wards in particular, being vacated; a deal was done by the NHS where private hospitals would supply more beds and ventilators; the government were promising to ramp up testing as this would ensure the movements of the virus could be closely monitored; there was talk of support for self-employed workers in light of what the government was doing for other workers on its Furlough scheme; there rumours of a possible postponement Tokyo Olympic Games due to start in August; worried parents were readying themselves to commence on-line classes with the closure of schools the previous Friday; and vicars were conducting church services virtually, as their would-be congregations were watching on their devices from home! The country was on a precipice and tougher restrictions were surely only days, if not hours, away.

Sunday's total deaths in the UK had now risen by a further 48, to 281, and cases by 600, to 5,681. Parts of Italy were fast becoming a disaster zones as hospital intensive care units were being completely overwhelmed with a 'tsunami' of new patient intakes desperately needing serious respiratory aid. Total deaths in Italy had increased by a further 651 to 5,476 and cases were up to 59,138. Meanwhile Madrid was fast becoming the epicentre in Spain as it battled mainland Europe's second worst outbreak of the virus.

As Britain closed its eyes on another week, Boris Johnson was preparing to unleash his most decisive set of rules and regulations yet, that would test the public's confidence and resolve more than at any time in over 50 years. 55 per cent of the nation were fully in support of him with his handling of the crisis thus far, but how would things look after the next 50 days?

Alexander Harry Ind: 'This is your Life', not forgetting Holly Francesca!

Alex and I were getting a little bit of cricket practice in on the front drive just prior to Boris's latest and most stern announcement. We were really hoping even at that stage that we would be getting a punctual start to our cricket season with our 'cricket family' from Oakmount Cricket Club, in early May. Cricket for us as a family is such an important part of our summer and we had been looking forward so much to this year after Alex's very serious ill health last year.

"Mark with little Alex on Deauville promenade with little Holly lurking in the background back right"

Alex was born in September 1998 and after five days at home, his limbs and lips suddenly went blue and he became extremely breathless. After being taken back to Winchester Hospital, where he was born, there were serious concerns amongst the medical team that he was suffering from a life-threatening cardiac problem, although nothing had ever been detected during ante-natal check-ups; very quickly afterwards I was following an ambulance, containing Susie, Alex and my father, with blue lights flashing and in full emergency mode, to Southampton General Hospital.

On admission, Alex was very quickly diagnosed with pulmonary atresia (a blocked pulmonary valve), ventricular septal defect (one functioning ventricle and two holes in the heart) and situs inversus (his major organs being the wrong way round) and given 20 per cent chance of survival. It was a quite extraordinary change of fortune to go from the elation of the birth of a son to complement our lovely daughter, Holly, to then within a week, have our world be turned completely upside down with the portent of losing our son within a week of his birth.

"Happy siblings Holly and Alex playing together as tots"

I remember to this day, reading through the consent forms that the senior infant cardiologist and senior infant cardiac surgeon required us to sign prior to Alex's first major cardiac operation. This was something that no 'parent craft' classes had ever prepared us for and the world suddenly felt a very dark and uncomfortable place.

Alex survived the operation thanks to the skill of the amazing surgeon, but we soon became aware that Alex's congenital heart issues were going to be something that he was going to have to live with, on and off, for many more years to come. The very same surgeon subsequently operated twice more on Alex when he was 14 months old and eight years of age respectively, with major open surgery lasting around 10 hours each time.

It was after this second operation that the aforementioned cardiac surgeon assumed demi-god status in our household as he had undertaken some of the most pioneering cardiac surgery on an infant that had thus far been performed anywhere in the country. Due to his unbelievable ability and extreme tenacity, our son had been given a real chance of living a reasonably normal life, though with some potentially serious limitations to physical activity.

I am sure I speak for many other parents of 'heart children', that one of the biggest challenges is not to focus so much of your efforts and energy on your sick child, at the expense of the attention you may not be giving to any other child or children in the family. Our daughter Holly had been born into this world in January 1995, as our first born and the 'apple of our eye', and also as my parents' first grandchild. Alex's arrival, three and a half years later, very clinically took some of the attention away from Holly with the seriousness of his long-term health challenges and I remember vividly, in the direct aftermath of Alex's open heart surgery when he was eight, the moment when I realised how we might inadvertently be neglecting Holly's feelings and her understanding of the whole situation.

"Holly and Alex in their favourite Deauville destination"

We had promised Holly that regardless of how ill Alex was, either Susie or I would return home from the hospital to be with her, despite the fact that my parents were staying with us and that fortuitously we only lived 15 minutes away from the hospital. Immediately after the operation however, Alex had to remain in the outstanding care of the team in the paediatric intensive care unit (PICU) as his condition was extremely serious after such major and pioneering surgery. We had to make one of the most difficult decisions in our near 28 years of married life, and that was that both of us needed to stay overnight next to PICU, in one of the special relatives' rooms - there was a genuine concern that Alex may not make it through the night.

We returned home briefly to tell Holly of our intention not to be with her that night; the image of her curled up in the corner of our bedroom, crying her little 11 year old eyes out, will live with me for the rest of my life. First of all, her beloved little brother had been taken away from her for a serious operation, then her little canine companion, Sully, had been carted off to my in-laws down in Bournemouth and to top it all off, she was not going to have the company of her parents to comfort her through the next incredibly stressful 24 hours. It was, for me, the moment the 'penny dropped' and that we had to see this situation through Holly's eyes and appreciate that her little world was in complete and utter turmoil.

As it happened, it took my father very forcefully to tell us to leave Holly with my mother and him that night, and that she would be absolutely fine, which of course she was. In that moment we needed to do what we needed to do, but it is something I often reflect on and hope that Holly understands the reason for our actions and that we never ever loved her any less.

As Alex's body grew there was always going to be the need to perform more surgery to replace some of the artificial tubing connecting different parts of his heart function, probably in his later teenage years. It was during the lead up to his A-Levels that he felt his physical strength diminishing and his breathing and general health and fitness worsening, so he duly underwent more major open heart surgery in July 2016; this was undertaken by another brilliant cardiac surgeon at Southampton General Hospital, and a former aide to and prodigy of his predecessor, Alex's original surgeon who had gone overseas to the US to share his expertise.

"Holly and Alex with baby Sully, our beloved first dog"

Up until that point and after his previous operation in February 2007, when he was eight, Alex had enjoyed much improved health and was miraculously able to play a couple of seasons of competitive football, something he had always wanted to do, but was told by the cardiac consultants that he would never be able to do. His courage and determination to prove the doubters wrong has indeed always been a theme of

Alex's inspirational story over the years and something that was very evident this May whilst we were in Lockdown, when he undertook an amazing physical endurance challenge. Throughout his growing up Alex had become a very keen cricketer and proficient opening batsman, a role in a cricket team that requires incredible mental and physical strength, something that he has gained through his copious amounts of suffering.

His recovery from surgery in the summer of 2016 was almost 'Lazarus-like', and he was back playing golf by the autumn and was probably in as good health as he had ever been. At that stage, we were not expecting any more lengthy hospital sojourns for a good few years, though we were mindful that he would still have some physical limitations. Two summers later and as a 19 year old in adult Hampshire League cricket, he duly became the leading run scorer for Oakmount Cricket Club in our promotion winning season, an absolutely incredible feat for someone who had been through so much and who still needed the use of a pacemaker to get him through any more physical exertions.

Alex continued to live a very active and normal life as he moved into his twenties and he commenced his degree in Physiotherapy at Winchester University, a very apt profession for him to study in, with the levels of empathy he had gained from being a patient and receiving physiotherapy himself on so many occasions. There was therefore no indication of what was about to befall him in the summer of 2019.

On the late afternoon of Wednesday 29th April I had just got off the train at Shawford station, where I parked when getting the train into London, and I was undertaking the 10 minute drive home when I received a call from Susie. It is rare that Susie ever calls me during the working day so I sensed something was not quite right. She went on to explain that Alex was experiencing a very high temperature, nausea and showing signs of lethargy and mild delirium and that we should take him to the hospital. Credit to Susie, she had always been mindful of symptoms that we had to be aware of in Alex that could be those of an infection, something that could be very harmful to Alex with his long-term cardiac challenges.

We ventured to Southampton General Hospital, a place we have come to know very well over the years, as fast as we could in what was at that time rush-hour, with Alex's behaviours manifested by the delirium, becoming more and more concerning. We eventually arrived at Accident and Emergency (A&E), and after mentioning Alex's background and history he was quickly rushed through for medical attention despite the lengthy queues of very sick and unwell patients.

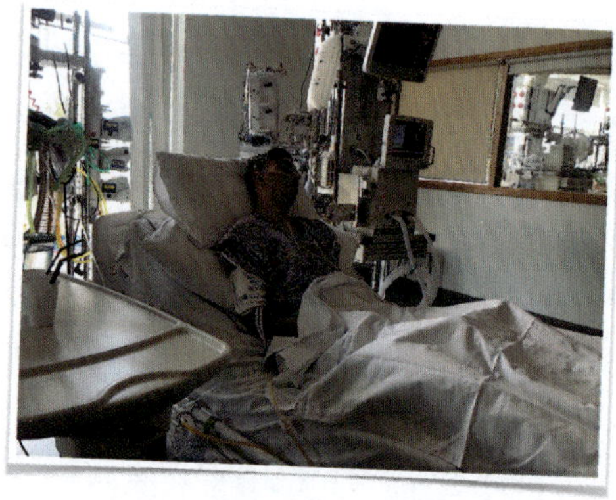

"Alex in intensive care having contracted sepsis in May 2019"

At this stage, I have to applaud those in our NHS who have chosen or been asked to spend time working in the A&E environment in any hospital. It is fast-moving and dynamic and I am sure at times, pretty grim and stressful, and this experience gave me a level of empathy and understanding of the challenges that A&E departments have had to endure particularly during the Covid-19 crisis, with the added risk of a deadly virus.

Alex remained under observation in A&E for nearly six hours all told and thankfully his very high temperature and general state of mind seemed to be improving, thanks to the magic of paracetemol. Although we were still waiting for someone from the cardiac team to give Alex the ultimate all-clear he made the decision that he wanted to go home because he was so fatigued but also to free up his bed and space in A&E, endemic of Alex's generally unselfish and thoughtful manner. At that stage it was thought Alex had contracted some form of infection that could be treated with ongoing doses of paracetamol.

During the next couple of days Alex showed no real improvement, in fact he became more fatigued and nauseous. Because we had not been able to see a cardiologist whilst in A&E on the Wednesday evening I had arranged as a precaution for a cardiology appointment in the hospital for just after lunch on Friday 1st May, which in hindsight was incredibly fortuitous.

On arrival at the hospital on the Friday Alex's condition very evidently worsened to the point that he became unable even to walk, so I located a wheelchair and transported him into the hospital, initially to have his blood samples taken, something he has had done on many occasions previously without incident. On this occasion, he passed out twice and started to look decidedly weak and frail.

By the time we got to the cardiology outpatients department I think the medical staff knew that something was seriously wrong. Within hours he was moved to the High Dependency Care unit where his delirium became so extreme that the consultant responded that he needed to be 'blasted with antibiotics'. This was the start of a battle against time to fight what we later found out was Sepsis, a very serious and life-threatening infection of the blood, caused originally by an uncommon form of eczema in his ankle. It was not long before he was then moved to the Intensive Care (ICU), where his condition became critical and his organs were starting to shut down.

I do not think that in those few critical hours that I realised how really unwell Alex was. Looking back at the delirium there were actually some mildly amusing moments, such as when he was talking to his girlfriend, Charlotte, who was in Sweden at the time, on his mobile 'phone and stating his name and address back to front whilst trying to speak in the earpiece!

My final memory of that evening was before I had left the hospital separately to Susie and Holly, Susie had given me a list of shopping to get from the late night Asda store. One of the items on that list was cress in order to make egg and cress sandwiches the following day. The severity of Alex's situation must have just dawned on me as I searched aimlessly for this cress, which I just could not find anywhere in the store. At that point, I just wanted to throw my shopping basket down and weep inconsolably; thankfully a very kind store assistant located the cress and I was able to pull myself together for what was going to be a very difficult and stressful night ahead for us all.

I woke several times overnight and in fact called direct to ICU at 3.10am stating that, in my humble opinion, I thought Alex probably just had a kidney infection. The nurse thanked me for my advice, stated that Alex was in a stable condition and that I should think about getting some sleep.

I was suddenly awakened at just after 7.00am by my 'phone ringing by my bedside. One of the biggest fears one has in these situations, is the call from the hospital that no-one wants to get, and one which I am sure many relatives and friends of Covid-19 patients have received during this dreadful pandemic. I could see that the number was that of ICU, and fearing the worst, I went into a cold sweat; the nurse that I had spoken to four hours previously, said, 'Good morning Mr Ind, I have someone who wants to speak to you', and with that, a coherent and seemingly wide-awake Alex spoke. It was probably the most wonderful thing that I have ever woken up to and the utter relief I felt at that moment was immense beyond words.

A word of gratitude, at this point, Alex's cardiologist who was thankfully on duty that day and who is extremely genned up on Alex's medical history and who took the swift action to ensure the correct medication was administered to him in the nick of time, and frankly saved his life. The dedication that she showed, putting

Alex's situation before anything or anyone else and not leaving his side until she was sure he was stable, was to be truly admired and we will be forever grateful.

Alex spent the next 10 days or so in ICU and the Young Adult's Cardiac Ward E2 (YACU), being cared for by the amazing cardiac team at the hospital, who are just so brilliant and many of whom we know from previous hospital visits. Unfortunately though, our worst fears were realised and the infection had become so bad that it had penetrated the tubing around his heart chambers and infected the main conduit to his heart that he had had replaced in his last operation in the summer of 2016. So on Monday 13th May, 2019, the same surgeon from his operation in 2016 once again and very skilfully administered another 10 hours of major reconstructive open heart surgery.

I know there must be many people who have experienced serious and lifesaving surgery themselves and their families have had to endure hours upon hours of anguish and worry, waiting to see that their loved ones had survived the surgery and that everything had been successful. I must say, having been through those anxious waits at least five times now as parents and of course for Holly as his sister, the nine or ten hours of waiting are just incredibly terrifying. We have developed coping mechanisms but it never gets any easier.

Alex remained in hospital for a total of eight very frustrating weeks for him, full of ups and downs, but he made little fuss throughout and he did make an extremely rapid recovery from the surgery as he had done in 2016. It was more the fact that he was still taking intravenous antibiotics for the infection which meant he had to be hospitalised for so long. Throughout that time, Susie, Holly, Charlotte, his girlfriend, and I were with Alex pretty much during every waking hour and our lives, were, as such, put on hold; to us, this had been our 'Lockdown'. One huge blessing throughout all the times we have had to go to the hospital with or to visit Alex, is how close we are in proximity to where we live – 15 minutes' drive on a good day and only seven miles.

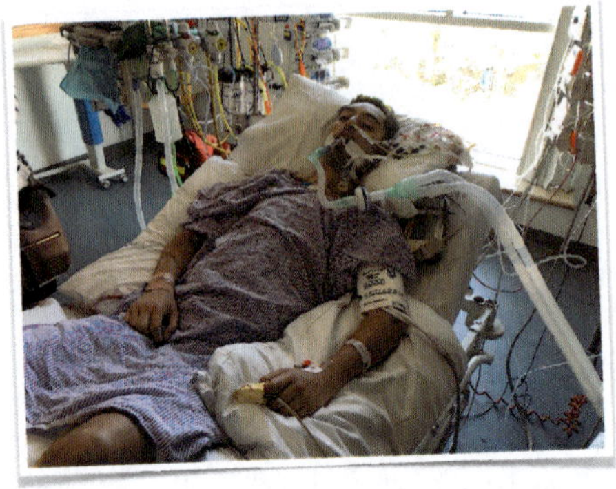

"Alex in intensive care just after open heart surgery in May 2019"

On Thursday 27th June, Alex finally came out of hospital to the sound of champagne corks popping in the Ind household; he did though remain under the watchful eye of daily medical homecare to continue to administer antibiotics intravenously, through a Periphally Inserted Central Catheter (PICC) line in his upper arm - and it was thanks to that daily medical homecare that Alex was helped through his next health scare.

It was the morning of Friday 2nd August, exactly three months to the day that Alex had originally been diagnosed with sepsis. John, the medical homecare assistant, had just connected up Alex's PICC line and started the next course of antibiotics, when Alex suddenly exclaimed that he could not move his left arm or leg. I could see also that one side of his face had dropped so I immediately knew these were the first signs of a stroke.

Thankfully John calmly and expertly stepped in to ensure Alex was in the right position and being a former Paramedic, he knew exactly what to do whilst we waited for the ambulance to arrive. As it happened, Alex's symptoms only last about 20 seconds and we later found out he had suffered from a transient ischaemic attack (TIA), otherwise known as a mini stroke, which is caused by temporary disruption in the blood supply to the brain resulting in a lack of oxygen. If not treated immediately in the way that John had done, TIAs can have very serious onward consequences.

So back we went and accompanied Alex to Southampton General Hospital for a less time-consuming period in A&E, followed by a night in the stroke unit. It was later thought to be the PICC line that caused the TIA but it was certainly another very scary moment for Alex, which of course he once again took in his stride, showing maturity beyond his years.

Quite miraculously and despite sepsis, major open heart surgery and a TIA all in the space of three months, Alex was back opening the batting for Oakmount Cricket Club on Saturday 15th August, barely two weeks after the TIA. His recovery continued to go from strength to strength thereafter and thankfully his three months of 'Lockdown' had at last come to an end.

So you see for him - and us on the side lines – to go through such a tortuous time 'incarcerated' in hospital as he was - and we were - in the summer of 2019, gave us a real perspective on what we were about to embark on during Boris's so-called Lockdown. Despite the impending gloom, we were going to make absolutely sure that we somehow enjoyed ourselves as much as possible to make up for the previous year and make sure Alex had a healthier and happier summer!

Monday 23rd March: Boris delivers a moment in a time

And so at 5.00pm on Monday 23rd March, 2020, the words that so many had expected for so long but hoped they would never hear, finally came out of Boris Johnson's mouth: 'YOU MUST STAY AT HOME!' was the instruction to the 27 million watching, and it was the first time during this whole crisis, that you could tangibly sense Boris's increased levels of anxiety and concern.

"Lockdown fruit and veg delivery"

Boris Johnson's defining announcement came after the latest meeting of the COBRA (Cabinet Office Briefing Room A) committee, a gathering of ministers and officials from across Whitehall, in response to critical events and crisis situations. This was of course not the first time that COBRA had met in direct response to the Covid-19 pandemic but it was certainly one of the meetings that was chaired by Boris. Later on in the crisis it was revealed that he allegedly had not attended some of the earlier meetings as he was predisposed with 'Getting Brexit Done'. His absence from these earlier meetings was a reason for much of the criticism that he received for being slow to respond to the pandemic from the outset.

Despite Boris's claims that he was rigorously washing his hands after each interaction, it certainly confused the message as in fact he continued to be seen in public shaking hands live on ITV's This Morning programme on 5th March, an England rugby international on 7th March and at an event with boxer Antony Joshua, on 9th March. Those decidedly questionable decisions by the Prime Minister would without doubt come back to haunt him when he himself tested positive for Covid-19 on Friday 27th March, eventually resulting in the country being rendered leaderless during the most serious national crisis since the Second World War, if not for a century.

Restrictions on one's daily routine and life's luxuries are something that none of us are used to and for our family there were indeed many activities and privileges that we were now going to be denied. For Susie, it was her not being able to meet her friends with dogs and continue Tizzy's puppy agility classes that had been so effective up until now; also her weekly Thursday catch-up with her friend, Caroline, were going have to be put on hold. Working in a school, Susie would still have some focus to her days and weeks as there were a number key workers, whose children would need tending to.

For Holly, she was going to be denied contact with her countless friends from school, college, amateur dramatics, music, dance and so on............! Friday and Saturday nights would just not be the same as she would not be able to go out to dinner, to bars and to her favourite haunt, Pop World in Southampton. But again like Susie, at least her work would continue, albeit from home.

For Alex, he would have to miss meeting up with his friends, playing golf, going to the gym and most frustrating of all, he would not be able to see his girlfriend of nearly two years, Charlotte, who had stuck by him throughout his serious illness last year and who has almost become part of the family. But at least he had his university course to focus on and particularly working towards his final year exam early in April, which would hopefully see him safely into the second year of his Physiotherapy degree.

And for me, the lovely breakfasts and long lunches out, gym visits, rounds of golf, evenings at the pub, Saints football matches and the like, would all come to a sudden halt – and worst of all, it was highly likely that any future job opportunities would have to be put on hold until further notice, and with international travel lessening by the day, it was looking increasingly likely that the hotel industry, particularly in London, was going to be hit very badly and for a lengthy period of time. Never was establishing a different set of routines so important for us all than now and with weeks, if not months, of isolation expected everybody's creativity and positive spirit would be required to keep us entertained and busy in Lockdown – and that is what inspired the posting of my 'Daily Tips' on social media.

In other developments on this historic day of Monday 23rd March: the race to obtain more ventilators had now consumed the business world as the government sent out rallying calls to companies like Dyson, Airbus, GKN, McLaren and Siemens for another 30,000 to be produced within the next fortnight, something that was greeted with great enthusiasm and zeal; stocks of hand sanitiser were in such short supply that gin distillers were drafted in to manufacture hand-sanitising products; the limit of £30.00 when using contactless to pay for items was now being increased to £45.00 as shops and supermarkets sought to reduce the reliance on cash, where bank notes were now thought to be another vector of the virus; it was thought that there were over one million British people abroad at this time and they were being encouraged to take a flight home as soon as possible, with air travel slowly but surely, shutting down although this was potentially going to present a big logistical challenge; police were being given powers to ensure the public remained at home and did not venture out unnecessarily or attend social gatherings in the way in which had been seen the previous weekend; as people were packed into trains and other public transport to try to make their way home as quickly as possible, ironically the virus was probably being passed on quicker and in greater numbers as they tried to avoid it; and finally, Gary Lineker was in the news as one of his sons had contracted the virus and reported symptoms of loss of taste and smell, something that many reported but they were not actually officially recognised as symptoms until nearly two months later on 18th May!

Over in Europe, Italy reported a lower number of deaths in any one day, than in previous days, although there was still an increase of 602 to a total of 6,078, over 62 per cent (3,776) of which were recorded in one region, Lombardy; this part of

Italy is thought to be where the virus was first detected and spread very quickly apparently due to the very high age demographic. Also in Spain, some of the first reports of deaths in care homes were coming out, something that would become a major challenge for and perceived oversight by the government in this country.

In the UK, and the main reason why Boris announced the Lockdown, was that the deaths and cases had now risen to 335 (an increase of 54 on the previous day) and 6,650 respectively, which was 18 days since the first reported death; there now followed the 'Fifty days of Lockdown'

Britain in Covid-19 Lockdown

Day 1, Tuesday 24th March: A brave new world

For those of us who are lucky enough to possess a garden, this proved to be an incredibly important factor in the feeling of relative freedom during the pandemic. Thus much of the first day of Lockdown was taken up mowing the lawn and tackling a couple of our very overgrown hedges in the back garden. What made it doubly beneficial was that literally the day after Boris made his infamous announcement the most incredible weather befell us.

"Lockdown is here! Let me out!"

During February Storms Ciara and Dennis brought very heavy rainfall and winds to many parts of the UK and Ireland, causing rivers to reach record levels in several parts of England. In fact the Met Office reported it as being the wettest February and the fifth wettest month on record, effectively rendering the ground absolutely saturated. For many who lived in flood plains or near rivers it was more misery to go with that of floods in recent previous years, where untold havoc had been wreaked. Suddenly to go from days and weeks of wind and rain to bright unbroken sunshine and clear deep blue skies was the complete antithesis and almost a reward 'from above' for our compliance to go into Lockdown.

As part of Boris's Lockdown criteria one form of exercise for one hour per day outside of the house was permitted. Having little Tizzy to walk gave us a very good reason to get out and about and therefore Susie and I alternated with the morning and afternoon walks, meaning Tizzy got a double dose of action.

I must say reading and hearing about Lockdown in other parts of the world re-enforced my feelings that our restrictions were nowhere near as severe as those in Italy, Spain and France, where, amongst other things, the fines were a lot bigger, people had to carry pre-authorised documentation as to why they were out and about and even threats of a period of time in jail. In fact in the Middle Eastern country of Jordan individuals were actually being incarcerated ruthlessly simply for not staying at home!

The garden also became a very useful cricket pitch from the very first day of Lockdown and Alex invented an exciting version of what he very amusingly described as the 'Ashes'; each player would bat twice until they were out, which would constitute the first innings and then the second innings would comprise of three further innings for each player, which lead to a result. We played several games at once which was great exercise and Tizzy even played a part by displaying superb fielding skills!

It was on this day also that Matt Hancock, the Health Secretary, made an impassioned plea to the nation to become part of a 250,000 strong 'army of volunteers' to help look after the 1.5 million vulnerable individuals 'shielding' from the virus in their homes for 12 weeks. This brought to mind army chief Lord Kitchener's iconic recruitment message during the onset of the First World War; the words 'Your Country Needs You' were replaced with 'Your NHS Needs You'. Interestingly Susie signed up on the government website as one of the many volunteers. There ended up being over 750,000 people come forward – and to this day, she has not yet been required to do any jobs at all!

Talking of the army, they were being more and more regularly deployed in trying to get PPE to the various hospitals around the country, as well as helping in the construction of a 4000-bed temporary hospital at the Excel exhibition centre in

East London, which was later named as the NHS Nightingale Hospital. This was one of the learnings from China, where a temporary emergency field hospital had been constructed in just one week in Wuhan, designed specifically to treat patients specifically with Covid-19 who required oxygen and to take the pressure off of the intensive care units in their regular hospitals.

One of the other processes that the army became increasingly involved in as the virus swept through the country, was that of testing – an unpleasant swab test in the back of the throat to see if one had the virus, although one might not be showing any symptoms even if testing positive. Countries such as South Korea, were very successful in keeping the virus under a degree of control because of their advanced capacity for testing and also due to its ability to track who patients have come into contact with resulting in targeted isolation of those individuals. With the threat of another coronavirus, MERS in 2015 and because they thought an epidemic of some sort was an inevitability at some stage in the future, the government ordered for the number of testing laboratories to be increased throughout the country. Due to this, South Korea was in a state of readiness when the virus hit and they had it under control within three weeks.

Unfortunately, in the UK we neither had enough capacity nor kits for extensive swab testing partly because we had not had the foresight to provide for research into new methods of testing. In Europe, the Germans notably had been wise to the imminent threat of the virus and the need for many more testing kits and hence got 'their towels on the sunbeds' before we did; a familiar tale, I hear you say!

Testing in this country had started reasonably well but as the cases increased disproportionately all around the UK, we simply could not cope with the demand. Initially there had been a target of 25,000 tests per day but presently only 5,605 were being done, so there was little hope in tracking accurately where the virus was most prevalent. Also there were front line NHS staff who were working closely with Covid-19 patients and not even being tested themselves. This was now becoming a desperately concerning situation which the government was under great pressure to resolve.

Meanwhile an antibody test was being checked and trialled by Public Health England which, if successful, could indicate whether someone has already had the virus, asymptomatically or otherwise, and thus provide the first steps towards immunity. This test would constitute a simple pinprick and was described by Boris Johnson as a potential 'game-changer' in the fight against Covid-19.

Spain's infection rate had suddenly doubled within the space of three days, and with that a record 514 deaths were recorded in one day, sparking the panic that had been seen in Italy during previous weeks. Spain's total deaths was now 2,800, with over 1,500 of these in the epicentre of Madrid. Much like London in the UK, Madrid was setting up an emergency hospital in a conference centre and poignantly an ice rink was being turned into a mortuary.

Unfortunately, in Italy the previous day's hope that deaths were slowing was quickly vanished as there were a further 743 fatalities taking their total to 6,820, more than double what there had been in China (3,277), a significantly bigger country with a population of over 1.4 billion compared to Italy's of over 60 million. There were already questions surfacing around the validity of China's statistics. Additionally India, the world's second most populous country with 1.35 billion people, was the latest country to go into Lockdown meaning about a third of the world's population was now in enforced confinement.

In the UK, another 87 people were reported to have died from Covid-19 with what was the biggest daily rise so far, bringing the total number of deaths to 422. There was also data coming out that nearly 20 per cent of Covid-19 patients using NHS critical care beds were actually aged 50 or less. Initially it was thought that the virus was affecting the frail, vulnerable and elderly but there was now a stark realisation that any age group could be impacted, although children were least at risk.

Day 2, Wednesday 25th March: Dangerous liaisons

"Lovely Lockdown weather"

The world awakened to another glorious morning with cloudless blue skies, enabling more hedge cutting and garden cricket. My daily walk with Tizzy, however, really revealed how concerned some people were about catching the virus: as I approached a couple from afar, and I am probably talking over 100 metres, they scurried across the road to avoid getting even remotely close to me, although cursory yet polite 'Good Mornings' and respectful nods were exchanged. Another individual was slightly more daring and actually remained on the same side of the road to pass me by but with his whole body facing inwards and almost being swallowed up by a large hedge. Did I smell or was it the dog – or was it just a nation completely consumed by a fear so great that by even walking along a pavement you were in the gravest of danger? As the ultimate social animals the most basic of interactions was being denied to us all.

Today also saw the inception of my 50 'Daily Tips' on social media, notably Facebook and Twitter. The idea behind these tips was to offer up helpful new ideas for some or reminders to others, which could be used during this period of Lockdown and that may then become future habits for healthier, happier and better living. They were also broadly centred on Stephen Covey's four key dimensions of renewal, namely the physical, mental, spiritual or social / emotional. For me, it was a great opportunity to share knowledge gained from my life in the business world as well as some of my own personal habits that have become part of my daily routine over the past few years. If just one person gained something from them and they provided a little bit of light entertainment to boot, then it was a worthwhile daily discipline for me to focus on in these slightly stranger times.

Someone who really used social media to its full was fitness sensation and personal trainer, Joe Wicks. Within days of going into Lockdown the nation had taken Joe to their hearts as he posted his daily fitness and well-being tips. I did think we might see a bit of 'Joe Wicks activity' in our household but ironically Susie and Holly only started working-out to his videos at the end of Lockdown, and then they only lasted a week!

As the virus continued to sweep relentlessly through the UK, it was reported that the Prince Charles, the Prince of Wales and first heir to the throne, had tested positive for Covid-19, although he was in good spirits and only displaying mild symptoms. Up until now, Tom Hanks the American actor, had probably been the most recognisable name to have contracted the virus, so for Prince Charles to have caught Covid-19 really brought it closer to home and a realisation that the virus did not discriminate against anyone. Reports also of the tragic death of a seemingly healthy 21 year old young lady further re-enforced that young people were susceptible to the virus.

People were very quickly realising the extent to which we were now being deprived of many of the niceties of life: amongst other things golf courses and national parks were off limits; children could not go for a 'kick about' with their mates in public parks; hairdressers and beauty salons were shut; and dentists and opticians were only available for emergencies. But you could still walk the dog, exercise for up to an hour locally each day, go to your allotment, play tennis with someone from your own household and even go to your workplace if it was deemed safe to do so. So was this really Lockdown in the true sense of the word and in the manner in which it was now being stringently enforced in Italy, Spain or France?

As supermarkets continued to try in vain to keep their shelves stocked up in light of the excessive and unprecedented demand, off-licences were given the 'green light' to remain open during the pandemic as they were deemed as essential. With the closure of pubs, clubs, bars and restaurants, demand for alcohol was such that supermarkets were running out of many items so off-licences and corner shops could remain open. This was just as well, as the pandemic seemed to reignite the nation's love affair with gin and tonic!

One of the many questionable decisions by the government was to allow construction workers to continue working on building sites where it was frankly nigh on impossible for workers to maintain a safe working distance, not only on the site itself but also travelling to and from their place of work. There was still alarming footage of many of these workers still cramming into tube trains on the London Underground and other methods of public transport. I even witnessed it at the end of our road where builders were in very close proximity to each other and sharing the front seat of their white van as if the world was operating in a very normal way. Maybe this was why London in particular became the initial epicentre for the virus.

Community spirit is always something that comes to the fore in a crisis, no more so than in good old Britain. Whether it was taxi drivers taking shopping and prescribed drugs to the elderly and vulnerable free of charge, hotels opening their doors to the homeless, 'haute cuisine' chefs preparing and donating meals to children of key workers or simply doing a neighbour's shopping, there was a feeling that a large proportion of the population was 'clubbing together' and / or combining their efforts to help those in need. Indeed Susie and I had three ladies who we looked out for, including my Auntie Heather who lives a short distance away. Although these ladies were fit and well, they were in the age category that were required to stay in their homes, so of course we were only too happy to do regular deliveries of essential items, much like I am sure many others would have done. Meanwhile, the number of registered volunteers enlisted to aid the NHS with various tasks to support the vulnerable and infirm had amazingly reached half a million, and more than double the original target, but how many of these would actually end up running any errands?

As medics learned more and more about the virus there were growing concerns amongst those at the sharp end of treating patients with Covid-19 as to how unprotected and unprepared they felt. PPE was perceived as either inadequate in quality or not in great enough supply to handle the demand of new patients. Morale amongst many NHS workers was becoming very low, and this was associated with a fear and anxiety about going to work and contracting the virus, either passing the virus on to patients without knowing it or rendering them useless in fighting the cause due to having to self-isolate; at worst, their own health and that of their families was at serious risk. And it was not just in hospitals that workers were fearful, but also those in care homes who were tending to the needs of many elderly patients with other serious underlying health issues. Coupled with this the government continued to promise that frontline workers would be in line for Covid-19 tests, but these were just not forthcoming – many felt like 'sitting ducks' just waiting to be picked off by this invisible enemy!

Spain recorded its highest death toll in one day (738) and now their number of total deaths had reached 3,434, becoming the second country to overtake China's total. Another 683 deaths were recorded in Italy, taking their total number to 7,503, over 64 per cent of which were now in the Lombardy region. As France's death toll was also increasing, the virus was ripping through the heart of Central Europe leaving a trail of destruction and heartbreak behind it.

In the UK, there were now 465 reported deaths with 9,529 confirmed cases but testing was now only really being done in hospitals on those who were being admitted. There were already very worrying signs that testing kits were in short supply and there was limited testing capacity, which was one of the very essences of keeping on top of the spread of the virus.

~

TODAY'S DAILY TIP: Having a strong immune system is one of ways in which one can remain healthy and well and keep Covid-19 at bay. Therefore adding foods rich in vitamin C to one's shopping list, most notably citrus fruits such as an orange, tangerine, satsuma, clementine, mandarin, grapefruit, lemon, lime or the like, and consuming a piece of this fruit daily, will aid our fight against the virus. (PHYSICAL)

Day 3, Thursday 26th March: Clapping for our medical heroes

"The colours of the rainbow were used to signify the 'Clap for Our Carers and NHS' Thursdays"

And as the sun continued to shine, the motivation to do various little jobs around the house and garden was growing by the day. We might have just entered this unfamiliar and uncertain period of Lockdown but it was quite a novelty and mildly exciting. I made sure I got up at a reasonable time on a daily basis and making the bed first thing ensured I had a very quick and early sense of achievement. So many of those seemingly mundane chores actually created some purpose to the day; even emptying the dishwasher of items, dried by its own heat, felt therapeutic and rewarding.

Today Alex accompanied me on the daily walk with Tizzy, who by now had become very accustomed to life with the Inds. Whilst on my walk I always made a point of buying a copy of the Times newspaper at the local Shell garage in order to keep abreast of the developments in this most fast-moving of crises.

As Rishi Sunak, the Chancellor of the Exchequer, continued to insist that the Treasury would do 'whatever it takes' to see us through this crisis financially, he announced a multibillion pound package to provide support to the self-employed, similar to that which he had done a week before for employed workers, whereby they would be able to claim a maximum of £2,500 per month for the ensuing three months. Although greeted enthusiastically by many, the scheme was only intended for those who had an average annual earning of less than £50,000, meaning a proportion of those self-employed would not be entitled to it. Mr Sunak was quick to point out that not everyone in the UK would receive financial support, which of course would have caused no small amount of stress and anxiety to a number of households.

I think it is important to give the government and the Treasury some credit for the several support schemes aimed at helping many stave off financial hardship. As previously alluded to, we were probably one of very few countries that provided such a level of support, which would hopefully preserve jobs. In fact in the United States, where this support definitely did not exist, there were reports that over three million American citizens had lost their jobs in one week, severely denting the US economy and putting a serious strain on the benefit system.

Certain members of the public had their own interpretation of Boris Johnson's rules around exercise, to such an extent that they were travelling to locations well away from their own homes to run, walk or ride their bikes. Boris had insisted that only essential journeys should be made by car and that exercise should be taken locally. Going by the numbers of people that police were telling to return home, the message had either been misunderstood or ignored; I would guess that the beautiful spring weather may have had something to do with it also!

The whole essence of Lockdown is something that divided and continues to divide opinion. Those who contracted the virus and became very seriously ill as a consequence, or those who had family, relatives or friends who suffered the very grave effects of the virus, in some cases resulting in death, were imploring us strictly to follow the government's advice. On the other side of the argument were the doubters and those who saw the virus as an unnecessary inconvenience that was impacting on their lifestyles and on their future financial stability. The government's ultimate dilemma of health versus prosperity would regularly re-surface and cause hours of debate within households, my own included.

One of our abiding memories of this crisis was the Thursday 'Clap for the NHS and Our Carers', an initiative which was the brainchild of Annemarie Plas, a Dutch yoga instructor living in South London. It was meant to be a show of appreciation for the sacrifices that our NHS frontline medical staff were making in caring for Covid-19 sufferers in our hospitals. Thursday 26th March marked the very first show of unity across the nation and I must say certainly for the first couple of Thursdays that we did it as a family, it was a truly surreal yet uplifting and proud experience. I know many supplemented the circa two-minute handclap or bash of a saucepan or frying pan with the shedding of a tear or two as it proved to be quite an emotional and heart-warming occasion, shared with families and distanced neighbours alike. For me on one occasion and as I also sought the attention of others over our wall on the other side of our close, I nearly fell off of a ladder and landed myself with what could been a very unwelcome visit to A&E!

In China, there were the first signs that the spread of Covid-19 was really slowing down with only 6 reported new deaths. In fact in Wuhan there were allegedly no new cases at all. Bearing in mind the very first death in China was announced on 11th January, 2020 and it was now 26th March, we at last had some sort of an idea of what length of time we might be in official Lockdown for: any time between two and a half and three months, or between 10 and 12 weeks, or approximately 50 days!

Sadly the UK reported its highest rise in the daily death toll, reaching over 100 (115) for the first time but this was in no small part down to the change in the way that figures were being collated from the Office of National Statistics (ONS). A further 712 and 711 deaths in Italy and Spain respectively was a stark reality check that the virus was far from over in Europe.

~

TODAY'S DAILY TIP: It is important to contact and/or reconnect with friends and acquaintances in your 'phone book that you have not spoken to for a while just to say 'Hi' and to check on their wellbeing. In these very difficult times that 'phone call may just be the tonic someone needs to keep their spirits up and fend off some of that loneliness in Lockdown. (SOCIAL / EMOTIONAL)

Day 4, Friday 27th March: Injury time

"Delivering one of my Daily Tips for Lockdown"

Britain woke to another beautiful morning and Tizzy's walk was once again an invigorating one. After the daily chores were completed, it was a day of reading, soaking up the sun and good old garden 'Ashes' cricket with Alex, which was fiercely competitive to say the least.

Now I am sure that many inter-family games create a significant amount of rivalry and will to win. Our family is no different, and some that will remain nameless (Susie!), will do everything possible to push the boundaries of the rules. Holly and Alex just want to beat their Dad because they know how much pain defeat will cause. That competitive spirit was ramped up another notch when Susie and Holly joined us for a late afternoon round of 'tip and run' cricket – you each face 12 balls and if you hit the ball you have to run to the bowler's stumps at the opposite end of the garden. I batted last, having been set a target total of 13 to win. The innings started well with three runs off of two balls and then disaster struck!

I 'tickled' a short delivery onto the leg side and as it passed between Holly and Susie I had to set off for what looked like a pretty easy quick single. As I scampered towards the grass at other end and almost in slow motion, I tripped and fell head first with my right knee smashing into the paved area; the pain was excruciating, but all I could see was my beloved family absolutely roaring with laughter at my misfortune. The ultimate ignominy was that our next door neighbours, the fantastic Browns (Mikey, Izzy and their 2 fun-loving boys, Max and Harvey), had been watching the whole incident unfold over the fence and apparently as the accident occurred they slid slowly out of sight, themselves guffawing at what they had witnessed. It was the image of me allegedly jumping around the garden like a kangaroo that caused the most amount of mirth.

Needless to say, the game was abandoned as an honourable draw, family cricket ceased for the foreseeable future and 'Nurse' Susie eventually showed a bit of compassion and sympathy and bandaged up a rather sore and bruised knee that took five or six weeks to heal properly, leaving a dark scar to boot. Family cricket may have stopped but the following day even more fierce rivalries would be resumed with the Ind Family 'Games Decathlon'!

One of the bigger news stories of the day was the announcement that Prime Minister Boris Johnson had himself tested positive for Covid-19 and was showing some of the symptoms of the virus, namely the persistent cough and the high temperature, and he was now in self-isolation. On a video message update, he described himself as having 'mild symptoms' but would be continuing to run the country regardless. In a dramatic twist of irony, Matt Hancock, the Health Secretary, had developed virus symptoms a day or so before his boss had and very shortly after the Prime Minister made his announcement, Chris Witty, the Chief Medical Officer, was reported as displaying symptoms – you simply could not have written it!

If nothing else, this sudden upsurge in high-profile cases illustrated how rapidly the virus could spread if given the opportunity. With the number of close interactions with his cabinet and populous public engagements that Boris had had over the previous couple of weeks, it was almost inevitable that he would be infected at some stage. In addition, the stress of leading the country through this almost unique situation, coupled with the pressures of imminent fatherhood – his partner Carrie Simmonds, who had also displayed symptoms, was only weeks away from giving birth to their child – were bound to act as catalysts to attack his vulnerability. Those who know Boris well would probably say that his stoic nature and tenacity are a huge part his defence against sickness and ill health. That is all well and good if you have a consistent and balanced diet, take regular exercise and are getting adequate amounts of rest and sleep.

I would probably say that from 24th May, 2019, when Theresa May, Boris's predecessor, announced that she would be stepping down as Leader of the Conservative Party to 31st January, 2020, when he 'Got Brexit Done', Boris Johnson had laboured tirelessly and relentlessly without any serious downtime. He will have often worked late into the night, risen in the very early hours of the morning, snacked on junk food and exercised irregularly with his diary overloaded with appointments and meetings about many pressing and urgent matters – and then Covid-19 came along; so no wonder his body just could not withstand the pressure anymore.

That aforementioned stoicism and bravado, some might say stubbornness, to carry on regardless in the early stages of his illness rather than rest, would prove to be his downfall. Unknowingly, through his actions, Boris was to become increasingly more unwell leading him to the brink of death resulting in a rudderless nation when we needed him most.

The UK reported its highest daily rise in deaths and cases yet, increasing markedly by 191 and 2,921 respectively. Italy also experienced its highest death toll in any one day and 35 days after their first death, with 919 fatalities, bringing their total to 9,134. Of further concern to the Italian government was the fact that Lombardy's percentage of the total deaths actually dropped in two days from over 64 per cent to 59 per cent, indicating that the virus was spreading throughout other parts of the country. Elsewhere, another 713 deaths were reported in Spain and there were concerns abounding that the virus was starting to take a real grip on the USA, with Florida cited as being at the greatest risk due to its ageing and retired population.

~

TODAY'S DAILY TIP: Running up and down the stairs in one's house, if indeed one has a staircase, 10 times consecutively can really get the heart pumping and lungs working. This could be timed to monitor progress and done daily or a few times in the week. The benefits to one's health and fitness are highly tangible. (PHYSICAL)

Day 5, Saturday 28th March: Games day

And so the sun continued to shine.......... and, despite my injured knee, I had to practice what I was preaching, so I decided to undertake the stair challenge from yesterday's 'Daily Tip'. A feeble and frankly poor time of 1 minute and 54 seconds was recorded and set the benchmark for future attempts; I am pleased to report a personal best of 1 minute 27 seconds has recently been achieved and I am sure there is further room for improvement! Alex also acquainted me with a couple of his new exercise regimes, which I kept up intermittently over the ensuing weeks – for the record, I did not subscribe to Joe Wicks' daily fitness programmes, though I know it became a very important part of many people's routines.

Throughout the period of Lockdown we were very conscious as a family about making the weekends feel different to other days in the week, so we would try and plan in something that involved a bit more fun and laughter. Being our first Saturday in Lockdown, we decided on a 'Family Games Decathlon' which started mid-afternoon, interspersed with one of Susie's cracking meals, and which included games like 'Uno', 'Knockout Whist', 'Happy Families', 'Frustration', 'Logo' and 'Scattergories'.

"Susie and Tizzy getting the board games ready"

One of the many features of this period for us was the opportunity to do things that we had not done either recently or since the children were a lot younger. Unfortunately for me, those children have grown up to be smarter and cleverer than me, both of them beating me into submission; sadly there were no takers for a soothing game of 'Scrabble'! Playing these games though evoked many happy memories and reminded us that there was life before video games, mobile 'phones and other technological inventions that have taken over our lives since.

It truly was an enjoyable day, only marred by the clocks going forward ('spring' forward meant we lost an hour's sleep) and another massive rise in the death toll in the UK by 259, taking the total over the thousand mark to 1,028, which was sobering to say the least. 938 of these deaths were recorded in England alone, with numbers from Scotland, Wales and Northern Ireland, also included in the UK statistics. The deaths in Italy rose again sharply by 889 taking their total to 9,134, and in Spain, things appeared to be worsening considerably as their death toll rose by an astonishing 954 in just one day; this took their total to 5,812.

At this stage it certainly felt like we were in this situation for the long haul, so we may as well try to make the most of it and try to enjoy it as best as we possibly could – let's face it, we were being asked to spend quality time with our family, in the most beautiful weather, with a full stocked fridge and plenty of toilet rolls!

~

TODAY'S DAILY TIP: It has become increasingly important to monitor one's 'use by' dates in one's fridge to avoid unnecessary food wastage, to ensure effective stock rotation so that the perishable items we bought first are used first. Also cooked meat needs to be stored above uncooked meat, in order to avoid cross contamination that could in turn lead to food poisoning. (PHYSICAL)

Day 6, Sunday 29th March: TV addicts

And so the sun continued to shine although the wind blew a bit too.........and after the physical exertions of the previous two days and an hour's less sleep, Sunday assumed a much more restful status. The limbs were aching, the muscles were stiff and the knee was throbbing; I certainly felt my 53 years and more!

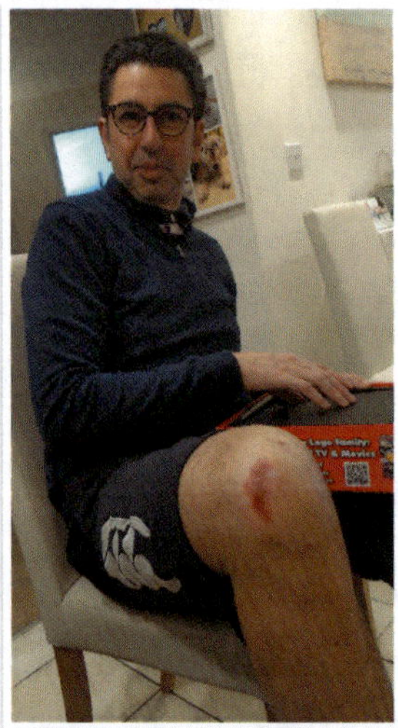

"Me nursing a bad knee from garden cricket!"

One of the many enjoyable routines that we established over the weeks of Lockdown was a long family weekend walk with little Tizzy through the Hampshire countryside. It ticked our daily exercise box and with the lovely spring weather and amazing scenery, it just re-enforced how much beauty we had on our doorstep. Bluebell Woods and the Quarry, both near Eastleigh, were our most frequent and regular haunts over the weeks.

I was very conscious during this time that I was not consumed watching repeats and re-runs on the television. Having Sky TV gives one access to so many different programmes and box sets, that one could just endlessly watch one episode of something after another. I was though mindful of a void that needed filling, particularly with no live sport – Alex and I would often spend our Sundays watching Football, Cricket or Golf.

Some of the most addictive entertainment that I have watched in the past, was Jed Mercurio's fictional 'Line of Duty', a gripping, fast-moving and incredibly dramatic series about corruption in the police force. Thus far, there have been five series in total, all with subtle sub-plots to try to uncover who is at the heart of the corruption. Though often surreal, and if one likes this sort of thing, it is a 'must-see' TV. Before we knew it, we had downloaded all five series and we embarked on a marathon binge-watching, viewing one episode after another – the irony was that we had watched all the episodes before!

On the virus front, we were starting to hear the first 'informal' advice in Britain from some scientists about the potential benefit to the public of wearing face coverings that could slow the spread of Covid-19, though the WHO still were not recommending the practice themselves. Later in the week Chief Medical Officer Chris Witty himself was actually quoted as saying: 'Wearing a mask if you don't have an infection reduces the risk almost not at all. So we do not advise that'. Of course in Asia, face masks have been commonplace for many years as means initially of countering the impact of the SARS epidemic. It is very interesting to note that they became a legal requirement in shops and shopping precincts in England on 24th July; this was to be one of Boris Johnson's many 'u-turns' during the crisis.

In light another high rise in the daily death toll in the UK, an increase of 207 to a total of 1,235, the government were now very concerned that there would a significant increase in deaths and infections over the ensuing couple of weeks. Sir Patrick Vallance, the UK's Chief Scientific Advisor, had stated on 17th March that 20,000 deaths or less would represent 'a good outcome', although these latest concerns created a degree of doubt around Sir Patrick's forecast.

Despite these warnings to the public, there were still many congregating in mass gatherings and enjoying the good weather, blatantly disregarding the government's social distancing rules, though a vast majority were not only becoming more compliant but also more fearful of what was ahead. The police were mindful of the need to offer up a 'softly, softly' approach to those flouting the rules, with fines held back as the last resort. I must say they must have been pretty chuffed at the closure of pubs, bars, and clubs and not having the habitual challenges that excessive drinking brought to some of the towns and cities of

Britain, particularly over the weekends. Sadly though there would be an increase in crime related to the impositions of the virus, most worryingly and notably, in serious domestic abuse.

Italy's death toll rose with another significant daily increase of 756, taking their total to 10,779, whilst Spain increased by another 716 to 6,528. As we were about to go into our second week of Lockdown, the country was bracing itself for what was going to be another dramatic week.

~

TODAY'S DAILY TIP: When a new week is on the horizon, take the time on a Sunday to plan what one is going to do each day. Tasks should be achievable and one should hold oneself accountable for getting what has been planned in, accomplished; the sense of achievement is very rewarding. (MENTAL)

Day 7, Monday 30th March: Media madness

"Alex with his new little sister, Tizzy"

And the sun continued to shine..........and Susie came off of Furlough for a couple of weeks to go back to working in her school, catering for the needs of children of key workers. Having Susie back at work meant I reverted to the early morning walk with Tizzy, establishing an even better routine to my week. Holly continued to work from home and Alex was revising hard for his end of year exam that was to take place on Friday.

My early weekday daily routine involved making the morning tea and putting the dog out, and I would then go around the house wiping every door handle and light switch with cleansing wipes in a somewhat paranoid manner, on the assumption that the virus may have somehow found its way into the house. So little was really known at this stage about how Covid-19 would impact everyone, though the newspaper and TV media was painting such a depressing picture, that it would lead you to believe that you were going to contract the virus, even in the enclosed confines of your own home. I was one of many in the nation who tuned into some of the lively debate and broadcasting on ITV's 'Good Morning Britain', who's presenters regularly divided opinion.

I believe the media have a responsibility to report any newsworthy story in the public interest with a degree of accuracy and a level of objectivity, whilst at the same time making it interesting and colourful enough to sell newspapers or generate enough viewers and listeners. I cannot help feeling that the overall reporting of this crisis was at times and from some sources, too subjective and negative, with the sole objective of apportioning blame, at every opportunity, to Boris Johnson and his government.

I continue to be critical of Boris and his team, for the delays and changes in and integrity of much of the decision making and their lack of preparedness, which could have prevented many deaths. This was brought about in some cases by the inexperience and naivety of a very new government led by someone not famed for his passion for detail, but I would say that this has been an unprecedented crisis that any government would have had challenges dealing with and hindsight is always a wonderful thing; I certainly do not think those in opposition, under the outgoing Jeremy Corbyn, would have necessarily been any better equipped but they may have done things a tad quicker.

But I do believe the press could have been a bit more supportive and less acerbic in their approach, and they often misplaced some of the nation's desire to see ministers and officials challenged about their actions by egoist journalists, and that it was more optimism, positivity and objectivity that was sought. The impact of the media on the mental well-being of many people could have been seriously underestimated.

One person that did demand much media interest was the Prime Minister's senior advisor, Dominic Cummings, who was the latest key individual to develop symptoms of the virus at such a critical time in the crisis. Weeks later he would be scrutinised for his own actions relating to poor decision-making that would severely compromise his reputation and the government's popularity.

Testing continued to be one of the government's main actions to try to control the spread of the virus, but with a global shortage of the kits and a lack of capacity, test laboratories were only really able to focus their efforts on the 9,000 patients, that were at that time, in hospital. Along with the lack of PPE and notably masks and gowns, front line medical staff were getting more and more concerned that they were not themselves able to be tested, leaving some of them woefully exposed to catching the virus. Meanwhile, Germany was reportedly testing a whopping 70,000+ people per day compared to meagre 8,278 in the UK, and I do not think there is any coincidence that their number of cases and deaths remained quite low throughout the crisis.

Another concern that was slowly 'rearing its head' was that, despite much of the airline industry being in shutdown, there were still many flights coming into the UK from parts of the world that were riddled with the virus. To make matters worse, there were no regulations around enforcing quarantine once passengers had arrived back in the UK; the only mild stipulation was that you isolated for two weeks if you were showing symptoms but this was not mandatory. With many of the infections, particularly in those of a more youthful disposition, being asymptomatic (i.e symptomless), this was a rather large loophole.

Several airlines were still being deployed to repatriate the 300,000 or so Britons that remained stranded in foreign parts. Dominic Raab, the Foreign Secretary, was preoccupied in round-the-clock discussions between airlines and the various embassies to try to negotiate for as many as possible to return home, but it was no easy task. Mr Raab would assume an even greater level of exposure and scrutiny at the end of the week, as his boss became increasingly more unwell.

Deaths in the UK strangely showed a lower increase than in previous days, rising by 180 to a total of 1,415. A few weeks later however, it was revealed that the statistics on a Monday would be lower than other days in the week due to the delay in gaining data because of the weekend lag. Italy had its lowest rise in new cases for several days, with just over 4,000 reported. The death toll was still alarmingly high at 812 - the same bizarrely as it was in Spain – and a total number of 11,591 in Italy, the highest in the world at the time.

Meanwhile across the Atlantic, President Trump stated that keeping their death toll at around 100,000, would represent a 'good job' done. As it stood, 2,817 deaths had been reported in the USA, a country with just over 328 million inhabitants, and the third most populous country in the world. Alarmingly though for Mr Trump, the US reported the highest number of new daily cases for any country in the world at 12,255. His leadership of America throughout the crisis would severely come into question as cases and deaths alike increased exponentially over the ensuing weeks and months.

~

TODAY'S DAILY TIP: With less opportunities for extensive exercise, one of the challenges in Lockdown has been how to do 10,000 steps per day. With the permissible exercise, it is possible to do at least 5,000 steps; to make up the other 5,000, it is therefore advisable to plan through the day what steps you can do when whether it is pottering around the house first thing in the morning, running up and down the stairs, exercising in the garden or through some other innovative method. (PHYSICAL)

Day 8, Tuesday 31st March: Toilet humour

And the sun continued to shine............and despite this, I embarked on what used to be a very popular pastime for me in my youth, a jigsaw puzzle. Having quite a detailed mind, doing jigsaws always came quite easy to me and the more I did them, the harder the better. This particular one was a colourful image of good old London Town consisting of 1,000 pieces, and rated quite low in the difficulty stakes. It was amusing to see that many suppliers of jigsaw puzzles were suddenly doubling or even trebling their weekly sales, as the nation attempted to fill their days with new or rediscovered hobbies.

"Toilet rolls in short supply"

The panic-buying in supermarkets seemed to be subsiding somewhat though stocks of toilet rolls were still in very short supply. In fact I got to a point in time, very worryingly some will say, when I actually started to monitor our toilet roll usage! What we had around the house in terms of whole toilet rolls would be my 'opening stock'; any new toilet rolls added after a weekly shop, would be my 'purchases'; and usually at the end of a fortnight, I would conduct a stocktake which would constitute my 'closing stock'. For anyone involved recording usage, they would know the formula:

Opening Stock + Purchases – Closing Stock = Consumption (Usage)

Thus I was able to work out exactly how many toilet rolls we were using in the household on a weekly basis, which worked out to be five and a half across four people. Imagine if the nation had adopted this method, how much less abuse supermarket workers would have been subjected to and how much less stress supermarket managers would have had to endure concerned about the provision of toilet rolls in the country!

Boris Johnson's cabinet convened for the first time digitally via an initial saviour of a limited business world, Zoom. Zoom, a web-based video conferencing tool that allows users to meet online with or without video, was actually founded in 2011 by a certain Eric Yuan; little would he have known then how valuable this form of communication would become nearly 10 years later, not just in business but also for leisure activities such as virtual pub and family quizzes.

Boris, who was by now starting to look and sound pretty rough, told his cabinet that things were going to get worse before they got better; for some, they had already: we were not testing enough people, a 13-year-old male had tragically become the youngest victim of the crisis thus far, many medics were contracting the virus and being 'threatened with the sack if they spoke about the shortages of PPE', the first deaths were recorded in care homes, police forces were struggling with the enforcement of the new rules on Lockdown, and there were still many Britons still stranded overseas some with no tangible hope at this stage of getting home – and to top it all, Llandudno in North Wales was overrun by a herd of Kashmiri goats!

On a brighter note: less people around the UK were using the roads and rail, the NHS Nightingale Hospital at the Excel exhibition centre had been completed amazingly in just over a week, good progress was being made on the vaccine front, the British public was finding innovative ways to entertain themselves and posting their 'work' on Facebook, and Prince Charles had successfully come through his period of isolation, unscathed – things were not quite so bad after all!

There was a thought amongst scientists that many people may well have contracted the virus already, thus potentially building up a level of immunity. In fact I have since spoken to several people who believed they were unwell for lengthy periods of time with the supposed main Covid-19 symptoms, as far back as December 2019. As we all know, winter brings about any number of viruses and illnesses, but it is somewhat thought-provoking that just maybe, Covid-19 was around in the UK earlier than February 2020.

The UK experienced a very dramatic rise in the daily death toll of 393, the highest increase yet, bringing the total to 1,808, and notwithstanding the extra deaths from the weekend lag. Italy was still in a desperate position with a further 837 deaths bringing their total to 12,428, whilst Spain's situation continued to worsen with a further 929 deaths and a total of 8,269. Nearly another 500 deaths in France, and a total of 3,523, gave every indication that Central Europe was firmly in the grip of the virus, although Germany's apparent preparedness and testing prowess was evidenced by only 682 deaths for the duration of the pandemic, thus far.

~

TODAY'S DAILY TIP: It is important in difficult times to find methods of relaxation that help relieve anxiety and stress levels. One of the best things one can do is focus on breathing exercises and one in particular that is proven to be very effective, is the 4-7-8 technique: breathe in for four seconds, hold one's breath for seven seconds and exhale for eight seconds, and see the difference. This can be done first thing in the morning when you awaken or just before you go to sleep at night. (PHYSICAL)

Day 9, Wednesday 1st April: Trouble with testing and paltry PPE

"Alex just loved his garden cricket against his Dad"

And the sun continued to shine......... and I was half expecting a raft of April Fool's Day pranks from someone in the family, but Susie, Holly and Alex were all so predisposed with their various roles and challenges that I actually got away scot-free. It ended up being a pretty routine day but with much of the afternoon taken up with a lengthy spell of competitive garden 'Ashes' cricket with Alex.

Having a rather enclosed garden meant that there was a great tendency inadvertently to 'smash' the tennis ball over the garden wall, as a batsman or bounce the ball over the fence into our neighbours' garden, as a bowler, but both came with penalties either with the loss of a ball or a loss of a wicket. I think we must have irritated the life out of the Browns, who were at the time doing a mixture of working from home and home schooling; little Harvey in particular was persistently on lookout for a bright green ball flying viciously into their back garden.

Britain loves its summer of sport each year. Annual events in tennis, cricket, golf and motor racing amongst other sports, fill the sporting calendar. Every four years, but not always in the same year, we are entertained by football tournaments and the pinnacle of all sporting events, the Olympic Games.

With gatherings of large amounts of people now very much off the agenda, sport was going to experience an unprecedented level of postponements and some cancellations. The first main 'casualty' was the Wimbledon tennis championships, which was first played in 1877 and due to take place during June and early July. It was cancelled for the first time since the Second World War between 1940 and

1945 and the first time during traditional peacetime. The much-loved Edinburgh Festival Fringe, due to take place in August, was also shelved on this day. The European Football Championships due also to take place during June and July, had already been postponed until 2021, and most disappointingly of all, so had the Olympics Games themselves – both the latter events had been re-scheduled for 2021 which at least gave some hope to many frustrated athletes.

Boris Johnson was now taking more of a hands-on involvement in speeding up testing and he deployed the support of many private laboratories to assist those in our hospitals. Testing kits continued to be in very short supply and capacity for testing was nowhere near where it needed to be.

One of the more futile sights that we observed during this crisis was that of empty testing sites, specifically set aside to enable the government to reach their ambitious targets. As Boris and his government really started to focus its efforts on getting more NHS frontline staff tested, large sites were created at relatively short notice. Unfortunately there were locations, such as the car park at the Chessington World of Adventures, which were 'by appointment only', which were almost deserted because people had not booked in advance or because they were just impractically too far away or too difficult to travel to; on the other hand, there was the Ikea Wembley's car park, which was completely inundated but some people were being turned away because their car number plates had not been recorded on the official list of authorised cars or other vehicles.

A lot of very good work had been done to set up these sites quickly but maybe a little bit more forethought could have gone into the practicalities and logistics. The policy and objective had been laid out but the execution was haphazard and in some cases chaotic, much like the logistical saga of getting PPE to hospitals and care homes. When introducing new systems and processes into any walk of life, I think it is so important to have regular and ongoing review mechanisms. Something I learnt in the business world was to 'Plan, Do & Review' endlessly to ensure an effective outcome and that those tasked to do the roles actually followed them through. If the government did have such methods in place it did not overtly seem apparent.

The demand for PPE was increasing by the day and there were continuing signs of discontent, not just amongst hospital employees, but also from those working in care homes. There was a general feeling that the NHS hospitals were being prioritised over care homes, and also where care homes are predominantly in the private sector, they were having to purchase their PPE at great expense; it was also thought that some suppliers were allegedly profiteering by increasing their prices, although these allegations were refuted.

A question that I saw posed several times during the pandemic was whether or not we would see a reduction in infections of Covid-19 in warmer weather. It is probably true to say that most seasonal flus and other viruses tend to be more prevalent in the autumn and winter months, with slow improvements to our nation's health beginning in springtime. Historically it would appear that we suffer our least ill-health during the summer months.

Scientists in China have studied virus trends in line with changes in temperature, both up and down, and their measurement criteria is based around something called the 'reproduction number' or 'R', which we became very familiar with as scientists were looking at ways of easing Lockdown. It is fundamentally interpreted as the number of new infections that are brought about from each previous one – in simple terms, if one person gets the virus how many more will become infected consequentially.

Going into Lockdown, the 'R' was probably between 2.4 and 4 in the UK, and the objective would be to reduce this to below 1. Each person then only passes on the infection to less than one other person, thus and in theory eliminating the epidemic almost completely. The essence of Lockdown was to reduce contact between people through social distancing and that would reduce the 'R' – and to be fair to the scientists, this is exactly what did happen. As to whether the virus reduces or even mutates to a milder form in the warmer months, this maybe the case because more people are outside and less in confined spaces, but this was more guesswork by scientists at this stage.

Despite the short-term financial support for many in the country there were increasing concerns about the long-term impact of Lockdown on the state of the economy. There was no doubt that there would be a significant number of job losses that in turn could very probably lead to more mental health problems and anxiety, particularly amongst the younger generations. It was bad enough for so many students to miss out on their graduation ceremonies, but difficulties gaining employment could be disappointment on a whole different level. The former Governor of the Bank of England, Lord King of Lothbury, stated that a prolonging of this situation could also 'trigger a rebellion' and serious public disorder. That disorder did of course come to our streets but caused by the events in America, with the killing of George Floyd resulting in the Black Lives Matter protests.

Prince Charles spoke to the nation to try and lift our spirits, after suffering mild symptoms of the virus himself. Although still not quite 100 per cent, he claimed that he was 'on the other side of the illness, but still in no less state of social distance and general isolation'. There was a real sense of a depth of feeling and empathy for the British public from the Prince in this crisis, not just because of people's loneliness or suffering of the illness, but also very much because of the loss of loved ones.

There were also rumours abounding that the Queen, herself, would be speaking direct to the nation, something that is extremely rare. Whatever anyone thinks of the Royal Family it is a very important and respected institution across the world that gives us a very necessary form of stability, and in Queen Elizabeth II, we have a real 'rock' for a monarch.

There was a further and very shocking rise in the number of deaths in the UK with a record increase of 563 in one day and a total now of 2,352. Boris Johnson was now being criticised by President Trump for the way in which the crisis had been handled in the initial stages, describing it as 'catastrophic', this despite the death toll in New York alone rising to 1,096, nearly a quarter of their total deaths. I think many Americans would severely criticise Mr Trump for the way in which he handled their crisis throughout, lurching from one bizarre change in policy and direction to another. His revision upwards of what he hoped the death toll might be kept to, from 100,000 to 240,000, was simply mind-blowing and evidence that his leadership had some serious misgivings.

Italy actually experienced a slight drop in deaths of 727, against the previous day's number of 837, but it still brought their total to a depressing 13,155. Health Secretary, Giulio Gallera, did however claim that, 'we are beginning to see a small light at the end of the tunnel'. In Spain, however, it was the fifth day consecutively that the daily death toll was above 800, at 864, taking their total to 9,053, although admissions to ICU's and hospitalisations had started to decrease. Nations across Europe were rallying round each other particularly in the provision of PPE, but was the UK now missing out on life-saving equipment because of its decision to leave the EU?

~

TODAY'S DAILY TIP: Post Covid-19, things may never be normal again but at least there will be things to look forward to, therefore it is important to write three or four things that one may want to do once we come out of Lockdown and when things that are shut re-open up again. Having something to look forward to really does enrich the soul. (SPIRITUAL)

Day 10, Thursday 2nd April: Welcome to Zoom

And the sun continued to shine..........and it was the second 'Clap for the NHS and Our Carers' Thursday. After another routine day of dog-walking, chores and garden cricket, we poured ourselves a nice gin and tonic and set about doing our first family Zoom call with the family in Bournemouth.

"Susie in her own version of PPE"

Luckily for Susie and I, Holly and Alex had already experienced Zoom and managed to navigate us through the challenges of Zoom connection, resulting in a really great catch-up call with the Bournemouth 'crew' (Mark and Joy, Craig and Sener, and Lisa and Kian), and some lovely chat remembering little Amelia. It was almost surreal seeing four groups of people in different locations all on the same screen, and a nice fore taster for us then to clap our hands in appreciation of what our frontline NHS and carers were doing for the country.

There were many heart-warming aspects of how our NHS have handled this crisis, one of these being how medics put aside their normal spheres of influence to care for patients in the ICUs. Where routine operations had been put on hold, many specialist surgeons who would normally deal with other aspects of medical care were now supporting the Covid-19 effort, having been retrained in procedures such as operating ventilators. This was in addition to over 4,500 retired doctors and nurses who had already come out of retirement to plug some of the staffing shortages, some literally putting their lives on the line.

Matt Hancock, the Health Secretary, returned for his first day of work since his seven day isolation ended after contracting Covid-19 the week before. After a barrage of criticism about the lack of testing, he was now promising that

100,000 tests would be carried out per day, by the end of April, via his 'five pillar' plan. This was an incredibly ambitious target considering that barely 10,000 tests were being carried out at present, and superseded his original end of month target of 25,000 tests per day. It was quite a first day back for Mr Hancock as he also took the opportunity to write off NHS trusts' historical debt of a staggering £13.4 billion, allowing hospitals to focus on dealing with the pandemic. And as Mr Hancock displayed his own version of things happening in 'threes', he proceeded to demand that Premier League players take a pay cut and make contributions to the fight against Covid-19; this of course 'went down like a lead balloon'!

Mr Hancock's boss however was still suffering from a persistent cough and fever symptoms, and although he was seen at the entrance of 10 Downing Street, clapping enthusiastically for our frontline medical staff, he did look decidedly 'under the weather'; things would go dramatically downhill over the next 48 hours.

We were now two weeks on from the Cheltenham Festival that ended on Friday 13th March and with the incubation period for the virus being 14 days, a number of attendees of the Festival were reporting Covid-19 symptoms. The government had allowed the National Hunt meeting to go ahead despite criticism that such a large gathering might spread infections and increase the 'R'. When challenged, the organisers of the event, the Jockey Club, defended their decision and claimed that they 'went ahead under government advice'. The government's answer to this and any criticism that came their way about their handling of the pandemic, was the stock reply that they were 'guided by the science'; this was an irksome response (true or not) so often used and possibly aimed at absolving themselves from any blame for any situation maybe for fear of legal action against them.

Strangely flights were still coming into the UK from countries seriously affected by the virus. Travellers arrived into Heathrow from both Rome and Madrid, but there were no rules on quarantine for these individuals on flights and our borders remained open as the government believed there was no evidence that by closing them it would control the spread of the virus. Further down the line, and in another bizarre and seemingly belated 'u-turn', similar to that of face masks, the Home Secretary, Priti Patel, announced on May 22nd that anyone arriving new into the UK from June 8th onwards, would have to self-isolate for two weeks – why we waited nearly two months for this announcement and a further 2 weeks afterwards to get the point of enforcing this rule, I still cannot quite fathom, especially when changes in policy more recently had been enforced with barely 12 hours' notice ?

Another record daily rise of 569 Covid-19 deaths, taking the total to 2,921, was reported in the UK, which included the comedian, Eddie Large, part of the comedy double-act with Sid Little in the 1970's and 1980's, 'Little and Large'. Mr Large, born Edward McGinnis, had been unwell for a while and had suffered with heart problems over the years, resulting in a heart transplant. He had tested positive for Covid-19, and having the virus probably accelerated his death, much like many of those with underlying health conditions who so sadly died after being infected. The question is often asked as to whether someone who died after testing positive died solely of Covid-19 or actually died prematurely of the illness that they already had because the virus took over their immune system. Either way, each and every death was a tragic loss to family, friends and acquaintances alike.

Spain reported the highest ever daily rise in deaths for any country globally, with a staggering increase of 950 in one day, bringing their total to a sombre milestone of 10,003 and the world's second-highest death toll, despite a slowing infection rate. Italy had a further 760 deaths from the previous 24 hours, and their total now stood at 13,915.

As the situation worsened in the USA, particularly in New York with grave concerns over a lack of ventilators, unprecedented job losses and a growing death toll, China was showing the first signs of an easing of Lockdown. Travel restrictions were being lifted between provinces, with Hubei, the alleged original source of the pandemic, being most closely monitored for signs of a second wave of the virus. Any so-called second wave and subsequent Lockdowns would likely be regionalised and would give us in the UK a further idea of what the post-Covid-19 era might look like here.

~

TODAY'S DAILY TIP: Creating new habits and maintaining ones already in place, are the cornerstone for a healthy and fulfilling life all round. If these daily tips can help establish better routines, then I feel they will have been worthwhile not just for the period of Lockdown but hopefully longer term. (SPIRITUAL)

Day 11, Friday 3rd April: Long live our noble Queen!

And the sun continued to shine……………and it was a big day for Alex as he sat his end-of-year examination on-line; a pass would pretty much see him through to the second year of his physiotherapy degree at Winchester University. Alex's studies had been somewhat hindered by his incapacitation and subsequent laboured recovery last summer, but he was certainly very much back in synch with the course and wanting to continue his studies wholeheartedly in something that he had so much empathy for.

At 9.55am Alex shut his bedroom door as he embarked on his 45 minute exam. It should have been longer and indeed was intended to be a practical exam. So much of physiotherapy is about practice on the patient, but with the restrictions on physical attendance in place his bedroom had to do. I sat anxiously downstairs, knowing how hard he had studied and how important the next 45 minutes were and when he appeared post-exam you could sense it had gone well and the relief was tangible. It was now a waiting game for his results which he would get at the beginning of May.

During the course of Lockdown Zoom quiz nights became a very popular way in which many friends and families alike could reconnect virtually whilst simultaneously improving their level of general knowledge. That evening we embarked our first Zoom quiz night aiding Holly and her friends in what became a regular Friday night occurrence. Alex and I also took the opportunity to order takeaway food from one of our local public houses, the Otter in Otterbourne.

Many hospitality businesses were forced to close their doors and furlough their staff during the pandemic, but the Otter repositioned their business to do takeaway traditional pub food and real ale in two pint cartons, all at very reasonable prices. In essence, you phoned through your order during the afternoon and you were given a very specific time to turn up to collect your order. We did this for seven consecutive Fridays and not only was it brilliantly executed from a logistical perspective each week, but it was some of the best fish and chips that I have had in a long time. Huge credit must go to Dave, Pauline and Nick, as they remained busy throughout serving our local community, and put themselves in a great position for when Lockdown was eased.

Amid calls for Boris Johnson to present a clear strategy for exiting the Lockdown, the announcement many had been waiting for was finally made – the Queen was going to address the nation on Sunday 5th April at 8pm with a special recorded address. Apart from her annual 3pm Christmas Day speech the Queen simply did not make a habit of talking to the British public unless it was in unprecedented circumstances. There were five occasions when this occurred, the most notable being when she attempted to heal the fractious relationship between the people and monarchy following the shocking death of Diana, Princess of Wales in 1997.

"G&T to toast our monarch, anyone?"

The wave of hysteria and emotion that swept the UK, in fact the whole world, in the immediate aftermath of Diana's death, completely took the Royal Family by surprise. The emotion quickly turned to anger as it was widely perceived that the Queen had not displayed the required level of sensitivity to the situation and that her lack of a public and sympathetic reaction was heartless. Her decision to speak to the nation on 5th September, 1997, on the eve of Diana's funeral, was both well-timed and necessary. Without doubt, her emotional address went a long way to healing the rift with the public and it was delivered faultlessly with emphasis on her utmost respect for what Diana had done during her life; arguably it was a watershed moment that ensured her popularity would prevail for many years to come. Sunday's imminent address was therefore now very eagerly anticipated.

There was now a very distinct possibility that we were heading for an even deeper recession than was seen in the 2008 financial crisis or the Great Depression of the 1930's. Our famed service industry, that includes retail, entertainment and hospitality and which the UK economy is so heavily reliant on, was on its knees and only heading one way despite Rishi Sunak's, the Chancellor of the Exchequer, positive interventions. These industries rely so heavily on social and face-to-face interactions and also provide many of the reasons why life can be so enjoyable for so many. With an ever deepening economic crisis comes further risk of greater job losses with the younger and lower-paid workers having the greatest concerns. There were already, for example, worrying tales of theatre workers and thespians not only having their main source of income taken away from them but also the opportunities to earn secondary income in bars and restaurants had now disappeared.

Some of the anxiety that people were experiencing in Lockdown was manifesting itself in some rather strange and surreal night time dreams. According to experts in sleep science, if you are anxious and stressed this can bring about more vivid and emotive thoughts that in turn can produce these anxiety dreams, particularly where some people may have been in bed longer due to not having to get up for work. Although my Lockdown experience was a very good one, I was not immune from the odd strange and anxious dream myself, a couple of which meant I woke up in a cold sweat feeling quite emotional.

The debate around whether we should wear facemasks continued to rage on but consistent with Chris Whitty's thoughts earlier in the week, Jonathan Van Tam, the Deputy Chief Medical Officer stated, 'there is no evidence that general wearing of facemasks by the public who are well affects the spread of the disease in our society'. And still the WHO was not recommending it as common practice for healthy people despite it being cultural in South East Asia for so long.

As we approached the end of the second week of Lockdown the reality of this situation that we found ourselves in was starting to kick in. That said and despite the restrictions, many people were spending more time with their families, embracing traditional hobbies such as gardening, baking and reading, clearing out cupboards and attics as part of mass de-cluttering missions, sharing their exercise and dance routines on social media and enjoying a much less polluted atmosphere, aided by some quite amazing weather.

Conversely one should never forget that there were many others grieving the loss of or worrying endlessly about the health of loved ones, as well as those that did not possess the open and private space of a garden, those that were alone without the company of family and friends or those that were stuck in high-rise apartment blocks or tenements with young children or sick relatives. The question was, how long would the British public remain tolerant of this situation particularly where we were starting to hear rumblings of discontent amongst Italians, Spanish and French, albeit with their much stricter regimes?

Over in the USA, over a quarter of their 6,786 Covid-19 fatalities were now from New York City alone. Things were so desperate that many refrigerated trucks were being parked up on pavements outside hospitals and being utilised as makeshift mortuaries. Medical staff were at breaking point at the constant influx of new patients and the images of those dying alone without their loved ones. 'You can't help but cry.......', Dr Craig Spencer, an infectious disease specialist at Manhattan hospital, said of having to turn off a patient's ventilator whilst thinking about a broken family back at home and himself sobbing in grief.

42 days after their first death was reported, Italy's death toll stood as the highest of any country worldwide, at a shocking 14,681, after a further 766 were recorded from the previous day. Another terrible daily rise of 932 deaths in Spain

brought their total number of deaths to 10,935; the USA was now the country with the third highest death toll and their rate was rising as sharply as any country each day. The UK's situation was certainly worsening by the day with another very concerning daily rise in deaths of 684 bringing the total to 3,605, the fifth worst hit country, and at this stage we were still a long way off of the peak.

~

TODAY'S DAILY TIP: As much as our mobile 'phones are incredibly valuable for communication purposes and great sources of information, there may be a tendency to be on them too long at the expense of doing something more useful or productive and even our mental health, with information overload. Therefore restrict the time on one's 'phone and take time out to live a fuller life by finding other things to do that take away the need constantly to use a 'phone. (MENTAL)

Day 12, Saturday 4th April: An evening at the races

And the sun continued to shine..........and the weekend was once again upon us. After a lovely morning walk to the Quarry and around Bluebell Woods with the family, I afforded myself one of life's luxuries for my breakfast – two slices of 'eggy' bread, two rashers of well-done bacon, baked beans accompanied by lashings of HP Sauce!

"One of the many breakfasts I cooked for Holly and Alex in Lockdow"

'Eggy' bread for me has endearing qualities and was one of those things that I used to consume quite regularly in my youth, in fact it was something quite synonymous with my boarding-school breakfasts. As diet and healthy eating have become more important in later life, my staple breakfast has moved away from 'eggy' bread and more recently has mainly consisted of poached eggs, mushrooms and baked beans on toast, Weetabix, a banana and a glass of cranberry juice, usually preceded by a cod liver oil capsule. Maybe there is no coincidence that thus far (fingers crossed) I have been blessed with reasonably good health.

It seemed that I had taken on the mantle of breakfast chef during the Lockdown period and I regularly cooked breakfast for Holly and Alex. Holly being more a consumer of poached eggs and Alex of scrambled eggs. Unfortunately eggs were one of the products that were becoming scarcer in our shops and supermarkets as demand grew in Lockdown due to changing eating habits and baking!

The Grand National is jumps racing's most popular and well-known race in the annual horseracing calendar. Many across the country partake in office sweepstakes or venture furtively into betting shops for their once-a-year 'flutter' on the horse they like the name of most or the jockeys' colours they favour most. Unfortunately for those people, this year's race was not to be run, or at least the usual format. Instead The Virtual Grand National, a computer simulated race created by a company called Inspired, played out at 5.15pm, on the date and at the time the actual race should have taken place. This was the fourth consecutive year that the race, won by Potters Corner, has been run in this format, but it took on extra special significance where Aintree was cancelled and attracted a television audience of nearly 5 million viewers.

Another family games night was planned for the evening preceded by one of Susie's outstanding culinary creations, her paella. Because our two offspring are non-seafood eaters, the prawns and mussels are prepared and added separately but her base of rice, chicken and chorizo sausage is as good as any paella that one might consume in Spain. It tasted even better washed down with a nice glass of Rioja. Many others also used Lockdown as an opportunity to experiment in the kitchen, but I must admit I have been blessed in my near 28 years of marriage with one of the most gifted cooks one could wish for, meaning that not only have I not had to develop my own culinary expertise, but also I have been fed like a king!

There was a significant change in the political landscape of the UK with the election of Sir Keir Stammer as the new leader of the Labour Party, replacing the much-maligned Jeremy Corbyn. Sir Keir, a defence lawyer specialising in human rights issues, received his knighthood in the 2014 New Year Honours, for 'services to law and criminal justice', though he prefers that people do not use his title. With his acclaimed legal background there was no doubt that he would provide robust opposition to the government but initially, and with the ongoing pandemic crisis, he stressed, 'I want to be very clear that I'm going to engage constructively'. In other words he wanted to be supportive to the government where possible, but how long that would last was open to question.

There were signs in Italy that they had reached or nearly reached their peak as the death toll increased by 681, their lowest daily growth for 10 days, but the total reached another depressing milestone surpassing the 15,000 mark. Spain was now reportedly the country in Europe with the highest number of Covid-19 cases at over 130,000 and their daily death toll rose by a further 809 with a total of 11,744. The UK's death toll rose dramatically again to 708 and a total of 4,313, and we were going to be rocked by a shock announcement the following evening.

~

TODAY'S DAILY TIP: Eggs, as referred to previously in this chapter, are a great source of high-quality protein rich in vitamins and minerals. What also makes them attractive as a super food is that they can be cooked and consumed in so many different ways: fried, scrambled, poached, boiled, as an omelette or part of a Scotch egg, eat eggs regularly as part of a balanced diet. (PHYSICAL)

Day 13, Sunday 5th April (Palm Sunday): A tale of two leaders

And the sun continued to shine................and out came the barbecue for the first time this year. This was one of many occasions during this period of restrictions that we had to remind ourselves why we were in Lockdown. Even though our Prime Minister had asked us to remain in our homes, it seemed so wrong that we should be enjoying ourselves safely in the bosom of our nearest and dearest, and blessed with some of most pleasant weather that we had seen consistently so far this year. Meanwhile our hospitals were being overrun with many very sick patients, some of whom might not make it through the next 24 hours; it was the classic paradox!

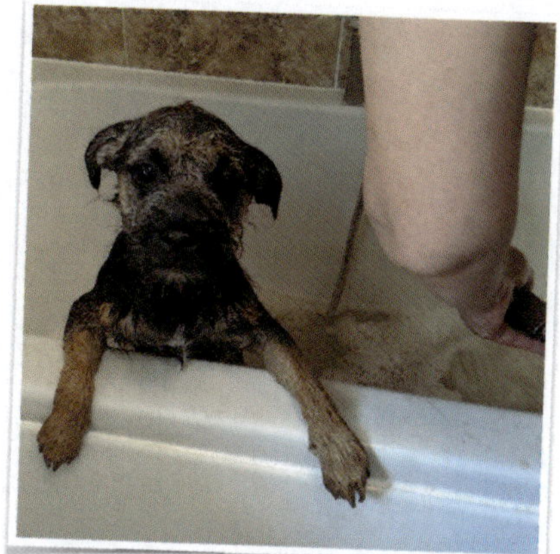

"'Oblivious to what was going on in the world, Tizzy was taking a bath"

But the drama of the day surrounded the country's two leading figureheads and one of Scotland's most public faces: Dr Catherine Calderwood, Scotland's Chief Medical Officer, naively flouted the 'STAY AT HOME' rules that she had been preaching about to the Scottish people, by visiting her second home for the second time in Lockdown, some 44 miles away from her main dwelling in Edinburgh. It resulted in her being removed from the public campaign in Scotland where she was presiding over the daily Covid-19 briefings to journalists and taking part in the various public health broadcasts. Although she offered an 'unreserved apology', the damage to her reputation and integrity was already done and it proved a great source of embarrassment to Nicola Sturgeon, Scotland's First Minister; after lengthy discussions during the evening between the two of them, Dr Calderwood stepped down from her role altogether.

At a similar time to Dr Calderwood's resignation came the second dramatic event of the day as the Queen, at 93 years of age, addressed the nation from the drawing room at Windsor Castle, urging 24 million of us, and even 2.4 million in France who tuned in, to lift our spirits whilst in isolation and in 'an increasingly challenging time', and remain 'united and resolute'. As she paid tribute to NHS frontline and care workers alike and thanked us for staying at home, she reassured us that '....better days will return' and when it came to seeing our loved ones, families and friends again she used those famously emotive words from the Dame Vera Lynn song from the Second World War: 'We will meet again'. Poignantly Dame Vera celebrated her 103rd birthday on 20th March this year, just prior to Lockdown, and died on 18th June, as Lockdown was being eased.

Many considered this to be one of the Queen's greatest speeches of her 68 years on the throne. Not only was her delivery perfect but the words were her own and they were very personal. The timing of her four-minute address was debated rigorously but it was thought that with the death toll continuing to rise exponentially, the British people needed their monarch to speak sooner rather than later and it would therefore have the maximum impact. But because it was recorded she would not be able to refer to the third and arguably most significant event of this Palm Sunday, Boris Johnson's admission to St Thomas' Hospital in Westminster.

Boris had now been suffering from the virus for 10 days after testing positive and whilst self-isolating, without his pregnant partner Carrie Symonds, in Downing Street. It was evident that his symptoms were becoming prolonged with reports of a continued high temperature and a persistent cough. On the rare occasions he had been seen in public or on video calls, he was looking decidedly more unwell, but the advice to go to hospital was more based around being precautionary and so that he could undergo tests. As scientists and medics learned more and more about the cycle of the virus, in general people have either recovered from it or take a turn for the worst by day 14, so one would could argue that Boris's doctor was certainly erring on the side of caution by advising the short trip to St Thomas', ironically at exactly the same time as the Queen's address was being broadcast.

And so the question on everyone's lips was 'who is now running the country'? Well the designated successor to the Prime Minister in the event of incapacitation, was the Foreign Secretary and First Secretary of State, Dominic Raab, who would now chair the 'war cabinet'. But he was quick to stress that Boris Johnson was still the Prime Minister and was very much still in charge of the government – and it was at this point that Boris may have started to realise that he should have listened to medical advice and rested more to get over his symptoms rather than continuing with his relentless schedule. With the best will in the world, trying to guide a country through the worst pandemic for over 100 years from a hospital bed when you are really not feeling well, is at best stoic and resolute, and at worst misplaced and foolish.

Health Secretary, Matt Hancock, was another of Boris Johnson's cabinet that became even more prominent with Boris's hospital admission, and his voice was sounding louder in the aftermath of a lovely warm weekend with many still flouting the social distancing rules. Mr Hancock was talking of introducing harsher restrictions and seemed to enjoy flexing his muscles in his attempts to control the movements of the British public. It was somewhat surreal that we were being threatened with even more draconian rules and regulations simply for walking, running, cycling or just sitting on a park bench in the open air! Mr Hancock was subsequently pressured into softening his tone.

As many doctors and nurses with Covid-19 symptoms were still not being tested, Professor John Newton of Public Health England, recently appointed to improve all aspects of both antigen and antibody testing, reported that the antibody tests were unfortunately not effective. Millions of these tests, to determine whether one has actually had the virus or not, had initially been purchased by government from

China in what seemed like an act of desperation and without actually knowing whether they worked fully or not; sadly the tests failed the tests!

Sir Keir Starmer's first meaningful challenge to the government came as he called for an exit strategy to be firmly in place and published transparently prior to the end of Lockdown. Matt Hancock's riposte was that it was 'too early', although there was allegedly a working party looking at several different options; surely it was not too early to formulate a plan that would at least retain some of the public's confidence.

Mr Hancock also had to answer questions surrounding his working relationship with the Chancellor Rishi Sunak, with the inevitable tension between the man responsible for the nation's health and the man responsible for the nation's economy and future prosperity; Mr Hancock refuted any rift and stated, 'we are working very closely together', despite Lockdown reputedly costing the nation £2.4 billion per day.

As cases in the USA rose to nearly 325,000, President Trump claimed that everything would be back to normal in the country by September, but not before 'a lot of death, unfortunately....' in the coming days and potentially in America's worst week. In Italy and Spain, however, they were starting to talk about a phased relaxation of Lockdown and people returning to work in the latter part of April and early May. Both countries reported their lowest daily increase in deaths, 525 (total – 15,887) and 674 (total – 12,418) respectively, further evidence that the peak may have been reached in those countries.

In the UK however, hospitals were becoming busier and busier with new admissions, with notable increases in the northwest of England. The death toll had risen considerably again by 619 and the total to 4,932, and things were about to get a lot worse for the Prime Minister.

~

TODAY'S DAILY TIP: With less pollution in the air due to the abandonment of the majority of air travel, why not open all one's windows in the morning and give the house a real good airing. Breathing fresher air inside and outside of the house can really aid lung health. (PHYSICAL)

Day 14, Monday 6th April: Boris in a spot of bother

"Plenty of cupboards were tidied in Lockdown"

And the sun continued to shine (although there was a sprinkling of rain overnight) .... and today I had planned to clear out a couple of the larger cupboards in the house. Having hoarding tendencies can make tasks such as cupboard clearing moderately challenging, so I had to have a quiet word with myself to be a bit more ruthless, otherwise the task would be rendered rather useless. Let us just say that cupboards were a lot tidier, but I am not so sure much was actually thrown away on this occasion. I do also have a habit of coming across something that I have not read or seen for a while and then get distracted with the perusal of said item and subsequent reminiscing, for example, old Southampton football club match day programmes and primary school reports!

My knee had healed sufficiently enough for me to resume more competitive garden cricket with Alex, although no running between the wickets! Little Tizzy busily continued her fielding antics, so we had to temper our power-hitting somewhat for fear of her being taken out by a half-chewed tennis ball. It was good to be able to practice our cricketing skills as normally we would be preparing in the nets with our teammates for the start of our league cricket season in May, with our fantastic cricket club, Oakmount.

The club was the brainchild of our amazing Treasurer, Nicky Miles, who was one of several parents of boys, including my son, Alex, who had become disillusioned with our previous club because the boys were not being given regular opportunities to step up to adult cricket. At least five of the boys started playing when they were 9 years of age and had continued to develop to colts' cricket at 16 years of age at which point, and if good enough, they would start to get exposed to adult cricket – and these boys were good enough.

So Oakmount cricket club was formed and we managed to secure a place in one of the lower Hampshire leagues, but it required some of the dads, myself included, to come out of 'retirement', to play cricket with their sons. This was something I had never expected to be able to do with Alex, partly because of his cardiac challenges, but for all of us dads it was something very special to be able to do and certainly something to be cherished in years to come, despite all the aches and pains one has had to endure!

In the five seasons since the club's inception, we have gained promotion on three occasions and sensationally avoided relegation last year with four consecutive wins in the final four games of the season. Of course winning is important and we have a very competitive bunch of cricketers, some who are very able indeed, but most important of all, we are inclusive of everyone including all the wives, relatives and girlfriends who avidly come and support us – everyone knows when Oakmount are 'in town' as we arguably possess one of the biggest 'away followings' of any lower league cricket team in the country!

The club is more than a cricket club and like one big family, I am sure much like many amateur clubs. In fact we mainly comprise of seven families with several very valued individuals who have joined along the way. I am very proud of the fact that no-one has yet left our club and there are friendships formed over the years that will no doubt last for a lifetime.

Very much away from cricket, and in a shocking turn of events, Boris Johnson, aged 55 and weighing over 16 stone, was moved into the intensive care unit (ICU) at St Thomas' Hospital, as he started to experience serious difficulty in breathing. ICUs are equipped with ventilators which aid breathing and usually patients remain conscious. In more serious situations patients are intubated, where a tube is placed in the windpipe before being ventilated; this will often require the patient to be put to sleep. Boris was initially given four litres of oxygen but remained conscious and in good spirits receiving many good wishes and messages of support from all around the world; one even came in from President Putin of Russia.

Carrie Simmonds, aged 32 and Boris's partner, was by now heavily pregnant but for obvious reasons had been apart from Boris for a while, particularly as she also had been displaying symptoms of the virus. Although there was no concrete medical evidence to support this, those who were pregnant were thought to be at greater risk of becoming very ill from Covid-19 and therefore were placed in the vulnerable category and required to shield themselves for the 12 week period. It was thought that she was staying in their South London flat with Dilyn, their two year old rescue dog and Jack Russell cross, well away from the flat above 11 Downing Street which she normally shared with Boris. It must have been an unimaginably stressful and worrying time for her, particularly where statistics told us that 46 per cent of those aged between 50 and 59, who were admitted to ICU suffering from Covid-19, ended up dying.

British Prime Ministers of the past, including Winston Churchill in 1953, have been unwell in office before so this was not an unprecedented situation. During the 1918 pandemic David Lloyd George nearly perished as a result of contracting Spanish flu.

The country was now without its leader if not in spirit, certainly in body at a time in the crisis that he was most needed. PPE was still not getting to hospitals and care homes quickly enough and in enough quantity, ventilators were still in short supply, testing was still way below where it should be especially for frontline workers, the economy was lurching deeper into recession, children and young adolescents were not receiving their proper education and tuition, British nationals were still stranded abroad and deaths from and cases of Covid-19 were worryingly still very much on the increase. Some television personalities were rightly or wrongly having a field-day challenging ministers for their apparent lack of action on their respective breakfast television shows!

So Dominic Raab, as First Secretary of State, stepped forward to deputise for his boss, although there is officially nothing in our constitution that states who should be in charge of the country in the absence of the Prime Minister. Being relatively inexperienced in government anyway was a concern for many when it came to Mr Raab, let alone 'leading' the cabinet in a crisis, and he certainly had enough on his hands still trying to repatriate many Britons from overseas. He did not appear to come across during the 5pm press conferences that he oversaw, as a charismatic and assured character that would instil confidence in those around him. He would surely have a few challenges trying to galvanise and exert authority on those who were up until now, his peers and his colleagues, a group of pretty inexperienced colleagues at that. It often is not just about members of the cabinet working together, but also the relationships between different departments and advisers beneath them in the hierarchy, who might have the same agenda but disagree on how to action policies and create new strategies in a very fast-moving crisis.

As the virus had ripped through the heart of the government - clearly a sign that the social distancing regulations that were being preached so vehemently by those in power, were not actually being followed - Mr Raab's first priority was to ensure he had enough key people in place to plug the gaps vacated by those affected by illness. The Prime Minister was wholly incapacitated, Dominic Cummings his senior adviser was still isolating, Sir Eddie Lister his other senior aide was shielding, as he was in the over-70's category, various other senior and junior aides were isolating with symptoms and Matt Hancock had only just returned from isolation – quite a challenge to say the least. It appeared it was even more of a 'baptism of fire' for Mr Raab as he revealed that the last time he had spoken to Boris Johnson about anything was on the Saturday, two days previously.

There were further indications from Professor Chris Witty, the government's Chief Medical Officer, that we would only come out of Lockdown on the understanding that certain criteria had been met. Professor Witty, another key individual who had himself only just returned from self-isolation, stated that we needed to be past the peak of hospital cases, to have enough testing capacity throughout the country, to have a way of knowing who had had the virus already and to know that the NHS would not be overwhelmed if there was a second wave of the virus. With the expectation that we were only going to reach the peak potentially over Easter the following weekend, there was clearly 'a lot of water that needed to pass under the bridge'; there was probably now a stark realisation amongst the British public that we were in this for the long haul.

Another of Professor's Whitty's concerns was the knock-on effect of the virus in terms of long-term mental health and financial issues, not to mention the increase in domestic abuse and suicide rates. Hearing this continually made us realise how lucky we were as family, firstly to be all together and secondly to be having fun and enjoying ourselves.

Professor Witty also stressed that the development of an effective and sustainable vaccine continued to be main weapon to combat Covid-19 and intense work on this was being undertaken across the globe. Interestingly, Bill Gates, founder of Microsoft, was pledging millions of pounds towards testing several vaccines and building factories for their manufacture, emphasising that a consistent approach was required between different countries all after the same thing.

In terms of treating the virus, reports were coming from the US that an established drug called hydroxychloroquine was being tested on Covid-19 patients and that anecdotally it could inhibit the virus. Although a ray of light, there were differing views across America, and indeed other scientists in China and France, as to its effectiveness. Not being a scientist myself, I am constantly baffled as to how long it takes to produce treatments and vaccines for supposed new viruses and diseases, which are actually strains of the same virus or disease which scientists have been working on for years already - maybe I should leave it to the scientists!

As the threat to the job market increased, many who had either already lost their jobs or who were on the government's furlough scheme were taking employment, temporary or otherwise, in jobs alien to those that they had trained in or had been doing before. As tends to happen in a crisis, some businesses were struggling whilst others were flourishing; supermarket delivery and warehouse jobs for example, for companies such as Sainsbury's, Waitrose, Argos and Amazon were suddenly in great demand as we headed for one of the biggest shifts in the labour market for many years.

Owing to the weekend lag, that we had now become accustomed to, deaths in the UK had increased by 439 and a total of 5,373, a smaller amount than had been expected, particularly with suggestions that we were not yet at the peak. Passing 5,000 deaths, however, was poignant and incredibly sad for all the families and friends of those who had perished as a direct or indirect result of Covid-19. It was also pretty alarming as it was only 31 days since the first death was recorded and represented over 10% of the 51,508 people that had tested positive for the virus.

Increases in deaths of 636 (total – 16,523) and 637 (total – 13,055) in Italy and Spain respectively, was a further indication that things maybe plateauing in those countries. What was still plain to see from their media coverage was that many communities, particularly in Northern Italy, would be impacted emotionally from these losses of life, for many years to come.

~

TODAY'S DAILY TIP: As referred to in a previous chapter, whilst out walking or on one's daily exercise and when you pass someone on the other side of the road, connect from a distance with a smile or nod of acknowledgment followed by a

'Good morning' or a 'Good afternoon', as you might just make someone's day. As social animals we are used to interactions with each other so we must try to continue this if we can, even with restrictions. (SOCIAL / EMOTIONAL)

Day 15, Tuesday 7th April: Jigsaw joy

And the sun continued to shine...............in fact it was becoming another scorcher of a week, something we have often seen in the month of April. It was therefore a very good excuse to spend a good amount of time in the garden 'tackling' a couple of fir trees which had grown rather too large for the area that they occupied. Although I say it myself, I think I did a pretty decent pruning job resulting in quite a stylish and symmetrical end result.

Once I had completed my 'work of art' in the garden, I sat down to start a 3,000-piece jigsaw puzzle of the Tyrol in Austria, and this one was probably right up there in the difficulty stakes. It certainly kept me occupied for a number of days and there was certainly a mildly frosty reaction from the family who accused me of being 'anti-social' and becoming a 'boring old man', which I found frankly insulting. The problem though with a jigsaw this size, is that it becomes addictive and every spare moment you have, you find yourself migrating back to the puzzle and into a deep therapeutic trance.

"I do love a jigsaw!"

Whatever political persuasion one was, it was probably hard to ignore that Prime Minister, Boris Johnson, was in a pretty poor and concerning state of health.

Although he was still able to breathe for himself with the help of a ventilator and without having to be intubated, he was still in a very critical condition. Of course there was also the irony that he was now seeing first-hand how important plentiful supplies of PPE and ventilators were in the fight against Covid-19 and how amazing much of the care was in our 1,257 NHS hospitals. It could be strongly argued that his experience in hospital, and especially in ICU, set the tone for his decision-making during the rest of the pandemic – would he now err more on the side of health rather than prosperity, as he sought to find a way eventually to take the country out of Lockdown?

Dominic Raab was now at the helm insisting that his boss, colleague and friend would be back in the near future to steer the country through these 'troubled waters'. In fact David Cameron, the former Prime Minister, who resigned after losing the Brexit referendum, talked in an interview of Boris Johnson's toughness, resilience and general fitness, as well as a 'tremendous zest for life and getting things done'.

Meanwhile, Mr Raab seemed a bit calmer and assured than he had been on previous appearances, maybe because Boris's condition was stable and he was more optimistic about not having to be the stand-in Prime Minister for longer than expected. In my world, it was a bit like a sous chef in the kitchen deputising for the head chef during his two-week vacation – he could deal with the day-to-day running of the kitchen and any of the challenges and issues that this brings but anything more long-term and strategic would have to wait for the head chef's return.

The Chief Scientific Advisor to the government during the pandemic, Sir Patrick Vallance, expressed a view that certain trends did 'begin to suggest things might be moving in the right direction', as the number of new cases of the virus were beginning to plateau. For anyone to have any degree of optimism about a Lockdown exit, a decrease in new cases would always need to be the first stage, followed by a drop in hospitalisations and ultimately a reduction in the daily death toll.

Unfortunately this was the day in the UK when we reached two new milestones: firstly it was the highest daily increase yet in the number of deaths (786); and secondly we passed 6,000 in the total of recorded deaths (6,159). The government's messaging was now becoming even more important; whilst recognising that there was some degree of hope, it was important to remember the heartache that so many people were still going through. To give credit to the government, at pretty much every 5pm daily briefing, ministers would offer their condolences and say that they were 'mourning the loss of each and every one of those who had died. The government of course were also very aware of the 'blame game' over the fact that many of the deaths might have been prevented by swifter actions in the first place.

Italy reported a further 604 deaths taking their total to 17,127, but their daily rise in new cases was only 2.3 per cent, the lowest growth since 13th March. They were also using antibody testing amongst their medical staff to see whether they had already had the virus, with the ultimate objective of creating immunity. Despite the UK's failure as yet to find an effective antibody test, the Italian authorities thought it was time to put faith in theirs.

Lombardy continued to be the worst hit region in Italy and so far there was a death toll of 9,484 out of a total in Italy of 17,127, which equated to 55.3 per cent. Although this percentage came down from a peak of 64.2 per cent on 27th March, there were clearly reasons why Lombardy, the country's richest region, still accounted for more than half the deaths in Italy. Being the most densely populated region with an ageing population and high pollution levels were certainly factors, as well as delays in Lockdown compared to other regions, where business and commerce had continued regardless. Interestingly close trade ties existed with China, which would have meant high levels of travel between the two countries. But it was also the region's lack of preparedness in their hospitals, supposedly some of the best in Italy, which meant that they could not cope with the Covid-19 patient demand. This was seen many times on our televisions as the story unfolded in Italy with patients being left to die in hospital corridors notably in Milan and Bergamo.

Talking of China, it was the first day since the virus outbreak that there were (allegedly) no recorded deaths at all in the country over a 24 hour period, with their total remaining at 3,331. This seemed very low for a country which had the largest global population of over 1.4 billion. As the Chinese were slowly trying to get their lives back to a degree of normality, criticism persisted from around the world that China had lacked transparency in failing to disclose the potential severity of the outbreak prior to it very quickly becoming a global pandemic, with wide ranging health and economic implications. But it was the World Health Organisation who bore the brunt of the criticism for their indifferent response.

~

TODAY'S DAILY TIP: One of the best ways to lift ones mood in difficult times is to listen to music, and in particular ones favourite tunes or albums. A mood of despair and negativity can very quickly turn into one of hope and positivity by playing the right melodies and as William Shakespeare said, 'if music be the food of love, then play on.' (SPIRITUAL)

Day 16, Wednesday 8th April: Let's play pool!

And the sun continued to shine.......and once again I could not resist the temptation of an 'eggy' bread retro-breakfast, this time with a couple of well-done Richmond sausages, a rather extravagant treat for a Wednesday. It certainly set me up well for the 'action-packed' day ahead.

I was working my way through the sorting of several cupboards this week and once today's was completed, I started on a mass hedge-cutting project. I initially cut the hedges on the first day of Lockdown and merely two weeks later, they had grown into uncontrollably dense thickets, probably because we were now at the heart of the growing season. There was no other option but to get completely stuck in and tackle the challenge head-on. So I donned the protective gloves and commenced 'Project Ambush'. One slight drawback was that our hedges contain rather a lot of brambles, so by lunchtime my arms and legs were covered in a plethora of scratches and mild skin tears, however I made some excellent progress.

"Thanks goodness we found the pool table"

Sport plays a significant part in our lives, and with no live football to watch or golf to play, garden cricket for Alex and me, had taken centre stage in Lockdown. That was until I discovered that, hidden under a rather large covering in the garage, we actually had a sizeable pool table that, although we had not utilised it for several years, was in pretty decent condition. So we set about lugging this great hefty item from the garage to the back garden, and we then gave it a good old wash down and finally set it up on the covered decking. Once erected, we got the spirit level out to address some of the inconsistencies in the rolling of the balls, and all of a sudden we had excellent all-weather form of Lockdown sporting entertainment to vie with garden cricket for our attention. Needless to say, the pool started in earnest and it would not be long before the table-tennis table and dartboard came out too!

In terms of sport on the virus front, Premier League football had now been suspended until at least 30th April. On 2nd April, Health Secretary Matt Hancock, had controversially asked for all Premier League players to take a pay cut, which was enforcedly rejected, particularly when Mr Hancock ruled out a pay cut for himself. Debate continued between the Premier League and the players' union - the Professional Footballer's Association (PFA), as to what the best course of action might be, whether cuts to players' wages should support NHS charities or be used to support clubs in the lower leagues or to ensure non-playing staff could still get paid.

The wealth in the Premier League is sometimes scorned upon and players are definitely rewarded handsomely, so it was somewhat surprising when some Premier League clubs used the government's furlough scheme to pay some of their staff. This was fiercely criticised and the clubs in question made a very swift about-turn. Credit to the players, they eventually formed a 'Players Together' campaign for Covid-19 relief, which was a means whereby players across all Premier League clubs would generate and distribute funds to the organisation, NHS Charities Together. In addition some clubs did agree to defer their wages but there were still grave concerns for the future of many lower league clubs, who were bound to find themselves in severe financial difficulty.

At last there was some better news coming out of St Thomas' Hospital as the Chancellor of the Exchequer, Rishi Sunak, reported to the media that Boris

Johnson's condition was 'improving' and that he was 'engaging positively' with the medical staff. I have a bit of soft spot for St Thomas' Hospital: firstly, because my brother, Hugh, was admitted there when he was very young and spent several months there with my mother, suffering from a very serious congenital stomach problem; secondly, I used to walk past it every day either on my way in to or way home from work, for over four years, as it was just around the corner from Waterloo Station. It always struck me how close it was to Westminster and I am sure like Hugh, Boris will have received the very best care from the NHS, especially as it is regarded as a centre of excellence for critical care.

Boris was in his third day in ICU and 14th day in hospital, and still receiving 'standard oxygen care', leading one to believe that he had thankfully avoided having to be intubated. We may never know how really seriously ill he was whilst in ICU but he did give a newspaper interview a few weeks later when he revealed that at one point it was touch and go whether he would have to be intubated and also that he was given 'litres and litres of oxygen' to keep him in the land of the living. In the emotional interview, he also stated that there was even a contingency plan in place in case of his death. Even if he did continue to recover over the ensuing days and exit ICU, many tales were being heard from those who had experienced similar trauma to Boris, who were either still in hospital two months later still experiencing symptoms, or having horrific flashbacks tantamount to post traumatic stress disorder (PTSD).

As the Easter weekend approached with a promise of more good weather, there were concerns that some people were still prepared to flout the 'STAY AT HOME' rules and venture away for a Bank Holiday break. The police were out in force on the main roads leading to the West Country amid fears that weekenders and second homeowners were about to descend on Devon and Cornwall 'en masse'. The message however had definitely been heard loud and clear in London with images of deserted streets around the many tourist attractions including Buckingham Palace, Trafalgar Square and Tower Bridge.

The fear and implications of getting the virus were certainly proving major factors as to why so many UK citizens were actually adhering rigidly to the advice. The message brandished on pretty much every current affairs programme or news conference on the television, of '**STAY AT HOME, PROTECT THE NHS AND SAVE LIVES**', was an abundantly clear one.

Suddenly that fear was notched up to another level with the announcement of the previous day's death toll – a shocking 938, bringing the total number of deaths in the UK to 7,097, with 6,483 in England alone and only 34 days after the very first recorded death. I do not think many people really thought that, after seeing all those dreadful images in Italy a couple of weeks previously, we would experience the same situation in the UK – the impact of Covid-19 was becoming graver by the day. The nation now waited with baited breath as to what the government's next steps might be as we prepared for their first Lockdown review that had been promised after three weeks.

~

TODAY'S DAILY TIP: Have a good rummage through and, if needs be, empty your freezer as there may be some real treats hidden away that you may have forgotten were there. Additionally, much like good fridge practice, it is important to rotate stock regularly and monitor those 'use by' dates. (PHYSICAL)

Day 17, Thursday 9th April (Maundy Thursday): Good neighbours become good friends

And the sun continued to shine .... and it was a day of playing pool with Alex interspersed with the continuation of the 3,000 piece puzzle challenge; it really was a hard life! With it being our third 'Clap for the NHS and Our Carers' Thursday, there was the stark reminder why we were being confined to our homes, particularly where hospital admissions and deaths were still so high. The Thursday handclap and banging of saucepans, or any other loud item for that matter, really brought many communities together. Stories were often told by and heard from people that had been neighbours for years but never got as 'close' to each other - albeit from a distance - as they were now; community spirit was very much alive.

We are lucky enough to have the Browns next door (Mikey, Izzy and their two young sons, Max and Harvey), who we have conversed with over a bottle of beer a few times during Lockdown, sharing tales of the past and much laughter too. We even discovered that we had a mutual connection we never knew about with somebody that we both worked with at different times of our careers; I wonder how many others made connections such as these during Lockdown. Even Tizzy has a little gap at the base of the fence that she sticks her nose through, demanding the boys' attention.

"Even the animals were good neighbours in Lockdown"

The news from St Thomas' Hospital about Boris Johnson was very positive as he was transferred to a ward from ICU after just over three days being ventilated. It was also day 15 of his illness, which for many is around the day that patients are either hospitalised initially after a turn for the worse or actually show the first signs of recovery from the virus. Boris clearly had his own whirlwind version of the virus which meant that, despite a worrying visit to ICU, he was already in the 'early stages of recovery' and reportedly in 'extremely good spirits'.

As an aside, I did once get the chance to meet Boris, albeit fleetingly, whilst walking back through Green Park, after watching the Victory in Europe (VE day) flypast on the Mall, in May 2018. At that stage he was not Prime Minister, and owing to the fact that I was fully suited and carrying one of my little black notebooks, he might have thought I was either a civil servant or someone who was employed in Westminster's corridors of power. Being surrounded by many civilian-clothed aviation enthusiasts, James my Deputy and I stood out in the crowd, and once we had established eye contact, Boris bid us both a very genuine and warm, 'Good afternoon, gentlemen, I hope you are well'. I have always thought he would be a joyful and humorous presence in social circles, though he often uses humour in his profession in equal measures, which can be both endearing and irksome, depending on the situation.

Had Boris Johnson ended up being intubated his chances of survival would have diminished greatly. As the immune system is working hard to fight the symptoms of Covid-19, it paradoxically then causes an overreaction of said immune system producing what is known as a cytokine storm, which ultimately can then be potentially lethal with severe damage to the lung tissue. Deaths from Covid-19 usually occur on average 27 days after contracting the virus, with survivors being discharged on average 23.5 days after the initial infection. This can of course differ in varying degrees, from person to person.

Harrowing stories were coming from all parts of the country where many families of those who were not so lucky in their fight against Covid-19 and living their last moments of life were, at best, being given only a few minutes to say their goodbyes, dressed head-to-toe in protective clothing. Some were even denied a visit altogether, having instead to rely on technology to bid farewell to loved ones; it was just such a desperately sad situation, not to mention the heart-breaking restrictions that had been imposed on funeral gatherings.

The UK police force probably had one of the more challenging jobs during this pandemic with the many new rules and regulations that they were expected to enforce. Where some were continuing to flout the rules, senior officers requested tougher measures to be able to deal with the persistent Lockdown offenders. The irony was that some of the offences being committed were not what one would call serious crimes against humanity. In a perceived back-down, the government in the guise of Home Secretary Priti Patel, appeared to warn officers not to be so 'heavy-handed' in their approach, particularly where some police officers had allegedly been challenging the public on what they had in their supermarket trolleys and their distancing whilst queuing. Ms Patel, who up until now had barely been seen during the crisis, was insistent that there would not be stricter restrictions and regulations to aid enforcement. Instead the friendly approach should be encouraged with fines and arrests being the last resort. From a police perspective, it seemed that they were between the 'devil' (the government) and the 'deep blue sea' (the British public).

Churches and place of worship continued to be complete no-go areas as we approached Easter and the most religious of weekends for those of the Christian faith. Clerics were becoming increasingly uneasy at being denied access to churches even just to film a special service or perform an act of solo prayer. As one Archdeacon said: 'Their closure inhibits us'. Some were even threatened with disciplinary action if they unlawfully entered their 'place of work' as we headed for the first Easter in the UK since the year 1213 without church services.

In other parts of the world, the US was not just seeing further increases in infections and deaths but their jobless number had reached 16.8 million in just three weeks; the number of claims for unemployment benefit had risen from around 220,000 per week pre-Covid-19 to now nearly 7 million per week! Also, in New York, confirmed cases increased by a mammoth 10,000 in one day, amidst reports that some doctors thought ventilators maybe inhibiting recovery and exacerbating damage to the lungs in Covid-19 patients. This was something British doctors also started to question over time.

Italy and Spain had continued to show slightly more positive progress in reducing infections in the past couple of days but the death toll in Italy was still at 542 and 610 on the 8th and 9th April respectively and a total of 18,279. In Spain, meanwhile, it was at 658 and 683 for the two days respectively and a total of 15,238. But there was some real hope coming out Wuhan province in China with an easing of their Lockdown, and New Zealand's Prime Minister declared, 'We are turning a corner', with only one death and 921 active cases – the formula to their success: one of the most stringent and early Lockdowns in the world.

With no sign yet of the curve flattening, the death toll in the UK rose by another grim number of 881, bringing the total number of deaths in England, Scotland, Wales and Northern Ireland, to 7,978. Would Good Friday see us hit rock bottom?

~

TODAY'S DAILY TIP: When clearing out a cupboard, drawer, an attic or the garage, try to be ruthless in throwing things away responsibly, particularly if you have had them lying around for over six months. This will be particularly difficult if you are hoarder, so be strong! (PHYSICAL)

Day 18, Friday 10th April (Good Friday): Hancock's half-hour

And the sun continued to shine........and a day that for many is a very a reflective and religious one, being Good Friday, started with a beautiful morning dog walk through the woods with the family. After a relaxing day playing pool and puzzle-making, our Friday evening ran its usual course with takeaway fish and chips from the Otter pub and a Zoom quiz night.

"Holly's Lockdown cocktail"

The Zoom quiz night craze seemed to take the nation by storm; it was quite incredible the number of people I had contact with during Lockdown who were going to be taking part, or had taken part, in a quiz evening at some stage. In fact this weekend we had three different quiz evenings planned with three different groups of people. What became a source of amusement was the number of times the same questions came up at different quizzes and we still got some of those answers wrong! And I must admit, being ultra-competitive, I was also amazed at how some people seemed to get the most obscure questions right!! I did though marvel at the wonders of technology and at how so many people could take part in the same quiz, all at the same time.

Boris Johnson's recovery continued to go in the right direction as he took his first steps since he was admitted to hospital. It would, however, be a while before he could consider anything like a return to work. Many Covid-19 sufferers would concur with Dr Chris Smith from the University of Cambridge, who suggested that Boris may well be feeling 'like he's been hit by several buses' and that he would be very tired and weak for quite a period of time. Rest and convalescence were a must, something very alien to Boris.

There was some more positive news on the vaccine front with an optimistic prediction that a vaccine for the virus might be available to the public as early as September. Vaccinologists from both Oxford University and Imperial College, London, had been leading the way to try to find a global solution to this pandemic, but it was Dr Sarah Gilbert form Oxford University who made this brave proclamation, stating that she was '80 per cent confident' about a positive outcome.

It appeared that the government were at last starting to make more consistent progress with the provision of PPE and an increase in testing amongst NHS and care home staff. There was, however, still a disconnection between the policy makers in government and those executing the policy on the 'shop floor', which was causing increased tension.

Matt Hancock had tried to reassure critics that 742 million pieces of PPE had been distributed to various organisations in spite of 'huge international demand', since the beginning of the pandemic, and if it was used sensibly that there was plenty to go round. The NHS's response to Mr Hancock's suggestion that PPE might be being misused was an angry one, replying that there were still several areas of the UK that were not sufficiently resourced and suggesting that Mr Hancock was not fully aware of how serious this situation still was for frontline workers.

It was a similar situation for testing, with Mr Hancock announcing that the capacity for testing had now increased to such an extent that all NHS and social care staff that needed to get a test would be able to. Although there were around 19,000 tests carried out the previous day, there were still many who most needed it on the frontline that could not get a test, especially those who were displaying symptoms and therefore were unable to work. The cynics could not fathom, at this rate, how exactly we would get to 100,000 tests per day by the end of the month.

The number of volunteers to sign up for the Royal Voluntary Service (RVS) had now reached 750,000, which was pretty impressive considering the original target set by NHS England, was 250,000. Frustratingly though for many that did sign up - my wife Susie included - having logged on, on a daily basis to offer their services, they waited in vain to be summoned. It was yet another example of a great initiative introduced in the proverbial 'boardroom' which was not working effectively on the 'shop floor'.

At around the same time that Jesus was supposed to have died on the cross, Good Friday at 3pm, the extremely sad news broke that the UK had experienced another record high number of deaths in a 24 hour period of 980, bringing the total of 8,958. This shocking news ensured that fear continued to grip the nation creating many negative and pessimistic thoughts. Some sources in Whitehall who had been monitoring very carefully the public's reaction towards all the measures that had been imposed, even suggested that the nation was 'very very worried.......' about the threat of the virus and that they would not be averse to even more restrictions. There was however one voice that I feel shone above the darkness throughout the pandemic, which was that of Professor Karol Sikora, an eminent oncologist expert of 50 years, amongst other impressive achievements.

His tweets were constructive and very often riddled with much-needed optimism and supportive messages, as he regularly advocated the importance of mental health awareness, particularly in the younger generations. He also challenged the decision makers and those in power, but in a respectful yet assertive manner. What concerned him most though was that, with all the focus on treating patients with Covid-19 with allegedly fewer than 10 per cent of the UK population having contracted it, we were going to be left with an even bigger health challenge post-crisis.

It is very possible that many cancers, heart problems and other potentially life-threatening illnesses were laying undetected for too long, meaning that early treatment was not possible. This in turn would lead to many more deaths than there had been as a result of Covid-19. As it was, there were already stories coming out of suspected heart attack victims, who were so fearful of going to A&E and catching the virus, that they were actually staying at home and putting their lives at even more risk; the poor and elderly were thought to be particularly vulnerable. The numbers of people attending A&E for reasons other than Covid-19 was at an alarmingly low level, in fact the lowest ever in March. Overcoming this fear would be one of the biggest challenges the government faced coming out of Lockdown.

A huge amount of sympathy has to go to the many school leavers and university under graduates who were denied the opportunity to celebrate precious years of hard work and friendship because of what the virus had done to the education system. Whether it was those last school assemblies, lavish Prom nights or clandestine parties, students all around the country were having to forego the opportunity to create special and lifelong memories. At least Zoom was able to fulfil another role and plug a gap for many final year university students, providing the backdrop for virtual graduation ceremonies in the bosom of their own homes and surrounded by their families. These individuals are our future leaders of industry and commerce, who may well be 'picking up the pieces' of a post-Covid-19 world, both physically and emotionally, for many years to come.

Even though cases were now falling slowly in Italy and Spain, their respective Lockdowns were being extended until May, although there was expected to be a partial easing of some of their economic restrictions A death toll of 570 and 605 in both countries respectively, was still too high, but at least it gave some hope to those in the UK that there could be a path 'out of the woods' at some stage in the distant future. But it was deaths in the USA that were on an increasingly sharp rise, now at a total of 17,005, second only to Italy at 18,849.

~

TODAY'S DAILY TIP: With a shortage of eggs during Lockdown, and the cake-making craze in full swing, an alternative ingredient to eggs in the baking process could be either oat milk, almond milk or soya milk. This produces an excellent end result and also is suitable for vegans. (PHYSICAL)

Day 19, Saturday 11th April (Holy Saturday): Let Zoom 'battle of the families' commence

And the sun continued to shine...........so after another lovely relaxing day out came the barbecue again. Our incredibly efficient 'Weber' barbecue unit was a godsend during Lockdown and incredibly we managed to survive for three months without having to change the gas. One of the benefits of the closure of restaurants and other food outlets was the availability of many meat and fish items at lower than average prices – and that included fillet steak. Needless to say, we made sure there was a regular weekly supply of this beautifully tender meat on our shopping delivery, which I would then cook medium on the barbecue, lightly seasoned and brushed with a little béarnaise sauce.

"The BBQ came in very useful in the lovely Lockdown weather"

Again we had to keep reminding ourselves of why we were being isolated from the outside world, yet living in peaceful, safe and mildly luxurious surroundings. For Alex especially, this was the opportunity to enjoy his freedom unlike the hospital incarceration of the previous year. One of the very heart-warming aspects of Alex's sojourn in Southampton General Hospital last year was the support he received from Charlotte, his adoring girlfriend. It does not bear thinking about, the stress and deep anxiety that she would have experienced during Alex's illness, particularly when she was in Sweden enjoying time with her cousin during the onset of his sepsis on Friday 3rd May. She managed to obtain an earlier flight back to the UK, meaning that she got to see Alex on the Saturday evening and a very emotional reunion ensued. Charlotte then had to endure three months of highs and lows, with the lowest ebb being in the immediate aftermath of Alex's 10 hours of reconstructive open heart surgery, but she stuck with him through thick and thin.

Tonight was the second of our three consecutive Zoom quiz nights, which was Charlotte's family, the Stones (Paul, Sam, Olivia, Georgia and of course, Charlotte) versus the Inds (Susie, Holly, Alex, Tizzy and me). I am sure she would not mind me saying it, but Holly generally dislikes quizzes, and Tizzy is a canine, so we were on a hiding to nothing from the start!

The Stones seemed to pull the most difficult, challenging and unanswerable questions 'out of the bag', yet answered many of our questions without any trouble whatsoever. Needless to say we were forced into submission and roundly defeated. But the Inds do not take defeat lying down and demanded a re-match, this would take place some three weeks later. Competition aside, we had great fun and it was a great way to keep in touch during Lockdown. It is easy to see why Charlotte and Alex get on so well, where both their respective families are so close and appreciate the whole essence of a loving family life.

With a further 917 more deaths, bringing the total to 9,875 and over 5,000 new cases, the UK was still in the grip of the virus. What appeared to be coming out from several sources as we got to know more about the virus was how Covid-19 was affecting males more than females. Research also had showed that if you were aged, already unwell with medical condition or obese, the chances of avoiding the virus decreased. Those who were also male stood at an even greater risk and the statistics bore this out, with 61 per cent of recorded deaths in the UK being amongst the male population. Italy and China also had higher male mortality rates than female. There are many schools of thought as to why females appear to be the 'stronger' gender when it comes to enduring and fighting off Covid-19, including generally healthier lifestyles. One medic had a theory that where there is more testosterone in males this represses the immune system, whereby oestrogen in females, supposedly liberates it.

Ethnicity was another factor muted as impacting the number of deaths. This was manifested particularly by the number of NHS frontline workers who had already died who were from ethnic minorities and who were also male. It was so sad to hear that some of these frontline heroes were in their sixties and seventies and had actually come out of retirement after Matt Hancock's 'call to arms', only to walk 'blindly' to their deaths.

~

TODAY'S DAILY TIP: Get up a little bit earlier, open the windows or patio doors and listen to the noises of nature be it the birds singing, the trees rustling in the wind or the tranquil buzz of a fly or a wasp. With the air having become much cleaner and fresher in Lockdown, nature seemed to be at its very best.
(SPIRITUAL)

Day 20, Sunday 12th April (Easter Sunday): Boris back from the brink

And the sun continued to shine................and on our family Sunday morning walk with Tizzy we continued to reflect on our inept and ignominious quiz performance against the Stones from the night before and started to plot our revenge. They had chosen the six categories on this occasion so now it was our choice and it was important we had a couple of categories that the Stones may not be so familiar with; we had three weeks to prepare to right the wrong of the previous day.

"We did love our family walks in Lockdown"

After another relaxing day incorporating my usual sporting 'scraps' with Alex on the pool and table-tennis tables, as well as continuing my tough jigsaw challenge, we embarked on our third quiz of the weekend, this time against a number of Holly's different friends.

I can honestly say I have not met anyone who I perceive to have more friends than Holly does, which is testament to her gregarious, kind and affable nature, which so many people find so endearing. That warm and caring nature extends to her workplace, where she is also highly respected in her Human Resources role for both her competence and skill in dealing with many different scenarios. Indeed I saw and heard this first hand with her having to work from home during the pandemic and I am truly proud of what she has achieved thus far. If she remains focused and continues to embrace new things in the way she has already, she has an extremely bright future ahead of her.

This latest quiz could not have been better timed as it inspired us with themes and categories that we could potentially use to defeat the Stones in the next family contest. Amusingly, several of the previous evening's questions came up that we still did not answer correctly! As human beings we all have an appetite for new knowledge, but sometimes with these quizzes coming thick and fast and being so fast-moving, it was difficult for some of those things that one had learned to stick in the mind. We did not disgrace ourselves though in this quiz, coming a creditable sixth place out of 20 teams.

Just as Good Friday had seen the terrible rise in the death toll in the UK, Easter Sunday saw Prime Minister Boris Johnson's release from hospital to recuperate at Chequers. Amazingly it was only eight days after he was admitted, and during which time he spent three days fighting for his life in the ICU of St Thomas' Hospital. Some might use the significance of the day as the theological analogy of his 'rise from the dead', but it was more akin to Lazarus's tale of recovery. Boris, very obviously fatigued and sounding husky, gave us the first indication of how very ill he had become in a video recorded at 10 Downing Street, but was effusive in thanking those who provided 'round the clock' care for him stating that 'things could have gone either way'. He called out several of the medical staff by name but was particularly grateful for the skill and care of two nurses and singled out Luis Pitarma from Portugal and Jenny McGee from New Zealand, who were there for him 'every second of the night'.

We also had a clearer picture of the stress and strain that his pregnant partner, Carrie Symonds, had been under as she tweeted, 'There were times last week that were very dark indeed. My heart goes out to all those in similar situations worried sick about their loved ones'. In other tweets one could just sense the relief and despite not seeing Boris for over a week, she had been buoyed by the many messages of support that she had received.

Boris's 'Easter message' almost served as a 're-gathering of the troops' to encounter the next stage of the fight against Covid-19. He expressed his gratitude for us all staying at home in isolation – some of us lucky enough to be playing pool, cooking fillet steak on the barbecue and 'Zooming' with our friends and families – but was very mindful of those mourning the loss of loved ones and the sacrifices that were being made by NHS staff, such as Jenny and Luis. What he made no mention of though was the crisis that was looming ominously in care homes, something that Boris and his government would be roundly criticised for, along with the delay in enforcing Lockdown, lack of consistent supplies of PPE and the ineptitude in all aspects of testing.

There was a perception amongst 'undervalued' care home owners, managers and employees that they had been 'hung out to dry' by the government, who had focused all their attention thus far on protecting the NHS. The 'STAY AT HOME.......' strategy and slogan appeared to be aimed solely at keeping enough capacity available in hospitals should the impact of the virus be decidedly worse than had initially been anticipated.

Data was starting to come out from Care England that almost 1,000 deaths related to Covid-19 may have already occurred in the 11,300 care homes around Britain, yet the official number mentioned by the government was only 20. In fact at this stage, deaths in care homes were not even being recorded as part of the daily death toll statistics. Additionally, much like we had seen in hospitals throughout the crisis, there were claims of a complete lack of PPE and testing for care workers. With little or no protective equipment in some cases, the risk and reality of a rapid spread of the virus was even greater in care homes than hospitals. So many of the residents were already very vulnerable due to other underlying and serious medical conditions, and contact with untested care workers was inevitable. Care homes were fast becoming the 'new' frontline and the government had to find a way to integrate the NHS and social care system to counter the perceived neglect.

Care homes, who are not funded by the NHS, were amongst several sectors that were also starting to experience financial difficulty due to extra cost pressures associated with the virus. There was also talk of impending financial crises in the UK's 210 hospices, as well as countless charities, many affected by high street shop closures. Despite the government's £750 million intervention to support all charities, long-term revenues from fundraising events would likely be impacted by the impending recession.

In light of continued concerns around the economic downtown, several ministers in the government were now calling for an easing of the Lockdown and a return to the workplace, as soon as possible. So many businesses were now struggling and contemplating cuts in their workforces, international trade was at a standstill with hospitality and travel being impacted as a knock-on effect and the long-term prosperity of our youth was being compromised as they were being denied their education. Those more concerned for the health of the nation though, including Health Secretary Hancock, were asking for caution against lifting Lockdown restrictions – would Prime Minister Johnson now be erring more on the side of health rather than prosperity, in light of his own health scare? Boris had serious thinking to do as he began his recuperation with his fiancée at Chequers.

The Pope, from the Vatican, and the Archbishop of Canterbury, virtually from his London home, delivered their respective Easter messages: the Pope focused on the importance Europe showing a united front in supporting the needy and those in poverty; the Archbishop called for compassion in treating every death with respect and individuality. This was in light of the vast numbers of fatalities in such a short space of time and the restrictions imposed on the numbers permitted at funerals.

Another depressing UK milestone was reached on this Easter Sunday, with an additional 737 deaths taking the total over the 10,000 mark, including more than 30 members of NHS staff. No wonder there was so much fear on the frontline, and anger at the continued lack of PPE and testing. Sir Patrick Vallance originally had asserted that 20,000 or less deaths would be a 'good outcome', but with half of that figure already reached and still doubts around whether we had reached the peak, there were grave concerns that the death toll could be very much higher than 20,000.

The USA reached its own dreadful milestone by overtaking Italy (19,899) in becoming the country with the highest death toll at 21,409, in fact every US state was regarded as being a disaster zone. As states 'fought' each other for medical supplies to fight the virus, it made one even more thankful in the UK for our conjoined National Health Service, which Boris Johnson described as 'unbeatable'.

Much in this pandemic was made of the number of cases, hospitalisations and deaths caused by Covid-19, but it is also very important to note that several people have actually made miraculous recoveries against all the odds, despite their age or underlying ill health. We witnessed some very heart-warming images of medical staff applauding their frail but alive patients, as they have been wheeled triumphantly from ICU to their recovery wards. It is, however, widely thought that as many as 7 out of 10 patients who have been in ICU do struggle in their recovery, suffering from long-term mental, physical or cognitive issues.

We had now been in Lockdown for nearly three weeks, most of us compliantly observing the 'STAY AT HOME' and social distancing messages, and this despite the best weekend of weather so far this year. There was still so much that we did not know about the virus and how it would affect our lives in the future, but lifestyle and freedom as we knew it had, for the time being at least, changed beyond recognition; with the government's update on the Lockdown imminent, what would Dominic Raab, Boris Johnson's stand-in, tell the nation the following week?

~

TODAY'S DAILY TIP: Easter is a time for new beginnings and with the nature of Lockdown, it is a time to learn new skills and habits, so why not read a new book, learn a new language or even learn to juggle! (SPIRITUAL)

Day 21, Monday 13th April (Easter Monday): The 10K Challenge

"The running shoes are ready on the day Alex announces his 10K challenge"

And the sun continued to shine (albeit with an unseasonal a chill in the air)..............and it was the day that Alex bizarrely announced to me that in a month's time we were going to be running a 10K together! I could barely bring myself to run a 5K, so to claim out of the blue that we were going to embark on a 10K was frankly ridiculous and completely random. Of course I begged the question of Alex, why we should be doing such a challenge? And the answer was as surprising as it was totally heart-warming, literally the 13th May, 2020 would be exactly a year to the day that Alex had undergone his last bout of major open heart surgery, and he wanted to prove to himself that he now had the physical endurance and mental strength to achieve something, that up until now, he had never been able to do – a quite staggering undertaking!

We all get inspired to do things in life by people, usually older than us, that have something that we crave for. I found Alex's courage and determination truly inspirational and needless to say, I was going to be with him every step of that 10K. So off we went on our first run together with a steady 1K up the road and the countdown to 13th May had begun.

With Boris Johnson now convalescing well away from the public eye, the British people were keen to know what the government's next step was in the managing of the pandemic crisis in the UK. It was widely expected that the man with the dubious honour of 'stand-in' Prime Minister, Foreign Secretary Dominic Raab, was going to tell us all on the following Thursday that Lockdown was going to be extended by another three weeks. This would probably be at least until 7th May, but would give the Prime Minister more time to reflect during his recuperation, on a long-term recovery plan.

As he spoke to us at Monday's press conference he praised everyone for their compliance over the Easter weekend. 'Your efforts are making all the difference', he stated and 'amidst this sobering death toll (there had been a further 717 deaths, described by Mr Raab as 'grisly') there are also some positive signs from the data'. As cases and hospitalisations were slowing down there was some evidence that the so-called peak may have been reached and that things were starting to plateau, something we had already seen happen in Italy and Spain. Scientists were still very cautious about this with Sir Patrick Vallance still concerned that the death toll may rise again in what could be a 'difficult' week ahead.

At this stage Mr Raab gave no real indication of what specifically may be announced on Thursday save to say that, 'If we let up, the virus will only take full advantage'. It was indeed interesting to hear from the public's perspective that nearly 75 per cent of the nation favoured further measures to limit the spread of the virus, which re-enforces the level of fear that had gripped the country, notwithstanding the fact that the daily death toll was still very high.

A small percentage were in favour of protecting the economy regardless of the impact of the virus, so at this stage the majority of the British public appeared to be in favour of remaining in Lockdown. It may also be argued that there were some people who were actually enjoying this new way of life, spending unexpected amounts of cherished time with their families and partaking in thoroughly enjoyable activities and pastimes in a much more relaxed and less stressed environment – would another three weeks of this necessarily be a hardship?

Rather than improving the PPE crisis seemed to be worsening, with reports of some gown shortages over the Easter weekend. One of the main problems with PPE in this pandemic was that much of it needed to be disposed of after use due to the very infectious nature of the virus. With just under 1.6 million NHS staff and around 1.4 million carers, demand was still outstripping supply with the number of very sick Covid-19 patients still in hospitals, and a mounting number in care homes. It was revealed that the government, for a number of reasons, had several opportunities to purchase PPE - namely gowns, masks and gloves, and some higher protection visors – as part of a deal with the European Union (EU), earlier in the crisis. Also there had been, allegedly, various batches of sub-standard equipment and issues with shipments from China.

I am sure that on occasions the media may well have blown elements of the PPE issue out of proportion. Sensationalist journalism claiming that some, not all of the 1,257 NHS hospitals were suffering from severe shortages of PPE and that some nurses were close to refusing to work, is aimed at selling more newspapers, creating hysteria and taking the government to task. There is absolutely no doubt that mistakes were made in our lack of preparedness and slowness to respond, as the perception was indeed reality, but it certainly was a monumental and never-ending task to keep up with the demand, described by Mr Hancock as a 'Herculean effort'. For now, Mr Hancock was urged to appreciate that there was still a huge problem and to up the ante even if it meant 'donations' of goggles from B&Q, masks from Airbus and Rolls-Royce or gowns from Burberry. Drafting in the army to aid with deliveries and logistics, particularly where there were large stocks PPE stored in Scotland, was indeed a good move.

The debate about whether people should wear face masks in public raged on, with the WHO now saying that they should be worn in every country across the globe, an assertion that was different to a week or so previously. Sir Patrick Vallance was not convinced when pressed, stating that evidence was 'much more persuasive for masks stopping you giving it (the virus) to somebody than it is for preventing you catching it.' So, for now, no face masks!

As supermarkets and corner shops were coping better, with demand nearly back to 'normal' levels, shelves were now filling back up with some of the key essential items such as toilet rolls, eggs, paracetamol and hand sanitiser. With bars, restaurants, cafes and pubs closed, however, over supply of some perishable produce was inevitable, as we had already seen with items such as meat and fish; these could in some cases now be purchased a lot cheaper than in normal times.

There were, however, stories from some of the 2,000 dairy farmers, who had such a super-saturation of unwanted milk on their farms and no way of changing from bulk to smaller packaging, that there was no other alternative than to throw away hundreds and hundreds of litres of milk every day. Many pub landlords had the same challenge with thousands and thousands of pints of lager, cider and ale being disposed of. There was a harsh realisation that it was not just the closure of a café or pub that was impacting livelihoods, the economy and our ability to purchase our favourite daily coffee or pint of beer, but it was everyone and every business in that supply chain also. Another three weeks of Lockdown may well control the spread of the virus, but in turn the resultant economic downturn would likely cut very deep.

As Italy's death toll rose by another 566, passing the depressing 20,000 (20,465) milestone, the total number of deaths in the US rose to 22,960, 10,056 alone being in New York – an interesting comparison is that 2,753 died in the attack on the Twin Towers of the World Trade Centre. In Spain things seemed to be improving a little more with a growth in the daily death toll of 517, bringing their total to 17,489, the third highest behind the US and Italy.

In France, President Macron announced a further four weeks of Lockdown, which had originally been imposed on 17th March. He was heavily criticised by the French people for his handling of the crisis in France but did at least admit that there had been errors, particularly in their lack of preparedness. There were still concerns that the unrest in the country could spark violent uprisings, something France and their people are famed for over many years. Their daily death toll rose by a further 574 taking their total to 14,967, the fourth highest so far of all the countries globally.

Germany continued to be regarded as the country in central Europe that was both the best prepared in their ICUs and the quickest to get on top of testing. This is borne out by the fact that only 3,022 deaths had been recorded in the country thus far, despite 128,092 cases.

The UK's total number of deaths now stood at 11,329, the fifth highest of all countries. With deaths in care homes not presently being recorded in the statistics and seriously on the rise, would this figure increase dramatically over the coming days and weeks, and credibility in the government start to dissipate?

~

TODAY'S DAILY TIP: As important as planning one's activities and jobs for the coming week is to carry out what one has planned to do, and avoid putting the things off that we do not really want to do. Procrastinating can cause unnecessary anxiety – as Nike say in their slogan, 'Just Do It'. (MENTAL)

Day 22, Tuesday 14th April: Anguish in care homes

And the sun continued to shine for the 23rd consecutive day............ and what a day to be outside. After a morning up a ladder in the spring sunshine pruning hedges, whose growth had proliferated over the previous couple of weeks, Alex and I set off for our run, which was part of a new daily routine. Alex had never really run any distances before, other than up and down a cricket wicket whilst batting. I usually made sure I umpired whilst Alex was batting in case of any sudden setbacks with his health and I was always on hand with water to ensure he was well hydrated, particularly on hot days.

“Many a hedge and bush were trimmed in Lockdown”

We of course took things easy for our first couple of runs, ensuring Alex’s heart and lungs got used to these increased levels of activity. During his operation last year the surgeon had replaced the infected conduit responsible for the flow of blood from the lower part of his body to his heart. Running for an extended period of time would be something that his key organs would take some time to become fully accustomed to, but the early signs of his levels of endurance were encouraging.

Having had a night off from our various Zoom quizzes, that evening we watched the first couple of episodes of the TV drama ‘The Quiz’, ITV’s portrayal of Major Charles Ingram and his dubious £1 million win on ‘Who Wants to Be a Millionaire’. This was another one of many re-runs screened in Lockdown that, in my eyes, seemed better second time around, and having done so many quizzes myself recently I am sure I got more of the answers right!

We saw the first signs from the Chancellor of the Exchequer, Rishi Sunak that the economic outlook for the country seemed to be much bleaker than had been originally anticipated. He admitted to being 'deeply troubled' by analysts' forecasts that predicted that the expected recession could be as bad as the Great Depression in the 1930's. With the economy projected to be shrinking by 6.5 per cent by the end of the year, the biggest drop since the mid-1920's; April, May and June alone were expected to be down by a shocking 35 per cent.

'These are tough times and there will be more to come', Mr Sunak said and despite the financial support that had thus far been offered to many in the UK, he solemnly stated: 'We can't protect every business and every household............our economy is going to take this significant hit..........people are going to feel that in their jobs and in their household incomes'. Reading between the lines, it appeared larger tax rises in the future were inevitable to pay back the government deficit, but this may take years and may seriously impact younger generations.

Despite this rather gloomy statement, he did remain resolute in wanting to get people back to work as quickly as was possible and that maybe the economy could 'snap back' to some degree of normality. There were of course going to be many employees who simply would not be able to return to work once Lockdown was eased, so the portent of mass redundancy and unemployment was very much on the horizon.

Deaths in the so-called 'forgotten' sector, care homes, were now very worryingly on the rise. It was claimed that there were now recorded outbreaks in two out of every three of the 11,300 care homes in Britain, which was leading to higher relative mortality rates in care homes than in hospitals. This situation was manifested by continued allegations that thousands of unwell elderly patients were supposedly discharged from hospitals back into care homes before being tested to relieve the pressure on those hospitals. There were continued calls for the Office for National Statistics (ONS) to include deaths in care homes as part of the overall daily death toll figures.

It was also still perceived that care assistants were being left without PPE and a robust testing process had not yet reached care homes. One former minister suggested that care home residents were 'being abandoned like lambs to the slaughter' because of a continued lack of support for management and staff in care homes. Rishi Sunak, during the daily press conference, wanted to reassure the sector by stating that, '.......you have absolutely not been forgotten.' Once again it raised the question as to whether there was a disconnection between what the politicians believed was being done to help those in care homes, and what was actually happening in reality.

I can only begin to imagine what it must have been like to be either in a care home as an employee, or as a resident during this pandemic. The care sector provides an extremely valuable and, in my opinion, undervalued and underfunded arm of support to the NHS, but with a 20 per cent rise in the number of people over 65 since 2010, there are just not enough care workers to provide a very different type of care from that in hospitals.

I have the utmost respect for each and every care and indeed hospice worker, who are often dealing with patients, not always the elderly, with very complicated and/or chronic, physical and/or mental illnesses. They also often must provide end of life care, witness residents dying, as well as need to communicate with families who end up losing cherished loved ones. Add to this a virus that most affected the elderly, often with prolonged illnesses, and a lack of protective equipment, testing and knowledge, and one can see how very special and caring these people are, especially with their poor level of remuneration.

From a resident's perspective, suddenly not being allowed to have family and friends to visit must have been completely soul-destroying. Many of these residents will have already lost spouses, and despite the company of fellow residents and care home assistants they would still be feeling the great pain of those losses. For many of them, now being denied the opportunity to see other members of their family, this may have just been the final straw; I often wonder how many of the Covid-19 deaths in care homes could actually have been attributed to 'broken hearts'.

We should also not forget the 1.5 million people that were forced to shield for 12 weeks, many of whom were elderly and lived on their own, and who would also have been denied visits from family and friends alike. I am sure for many of these people also, the loneliness and isolation would have been quite unbearable; at least there were volunteers and good neighbours to keep an eye on them.

One of the names that became so synonymous with the Covid-19 crisis, was that of Captain Tom Moore, a 99 year-old Second World War army veteran, who set himself a target of walking around his garden 100 times to raise £1,000 for the NHS. He aimed to do this by April 30th, the day of his 100th birthday. News of Captain Tom, as he became affectionately known, and his compelling challenge, spread around the nation at great speed as benefactors migrated to his fundraising page. Amazingly his total had already reached over £2 million – by the time 30th April arrived, the amount had gone through the roof and he had become the nation's 'darling' and an inspiration to everybody.

There had been serious fears in March that intensive care units (ICUs) in London hospitals may be overwhelmed by Covid-19 patients, necessitating more ICU capacity than the existing 770 beds. Consequently, and at no small cost to the taxpayer, the NHS Nightingale Hospital was erected in just nine days at the site of the Excel exhibition centre in Docklands, East London, and opened on Friday 3rd April. The hospital had now been open nearly two weeks but only 19 patients had used it over the Easter weekend. With a capacity for 2,900 ICU beds and talk of the peak of the virus about to be reached, would this temporary facility ever attain anywhere near capacity?

Where the government had been criticised for its lack of preparedness at the beginning of the crisis, having this extra capacity meant that they were well prepared now to avoid some of the scenes that we saw in Italy, with patients suffering in corridors. If, however, this hospital or any of the others around the country remained at low occupancy, they might be regarded as a waste of money and as 'white elephants'; the government were damned if they did and damned if they didn't.

The daily death toll in the UK had now risen by a further 778 taking the total to 12,107. The UK's figures included Northern Ireland's but not Ireland's, where the total number of deaths was still below 400. The Irish Prime Minister, Leo Varadkar, was reported to have criticised the UK's delay in locking down. He asserted that schools and pubs in Ireland had closed on March 12th and 15th respectively, over a week before the UK, and maybe he made a fair point looking at the comparative numbers.

Meanwhile, the German Chancellor, Angela Merkel, was planning to open primary schools and Italy was beginning a limited easing of Lockdown; were these signs that the virus was mutating into a milder form, and that Central Europe was trying to get things going again?

~

TODAY'S DAILY TIP: The more colour on your plate usually means that the meal you are eating is that much more likely to be healthy and provide the necessary goodness for both a balanced diet and to protect your immune system. Whether it is the green of lettuce or an avocado, the orange of a carrot or pepper, the red of a tomato or radish, or the purple of beetroot or 'red' cabbage, get that colour on your plate. (PHYSICAL)

Day 23, Wednesday 15th April: Virtual concert time

"Another stunning day in Hampshire"

And the sun continued to shine and it was another stunning day.............and this was the day I should have gone to a Simple Minds concert in Bournemouth with Alex and my very good friends, Chris Sherman and Steve Wilson. Needless to say, this was one of many events that had been cancelled or postponed owing to the pandemic, with the risk of the spread of the virus at its greatest in crowded and enclosed venues. For those who have not heard of Simple Minds, they are an 'Eighties' Scottish rock band famed for hits such as 'Don't you forget about me' and 'Alive and Kicking'. Their lead singer is Jim Kerr who was married at one time to the lead singer of the Pretenders, Chrissie Hynde for six years and to actress, Patsy Kensit, for four years.

I met Chris (Sherman) and his wife, Alison, when I worked for him as a graduate trainee hotel manager at the Caversham Hotel (now the Crowne Plaza run at present by my good friend, Nick) in Reading in 1989. The same hotel where, during the following year, I met my wife, Susie. Chris is a true leader of people who became one of the biggest influences on my career and taught me so much about running a successful hotel.

I met Steve in the same establishment when he was working in the hotel's restaurant. He was to become the Night Manager a year or so later and we became great friends, both reporting to Chris. Chris certainly worked us hard, but we also learned a lot under his tutelage - and he did reward us for our hard work with some excellent meals out with TGI Fridays being a regular haunt.

During this memorable time of my career we all discovered that we had a mutual appreciation for Simple Minds and have since attended many concerts around the country. They have made many albums over the years, some politically motivated, and are still an exhilarating and impressive band to watch live; this concert was meant to be part of their 40 years anniversary, and thankfully has been re-scheduled for February of next year, Covid-19 permitting!

To mark the concert, Chris and I, and our respective sons, Tom and Alex, both now avid fans, listened via Zoom to a compilation of Simple Minds' greatest hits over a couple of beers; sadly Steve was unwell but we raised a glass to him. It was not quite the real thing, but it was a great night of reminiscence in excellent company.

One of the things I reflected on a lot on during this pandemic was how families with young children were coping, particularly if they did not have their own outside space and if there was some form of conflict between the parents, meaning that the children suffered. I imagine at times it must have been a 'pressure cooker' environment with so many of our usual routines and habits denied to us. There was at least for many the opportunity to get out of our domestic surroundings for exercise and to enjoy the fantastic weather. I cannot help thinking though, that for some, poor mental health and depression were huge factors during and even after Lockdown.

One of our next door neighbour's sons, Max, celebrated his birthday on this day, which I am sure must have been hard for him not being able to see his friends. Many young children will have been denied contact with their friends, particularly where schools were closed, and the levels of anxiety experienced in relation to the virus should not be underestimated. That said, I am sure he had a great time with his family, even though the delivery company erred with his main present, sending him the wrong bike!

There would have been so many people who had plans in place to celebrate birthdays, weddings and other special occasions, but their excitement would have turned to disappointment as Lockdown got a grip on the nation. Many will have made the best of a difficult situation, and for others, I guess there is always next year. Poignantly for many, there would be no more celebrations.

There was a continued sense that the UK was now reaching the peak of the crisis with cases of infection and the death toll, which had stayed below 700 for the fourth day running – a figure still far too high - starting to plateau somewhat. Even though it was likely that restrictions were going to remain in place for another three weeks at least, the Labour leader Sir Keir Starmer, was calling on the government to set out a plan as to how we were going to exit from Lockdown. The government claimed that it would be too soon to communicate an 'exit strategy' as it may confuse the 'STAY AT HOME' message.

There was general consensus across all parties that our children's mental health and long-term prospects were being compromised by the Lockdown and that to get schools open needed to be one of the key priorities to an easing of the restrictions. This of course sounded easier in theory than in practice, particularly with how much fear there was still across the country of catching the virus. The theory was that if children could go back to school then parents could go back to work and aid the recovery of the economy. It was also assumed that children were the age group least affected by the virus.

On the other side of the argument, opening schools too quickly could increase the risk of a so-called second wave, as children could still transmit the virus asymptomatically to teachers and parents alike. There were also factors such as social distancing, school meals and sanitisation, amongst other things, that needed serious consideration, and much collaboration between government and school officials. It may have been less complicated to close down schools, but it was certainly not going to be straightforward reopening them or returning to any other aspects of what one might regard as 'normal life'.

Many British businesses got involved in the fight against Covid-19, manufacturing key equipment for the NHS in particular and proving that the UK is one of the world leaders in innovation and industry. One of the main areas of focus had been in providing ventilators, which had been in quite short supply and would need to be used for Covid-19 patients in an ICU who were experiencing very serious breathing difficulties.

A consortium had been set up called VenilatorChallengeUK, after Boris Johnson's rallying call back in March, for industry to produce as many ventilators as possible but in doubly quick time. Companies in the consortium included Siemens, Airbus, Rolls-Royce, BAE Systems, Ford and Dyson, and there was encouraging news that the first newly adapted ventilators built by the consortium had been regulated and approved, so that the production of around 5,000 ventilators could start imminently; the government would subsequently come in with an order of 15,000, half the number they had originally advocated. One industry source asserted: 'We are not in this for the money, we want to help the NHS....'

Meanwhile Captain Tom Moore's mission to raise as much money as possible, now that he had smashed his original £1,000 target, was gaining momentum in a quite incredible fashion. In just 24 hours he had managed to raise another £7 million, bringing his total to just over £9 million, money that would go to the organisation, NHS Charities Together. Captain Tom, who had served in Burma and India in the Second World War, was being showered with plaudits with some were even calling for him to be knighted.

The daily death toll in the UK rose by another 781 bringing the total number of deaths in hospitals only, to 12,868, and at last, Health Secretary Matt Hancock was going to be introducing new ruling whereby close family members could say goodbyes to their loved ones 'where possible', which would be so much more dignified than having heart-breaking conversations over the telephone or video links. To facilitate this there were going to be new measures and stringent regulations to 'limit the risk of infection'. Meanwhile there was mounting pressure on the government to provide statistics that included those who had sadly died in the care sector. Deaths in care homes were fast on the increase as a horrible crisis loomed large.

~

TODAY'S DAILY TIP: One of my great passions and hobbies in my youth was to do jigsaw puzzles, something I re-acquainted myself with throughout the Lockdown period. They are a great way to relax, have therapeutic tendencies and are beneficial to one's mental health. One may have puzzles in the loft or stored away in cupboards but if not they are readily available on-line. (MENTAL)

Day 24, Thursday 16th April: Three more weeks of Lockdown at least!

And a hint of rain in the air, the first time for nearly a month......................and whilst doing my routine early morning chores, I watched a rather spicy exchange of views between Health Secretary Hancock and one Piers Morgan. What I like about Mr Morgan is that he is not frightened to ask the questions that others shy away from and he will challenge politicians, fiercely holding them to account – I have witnessed Kay Burley on Sky News adopting a similar stance.

What consistently irked me though, particularly in this exchange with Mr Hancock, was Mr Morgan's persistent 'butting in', not ever allowing Mr Hancock the opportunity to answer fully a question that had been posed. I do appreciate that many of our politicians' answers, particularly when challenged, are frankly waffle and rarely answer the questions properly, but I just wish, talking as a viewer, that Mr Morgan would do a little more listening and a little less talking. That said, there is a reason why GMTV's ratings went through the roof and that is because of Mr Morgan; he may be divisive at times, but he is a good watch.

"The training for Alex's 10K challenge starts in earnest"

Alex and I resorted to the morning for our daily run, as we built up to the 10K, scheduled for 13th May. We changed the mode from road-running to a bit of 'cross-country', taking in a lovely rural route adjacent to the M3 and popular with dog walkers. About 20 minutes into the run Alex suddenly stopped and I feared that this was the end of the challenge, with his body telling him, 'thou shalt not run long distances!'

Extended periods of running create significantly more blood flow around the body than other less strenuous exercise which Alex had been used to doing up until now. During his operation last year, the surgeon had replaced the infected conduit tubing, taking blood from the lower part of his body into the heart and where he was suddenly exerting himself more intensively, the blood was taking more time to get through the conduit. This resulted in pain and discomfort in his stomach, and as we later discovered, was what caused him to stop. After taking on water and walking for a short period of time, the pain subsided and he began running again, but this time a little more tentatively. The rest of the run passed without incident, although inwardly I began to suspect that a 10K was just going to be 'a bridge too far', a thought that I was of course reticent to share with Alex.

As expected, Foreign Secretary and 'stand-in' Prime Minister, Dominic Raab, announced a three week extension to the period of Lockdown for review on or around 7th May, but with words of hope indicating that there was 'light at the end of the tunnel'. To be fair to the government, Boris Johnson had said on 19th March, that it would take 12 weeks for the 'tide to turn', and we were only a third of the way into that timeframe.

There was a proviso that five key criteria needed to be met and he was keen to stress that if restrictions were eased too soon that we would 'risk sacrificing all the progress we have made'; this could in turn could lead to a second wave of infections. Of course, as was the government's usual tactic of absolving themselves from blame when making any potentially divisive announcement, they were being wholly guided by the science.

The five-point plan was as follows:

- That the NHS could cope across the UK

- That there was a sustained and consistent drop in the daily death toll

- That it was evidenced that the rate of infection was reducing to 'manageable levels'

- That there were enough testing kits and PPE to meet the demand in all sectors

- That there was not a risk of a second wave that may overwhelm the NHS

The optimism that the government had was borne out of the fact that the 'R' number, the reproduction rate of the virus, had now fallen below one. We had now been isolating ourselves from others for over three weeks and, when we did come into contact with people in supermarkets for example, we were keeping our distance. This in turn meant that, if we were infected, we would be passing the virus onto less than one other person. Only three weeks ago this number had been at between 2.4 and 4.

Testing was still a major talking point, especially as Health Secretary Hancock had optimistically, in many people's eyes, set an end of month target of 100,000 tests per day. Only 18,665 tests had been carried out the day before even though there was a reported capacity of 35,000; this was barely 4,000 more tests than had been carried out three days previously. Germany, meanwhile, was reportedly up to nearly 100,000 tests per day. Health officials continued to blame the government for confusion around eligibility for testing and also for the inaccessibility of some testing sites. The government responded by claiming that there was plenty of capacity for all frontline staff. Either way, to be nearly four weeks into Lockdown with so few tests having been carried out would undoubtedly lead to criticism of the government.

Mr Hancock was also in the 'firing line' answering criticism as to why an alleged 15,000 flights were still coming into the UK per day without testing or having to quarantine. Some of these passengers were travelling from very affected countries such the US, Spain and Italy, and I must say it was incredibly baffling that this was being allowed to happen. When challenged on this, Mr Hancock gave the bizarre answer, 'We don't test at airports because the number of people coming through has dropped dramatically.' He strangely seemed to think that 105,000 new people per week did not pose any Covid-19 health threat. Other countries had closed their borders and the US had banned entry for people from the UK very near the start of Lockdown. Had the government just been naïve and was this another policy that would end up in a 'u-turn'?

With the challenge around care homes increasing daily, Mr Hancock was quick to play the political card and ask us to clap for carers as well as the NHS. The focus in previous weeks was very much centred around paying our appreciation to frontline hospital staff and the government were acutely aware of the public's perception of their handling of the virus in care homes; Mr Hancock even replaced his NHS badge with a new 'Care' badge signifying that he was bringing the NHS and social care together as a 'single brand'.

Meanwhile Dominic Raab was 'flexing his muscles' with China stating that they needed to face 'hard questions' about the source of the virus. In the same breath he stressed that: 'We ought to look at all sides of this.......' whilst emphasising that relationships with Beijing were 'very good'. This was going to be a tricky one to untangle and Mr Raab would need all his powers of diplomacy as should befit a Foreign Secretary.

As America recorded another near 19,000 new cases of the virus and with their total death toll still rising dramatically to 33,875, President Trump controversially announced that he was going to be unveiling plans to ease restrictions saying that the US had 'passed the peak' of the pandemic. Mr Trump appeared intent on getting the economy back up and running and America back open for business, although state governors were insistent that restrictions should remain in place for many more weeks to come. It is actually the governors that have the power to re-open states, and the governor of New York duly announced that Lockdown would remain in place until at least 15th May. Protests against Lockdown in some states indicated that the country was split.

Proud Yorkshire man, Captain Tom Moore, continued to endear himself to the nation and finally completed his challenge of walking around his garden 100 times to a guard of honour from the 1st Battalion Yorkshire Regiment. His fundraising efforts had now passed the £15 million mark and he was fast becoming an international superstar. He even 'sang' a few words of Michael Ball's version of 'You'll Never Walk Alone', and reassured the nation: 'To all those finding it difficult, the sun will shine on you again and the clouds will go away'

A further 861 deaths from Covid-19 were recorded in the UK bringing the total to 13,729. Of these, 12,395 were in England, 699 in Scotland, 495 in Wales and 140 in Northern Ireland. One of the big concerns was the number of excess deaths that were being reported that were not attributed to Covid-19. Were we now on the brink of even bigger health crisis with a backlog of cancer, heart and liver patients waiting too long for treatment and in the case of very serious illnesses, too frightened to go to A&E for fear of contracting Covid-19?

~

TODAY'S DAILY TIP: Those of us who possess a loft will know that this space can become cluttered with all the things that we cannot bring ourselves to throw away which are then forgotten. So, get up in that loft, you never know what you might find. (SPIRITUAL)

Day 25, Friday 17th April: Rain, rain, glorious rain

AND TODAY THE RAIN CAME POURING DOWN AND PRETTY MUCH PERSISTED ALL DAY.......and the garden, that had started to look like we back in the drought of the summer of 1976, got a much needed drenching. Needless to say, there was no walk with Tizzy or run with Alex! Instead I had a good day to focus on the 3,000 piece jigsaw puzzle that was proving to be a little more challenging than I had expected. The usual Friday night visit to the Otter pub, for a traditional fish and chips, and quiz night, followed.

"Holly and Alex try a bit of Tik Tok"

Having a routine to one's day was an important way in which the daily boredom of Lockdown could be countered. There were many tales of bored people creating their own videos of a variety of topics and posting them on the various forms of social media. As quickly as they were posted numerous videos were then going viral, providing an amazing assortment of material for a nation hungry for innovative entertainment. Holly and Alex jumped on the 'bandwagon' performing a rather amusing dance and posting it on Tik Tok, a social media platform for creating, sharing and discovering short music videos, that became synonymous with Lockdown. It was especially popular with the young as an outlet to express themselves through singing, dancing and comedy. Some were becoming internet sensations overnight though I am not sure Holly and Alex gained more than 40 likes, but they certainly caused a huge amount of mirth within family circles!

The government were adamant that they were not going to be drawn on what an exit plan from Lockdown looked like as it may undermine the 'STAY AT HOME' message. Senior Tory MPs accused ministers of 'treating the public like children' as pressure grew on the government to publish their exit strategy. As one MP and former cabinet minister urged: 'The government must use this period of extended Lockdown to develop a plan…….' Another said: 'Communication is critical in keeping people on board. You need to educate the nation about what to expect in the next phase.'

Although it was important to see what was happening in other countries ahead of us in the easing of Lockdown, what we were probably seeing from the government were delaying tactics in the absence of the Prime Minister. An organisation can function pretty efficiently for a period of time without its leader, but after a while a hiatus can appear and in this case one cabinet minister summed it up perfectly by saying: 'We are in a holding pattern until Boris gets back'.

Reports of in-fighting between senior ministers were now becoming commonplace and this was very much symptomatic of a leaderless cabinet that was caught between the advice of confused scientists and the ebullience of Dominic Cummings, Boris Johnson's most senior advisor. The latter was very much back from his lay-off due to the virus and as a number 10 figure observed: 'Back to his forceful best….' Foreign Secretary Dominic Raab may have been the 'nominated' stand-in for Boris, but it was the other Dominic who was seen to be calling the shots. With the sometimes petulant Health Secretary Hancock, the suave Chancellor of the Exchequer Sunak and the old-stager Minister of the Cabinet Office Gove, all with differing views, there was mounting friction as to what the cabinet should do next.

Scotland's First Minister, Nicola Sturgeon, was much more committed to treating the 'public like adults' as she assured the Scottish people that she would produce a 'decision-making framework' the following week to ease Scotland out of

Lockdown. It became a slightly confusing aspect of Lockdown, where we are supposedly governed and legislated by a UK Prime Minister, yet the first ministers of Scotland, Wales and Northern Ireland could willingly make their own and different decisions from those of Boris Johnson and his cabinet.

The politicians and scientists continued the debate around whether face masks should be worn in public confusing us all as to what the right approach might be. The Mayor of London seemed to think the UK was 'lagging behind the international community' by not imposing them on the British people. Leading scientists though were still telling us at the daily briefings: 'We do not recommend face masks for general wearing by the public....', and: 'the evidence is weak and the effect is small......' Several doctors meanwhile, were petitioning in favour of those in Britain wearing a face covering in public. Grant Shapps, the Transport Secretary, made the situation even less clear by saying: 'It is not the right moment to instruct people................to wear them if we are not certain yet that they are going to be advantageous', almost insinuating that we may be asked to wear them in the future.

With some Hospitals still allegedly running low on stocks of PPE, one wondered whether this may have been one of the reasons that the government wanted us to avoid the use of face masks at this stage. But it was full-length gowns that appeared to be in most short supply with a concern that several hospitals would run out of them over the weekend; the issue of PPE would just not go away for the government.

There was some good news on the Covid-19 treatment front as 100 of the most unwell UK Covid-19 patients were exposed to a US antiviral drug called Remdesivir, produced by a company called Gilead Sciences. As usual with anything that came out of America that was endorsed by President Trump, UK scientists and medics were urging caution, despite the reports of US Covid-19 patients making a rather rapid recovery from the more serious elements of the disease. Remdesivir had originally been used to treat Ebola but was also advocated enthusiastically by the WHO back in February, as a potential treatment for Covid-19. Other drugs that we were starting to hear about as possible treatment to reduce the severity of the symptoms, were hydroxychloroquine and dexamethasone but clinical tests were still very much ongoing.

Rushi Sunak's popularity increased another notch with the announcement that his much-celebrated Furlough scheme, effectively a £40 billion wage subsidy to those in paid employment, was to be extended until June. The commitment was to pay up to 80% of an employee's monthly salary up to a cap of £2,500.00. Whilst this was great news for many, was it delaying further the inevitability that many would actually lose their jobs when the scheme eventually ended?

As Captain Tom Moore's fundraising efforts incredibly topped the £19 million mark, many of the British public were becoming more and more at one with nature as they were spending more time out and about walking in the fresh air, and/or their local rural communities. Despite the closure of pubs, restaurants, non-essential shops and the like, some people were reconnecting with simpler less stressful lifestyles with cleaner air and a greater interest in wildlife; one expert described it as the 'Captain Tom effect', as Britain continued to take the modest and humble 99-year-old war veteran to their hearts.

As industry and business continued to creep back to life in Wuhan, the supposed source of the virus, after a 76-day Lockdown, it was revealed that the death toll in Wuhan was as much as 50% higher than had originally been reported. President Trump was continually critical of China's whole culpability for the pandemic which in turn had wrecked the US economy. The apparent lack of transparency in the reporting of their numbers of Covid-19 cases and deaths just fuelled his fire even more. China's response was that they had innocently neglected to include those who had perished in their own homes and that the revision of their figures was purely an oversight. To be fair to China, the countries of Italy, Spain and Britain all increased their death tolls once non-hospital deaths had been recorded. That said, there were still many unanswered questions surrounding China's initial lack of communication regarding the virus and that the spread could have been stemmed earlier. A poll indicated that there were many Britons who wanted answers. Meanwhile, China's own economy had shrunk to its lowest level in four decades.

As a further 847 deaths were recorded in the UK, bringing the total to 14,576, there was increased hope that the spread of the disease had finally plateaued. In Italy, 575 deaths were reported meaning they were still the country that had the second highest death toll of 22,745, behind the USA at 35,944. Italy was now really seeing a drop in new cases and less beds in ICUs were being occupied; maybe things were starting to improve throughout Europe, but a leaderless UK government was still lurching from one mini-crisis to another.

~

TODAY'S DAILY TIP: Why not delete any unwanted and unneeded photos or videos on your mobile 'phones as this will not only free up space in the photo library but also may mean that you are not having to re-charge your 'phone so frequently. (SPIRITUAL)

Day 26, Saturday 18th April: Dressing-up for the dinner

The grass already looked a shade greener after the previous day's downpours and after a moderately inclement day of gloom and cloud, the sun came out in the evening for what was to prove to be one our most enjoyable evenings in Lockdown. Prior to that, Alex and I managed to convince Holly to come for a run with us as part of our 10K build-up, something she duly did with great vim and vigour. Convincing her to actually run the 10K was to prove a 'bridge too far'!

"Everyone dressed up for the 'Ken Wilde' dinner"

During the evening we were meant to have supported our good friend, Ken Wilde, with his charity fundraising evening. Much like many similar events, Ken was forced to postpone the charity function to a later date in the year. Instead of abandoning the evening totally, Ken asked would-be attendees to hold their own virtual dinners, posting updates and photos on social media. Now our family do not need a second invitation to dress up; out came the fancy frocks and ironed shirts and we headed to the patio in the evening sun, for photos, champagne and Susie's sumptuous homemade canapés. Even little Tizzy joined in, donning her fetching new dickie bow and posing for the camera with her cute canine smile.

We set the table with the best cutlery, mats and glassware and Susie produced one of her special Lockdown meals: camembert, mixed olives and assorted breads to start with, followed by chicken schnitzel, pesto fusilli and salad, and finished off with her legendary homemade chocolate brownie and clotted cream; it was all washed down with a lovely chilled Sauvignon Blanc. We of course raised a glass or two to those not so fortunate as we were and once again reflected on the underlying serious reason as to why we were all isolated from other family members and friends.

The evening continued with many of our favourite games including 'Happy Families', 'Uno' and 'Scattergories', as well as an excellent interactive game called 'Knowledge is Power', a clever general knowledge quiz played on everyone's mobile phones, where each person has their own quirky character. As usual, competition was fierce with Holly and Alex as the habitual winners. We rounded off the evening with dancing and 'Sing star', a form of 'Karaoke', in the orangery. It was undoubtedly a truly enjoyable and uplifting evening and we hope we did Ken proud.

Back in the crazy and uncertain world of Covid-19, the rate of infections and deaths continued to plateau, and there was a real belief amongst some experts, that the peak of the epidemic in the UK had at last been reached. In areas of China, however, there were reports of a surge in new cases of the virus; were these the first signs of the so-called second wave that everyone feared so much?

~

TODAY'S DAILY TIP: One of my most therapeutic activities during Lockdown was cutting down or pruning hedges. Because of the growing season and despite the dry weather, as quickly as the hedges were being cut down, they were growing again. To engender a real sense of achievement it is a good idea to take pictures before you start and when you have finished the job. (PHYSICAL)

Day 27, Sunday 19th April: Remembering Dear Uncle John

As the beautiful spring weather re-appeared after the much-needed recent rainfall, our weekend morning walks with all the family became even more cherished. The usual route took us to the Quarry followed by an amble once again through what we know locally as Bluebell Woods – and with sunlight glinting through the trees and the bluebells in full flower, it was quite a picture.

"Loving the family walk in Bluebell Woods"

Throughout the Lockdown, I was acutely aware of several people I knew who were living on their own, who although in adequately good health mentally and physically, would no doubt have been feeling a great sense of loneliness on a daily basis. One of those people was my Auntie Heather, who lives barely a 15 minute walk away. She had lost her husband, and my much-loved Uncle John, to Alzheimer's disease last year. Uncle John – it appears many people I know have or have had an Uncle John in their lives - was hugely influential in my life, taking me to my first ever Saints game at the Dell in 1977, when I was 10. He also loved his real ale and cricket, playing for and watching St Cross Symondians over the years, one of the area's most celebrated clubs. Professionally, he was a well-respected Doctor of Sound at Southampton University. His passing left a big gap in the lives of Heather and my three cousins Pippa, Susanna and Veronica and all of theirs and our respective families.

We regularly contacted Heather by 'phone throughout Lockdown and Susie would often place essential items such as eggs, on her doorstep. On the way back from today's walk we thought we would try to see her in person so made a point of knocking on her door and retreating back to the pavement, so as to be a safe distance away. Although she has become very independent since she lost John, I could tell she was so pleased to see us, albeit from 20 metres apart, and just have that little bit of 'face-to-face' social interaction that probably made her day.

As Boris Johnson continued to follow the advice of his doctors at Chequers, the Prime Minister's country home in Buckinghamshire, and stay away from number 10 Downing Street, he was reported to have told some of his cabinet colleagues that he was very cautious about the easing of the Lockdown restrictions. Because he had suffered so badly with Covid-19 himself there was clear reticence even to consider changing things as his 'over-riding concern' was to avoid a second wave of the virus, something that China had started to see signs of. Although a different disease and in a different era, more people died of the 1918 Spanish flu outbreak in the second wave, than the first – an estimated 50 million were thought to have died in total.

It was critical to Boris that the 'R' number, the rate of reproduction of the virus, was well below one before restrictions were eased, which supported Health Secretary Hancock's agenda. Cabinet Office Minister Gove and Chancellor of the Exchequer Sunak on the other hand, who both believed the peak had been passed and that the 'R' rate was well down, wanted to start easing things as soon as possible; Foreign Secretary Raab and Boris's supposed 'shoe-filler' was 'sitting on the fence'.

One of the government's leading advisers on the pandemic throughout, was Sir Jeremy Farrar. He was 'fiercely' in favour of a speedy easing of Lockdown telling the media: 'The damage it's (Lockdown) doing to all of our health, our wellbeing, our mental health, is disproportionately of course affecting the most vulnerable. I hope we will get there in three, four weeks' time because it is clear that the Lockdown can't go on for much longer'. If there was a time for decisive, energetic and resolute leadership, it was now, but with Boris so far away from 'the action' and still very weak from his near-death experience, the government would have to continue to 'fumble their way through the dark'. Was it now time to consider the possibility of appointing a deputy to the Prime Minister, who had the true power to make decisions, rather than the ineffective 'stand-in' role that Dominic Raab was supposedly performing?

One of the many important debates still raging was when school pupils might be able to resume their full-time education. Although there were countless parents offering alternative and very impressive methods of tutelage, it was not quite the same for children as being taught in a classroom by trained teaching professionals. Notwithstanding the fact that many parents were experiencing untold levels of stress themselves trying to 'teach' and do their own jobs from home simultaneously. There were some children that were receiving no education at all, which was incredibly concerning for their future prospects.

Over 60 per cent of schools were still partly open, providing an opportunity for the children of key workers or vulnerable children to continue their education or to gain respite from various domestic challenges. Parental fear around the virus was keeping some eligible pupils out of school, but of greater concern, were the number of entitled vulnerable children that were not attending school. Raising fears that they were confined at home, surrounded by domestic abuse or other very frightening situations.

Worryingly Gavin Williamson, the seemingly rather inept Education Secretary, appeared himself unsure of when schools were likely to reopen at the 5.00pm daily press conference. There were reports that they may open their doors at the beginning of June after the official half-term break, but it may only be for a few pupils in certain year groups. The issues of fear amongst parents and of social distancing were going to be key, as distancing particularly would not be the easiest thing to do with young children. Education Secretary Williamson would come under increased scrutiny in the coming weeks and months.

As positive news of potential vaccines continued to filter into the public domain, it was tempered by Chief Scientific Adviser Sir Patrick Vallance's words of caution that we should be careful not to bank on a vaccine to pave the way out of this unprecedented global health crisis. 'All new vaccines that come into development are long shots. Only some end up being successful........This will take time'. He added: 'A vaccine has to be safe to work........With Covid-19 we need to understand more about the immune response.' By exercising caution in this matter, Sir Patrick clearly wanted to under-promise, which would leave him and the many scientists and researchers involved in creating a vaccine, in a better position to over-deliver. He was also concerned that if and when an effective and safe vaccine was eventually ratified, that we would have enough manufacturing capacity to produce doses of the vaccine in the large quantities needed and quickly enough to try to get us back to a semblance of normality. With good progress still being made by Sarah Gilbert at Oxford University's Jenner Institute and talk of a vaccine being readily available by the end of the year, these were indeed wise words.

A further 596 deaths were recorded in the UK and 16,060 in total, although this was still a painfully high number, it represented the lowest daily figure for a fortnight. In Spain, there was talk of children under the age of 13 now being allowed outdoors from 27th April for the first time since Lockdown five weeks previously. In France, some schools and retail outlets were being planned to open from 11th May. Slowly but surely it looked like Europe was starting to open up again, although Sweden never even enforced Lockdown in the first place, instead allowing their citizens to roam free and go to bars and restaurants, whilst observing social distancing; eye-catchingly, their death toll has never got above 6,000.

~

TODAY'S DAILY TIP: It is important in tough times to keep the mind challenged which in turn can help relieve the boredom. I find that a daily crossword and/or a Sudoku are very good for the brain. I have even managed to complete a 'Super Fiendish' Sudoku from the Times, something I have never done before. (MENTAL)

Day 28, Monday 20th April: Fundraising for fun

"The 2019 annual charity event for Wessex Heartbeat"

It was a lovely fresh, breezy morning in Hampshire as Alex and I embarked on our morning run, something that was becoming more routine by the day, as we were building up to his 10K scheduled for 13th May. At this stage, the planned run was purely aimed at testing Alex's endurance and proving to himself that he could achieve something he had never done before in his life. It was only after a brief chat from afar with a lovely lady in our road called Sue that another focus for the run arose. During Lockdown, usually on a weekly basis, I would check that Sue was okay and whether she needed any essential items as well as engaging in brief conversation with her from afar. On one occasion, after I had finished my morning run, I called on Sue and we got talking about Alex's planned run. On hearing about his compelling story, and being an ex-nurse, she rushed to grab a crisp £20.00 note and generously handed it over, suggesting that we used it for any fundraising we might be doing.

Now fundraising is something we have done a lot of as a family over the past 18 years, initially for Wessex Children's Heart Circle, but mostly for Wessex Heartbeat, and our inspiration was Alex with his many cardiac challenges over the years. With the support of so many people, and an annual fundraiser, we have raised thousands of pounds to support children and young adults with serious cardiac issues.

"Winning the Wessex Heartbeat fundraising award for 2019"

Although there are too many people to mention individually, certain individuals have been key to these fantastic evenings that have taken place over so many years. Firstly, Sue and Jon Smith, and Mike Wilson whose respective sons Callum and Jack died far too soon as toddlers, having suffered very severe heart conditions; we continue to remember them at our events and their parents are so brave and inspirational. Then there is the inimitable, witty and local legend Denis Bundy, who has compered the evening so professionally as well as conducting the main auction. Next is our suave and crooning entertainer Martin Murphy, who has sung so ably for us and kept everyone dancing until the end. There are our great friends Antony and Lisa Jackson, and Andrew and Leann Griffiths who have supported us so much with the fundraising on the night. Then there is Pete Vickery who's company SOS based in Southampton, have so kindly sponsored the event pretty much every year. Last but not least is the amazing Geoff Smith, whose annual golf day and dinner in aid of the debilitating lifelong condition that is multiple sclerosis, which he himself suffers from, was a great inspiration for me to do my event in the first place. I must also mention Susie, Holly and of course, Alex, who have all done more than their fair share over the years. We have been so grateful to EVERYONE who has supported our fundraising efforts over the years and hopefully we can continue the event for many years to come.

Needless to say, with our neighbour Sue's initial £20.00 contribution, the next stage of fundraising for Wessex Heartbeat was underway. It would be a couple of weeks before Alex conceived his 'Just Giving' fundraising page and within hours of launching it very generous contributions came flying in from kind benefactors. There was now going to be even more purpose to Alex's incredible physical undertaking.

As Alex embarked on his fundraising mission contribution to Captain Tom Moore's fundraising page now topped more than £27 million, a simply extraordinary achievement. He was in turn inspiring others to challenge their own limitations. A six-year-old boy who suffers from spina bifida particularly comes to mind who, on seeing Captain Tom's resolve, undertook to walk 10 metres per day using his walking frame raising over £100,000 for the NHS. As much as one marvels at such personal courage in completing these challenges, so should the many people's generosity in contributing to charitable causes in difficult times be admired and applauded.

With at least another three weeks of Lockdown economic forecasts for the future prosperity of the nation were looking even gloomier by the day. The high streets of our towns and cities lay empty of shoppers, the hospitality, entertainment, and travel industries were at a standstill and many other businesses were starting to struggle. Global oil reserves were at an all-time high because so few cars were now on the road and planes in the air, thus reducing demand and consumption, bringing petrol prices plummeting. With nearly 12 million workers expected to be furloughed over the next three months at a cost to the taxpayer of around £40 billion, many jobs were being protected for the time being at least. Chancellor of the Exchequer Sunak certainly had his work cut out and no wonder he wanted to get Lockdown eased as soon as possible. And even if and when Lockdown is lifted, how much will consumer confidence have been shattered with so much fear still circling around the country? Then there is that thing in the background that no-one seemed to have mentioned for weeks, Brexit!

Health Secretary Hancock was still intent on convincing us that he was going to reach his optimistic 100,000 tests per day by the end of April, even though only 19,316 were carried out the previous day. Convinced that all the relevant NHS and social care workers had been given every opportunity to get a test, testing was now being expanded to supermarket, train and bus staff. By increasing capacity to 36,000, Mr Hancock thought that was the answer to the problem, but it was actually getting people tested which was what he would be ultimately judged on.

With PPE being utilised at an astonishing rate demand in some areas still seemed to be outstripping supply. With gown shortages being the latest challenge from the weekend, one can imagine the government's excitement when it was announced that a large shipment of gowns would be arriving from Turkey before the start of the new week. That was until they discovered that the order had not been properly placed and as a result the consignment did not arrive on the Sunday as expected. This appeared to be a case of over-promising and under-delivering, which did not go down well with the already disgruntled frontline medical workers, some of whom were threatening not to work due to PPE shortages. Who would be a Health Secretary at this time?!

Although not known for definite, as there were no records in the daily figures, it was thought that there had up to now been well over 4,000 deaths in care homes as a result of Covid-19, a number that had doubled in four weeks. Whether these deaths were directly due to the virus or because the virus accelerated death in those who already had very serious medical conditions and had tested positive, is debatable. Whatever the case, deaths in the care sector were rising as hospitalisations were coming down, a further indication that patients may well have been sent back inadvertently to care homes to die and spread the disease. Many were dying in care homes in undignified circumstances and probably in extreme pain. We may have reached the peak in hospitals but the crisis in care homes had now reached alarming levels.

The daily death rate was down with a further 463 recorded deaths, but this may have had something to do with the weekend lag in updating the data. This brought the total to 16,509, and amongst this number were an estimated 100+ health workers, although the official figure at this stage was 49. Mr Hancock seemed to think it was a lot less, as the disconnection between the government and what appeared to be happening 'at the coalface' persisted.

As the daily death toll in the USA rose by an alarming 1,705 to 41,356, Italy and Spain recorded lower daily death tolls again with 454 and 399 respectively, indicating that things were now really heading in the right direction. There was though unrest on the streets of Paris as frustrated youths battled police's continued heavy-handed enforcement of Lockdown. In Brazil, the country's leader Jair Bolsonaro was nonchalantly dismissing the virus as 'the little flu'; little did he know that Brazil would end up with well over 100,000 deaths, as South America was about to be hit in devastating fashion.

~

TODAY'S DAILY TIP: Just as regular 'doses' of citrus fruit help strengthen our immune systems, there are foodstuffs that aid the fighting of infection, particularly in the lungs, a place that Covid-19 can harm us the most. So why not add chilli, ginger or garlic products to your diet as these have proven ability to fight infection. (PHYSICAL)

Day 29, Tuesday 21st April: Mission accomplished

"Eggs were in very short supply during Lockdown"

Whilst most items, especially the essential ones, were back on our supermarket shelves after the March madness, eggs and flour were in particularly short supply. With baking crazes sweeping the nation these seemed to be the two products that were in the greatest demand. Having tried, mostly in vain at the beginning of Lockdown, to do our weekly supermarket shop on-line, we were now managing to secure delivery slots with better supplies of eggs and flour. Those same supplies, however, were becoming decimated, partly because of our poached egg consumption and partly because of Susie's great penchant for making delicious bakery treats – her chocolate brownies have become something to behold!

As quickly as the supermarkets were filling their shelves and delivery vans with eggs and flour, stocks were disappearing at an even faster rate, so I needed a plan B. Now, when I used to drive to Shawford station to park my car and commence my daily commute to London, I passed a local Nisa shop that always seemed to be stocked up with all and sundry. I also knew that they had an early morning delivery and, allowing for shelf-stacking time, I knew pretty much when the more in-demand items might be on the shelves. So the plan was hatched (excuse the pun!) for the following morning.

Another lovely morning greeted me as I rose early and jumped energetically into the car in a state of mild apprehension, but intent on successfully implementing the plan. As I pulled up to Nisa, there was only one car in the car park, the delivery had been and gone as expected, and I was at last able to buy eggs and flour which were both in bountiful supply.

Although the mission had been accomplished there was a poignant footnote: the shop assistant who took my money at the till was in the process of opening an envelope with a card in it, and as she saw me approaching she apologised profusely for her inattention and explained that her husband had very recently passed away. She was close to tears but stoically continued to serve me, as I stood with a lump in my throat and offered my heartfelt condolences – I am unsure to this day as to whether the death was Covid-19-related or not, but it was a stark reminder that Lockdown would have been a terribly sad and painful time for so many.

On returning from Nisa in a more sombre mood, Alex and I set off at a steady pace hopefully to accomplish something he had never done before, complete his first ever 5K run. The first half of the run took us through the woods and as we jogged on rural pathways we passed by many timorous dog-walkers and ramblers, clearly worried that we were vectors of the virus, if their body language was anything to go by. After a very brief water stop, which we learned was a way in which we could alleviate the stomach pains that Alex usually experienced at the start of his runs, we continued, this time pounding the pavements of Eastleigh and its surrounds. The last kilometre and a half was mostly uphill, which proved a real test for Alex, but his dogged determination saw him complete the 5K in just over 44 minutes, which was a pretty decent effort. By doing this 5K, we had started to plot the route for the 10K and recording the time set a benchmark for future runs. Most importantly, Alex had completed and enjoyed his first ever 5K and felt absolutely fine at the end of it.

Following a morning of accomplishment, I spent the afternoon tackling a very large hedge located in front of the house and adjacent to where we park our cars. Like doing puzzles, I find cutting down hedges extremely therapeutic and I became so engrossed in the job that I just kept cutting. Before I knew it, a rather large pile of foliage had suddenly appeared and there was only so much room in the garden re-cycling bin. With no recycling centres open due to the virus, the pile was to remain in situ until the bin was eventually emptied a week or so later; at least I now had a very nicely manicured hedge!

'**STAY AT HOME**', '**PROTECT THE NHS**' and '**SAVE LIVES** – if we did not know it already, these were the government straplines that we had had drummed into us at the inception of Lockdown. And if one were to evaluate the effectiveness of these slogans, one might say that the first two had achieved relative success. The 'STAY AT HOME' message was abundantly clear and apart from a few that were still flouting the rules, most of the nation appeared to be compliant. If anything, it may well have instilled the fear of God into many people, as the virus appeared to be living up to its reputation as the 'invisible killer'.

As far as 'PROTECTING THE NHS' was concerned, there was still enough spare ICU bed capacity in the NHS hospitals, despite the peak of the crisis having supposedly been reached, and notwithstanding the fact that the 10 Nightingale Hospitals around the UK still had plenty of spare critical care beds. Although under severe pressure at times, hospitals had never really reached a position of being completely overwhelmed. With persistent concerns that elderly patients with Covid-19 were being sent back to care homes from hospitals, either to die or spread the virus – or both – this was also likely to have taken the pressure off of hospitals, but at the expense of care homes.

As to 'SAVING LIVES', which would surely be the main objective in any health crisis, the UK had the fifth highest death toll in the world, with a further 828 deaths from the previous day and a total of 17,737. This figure still seemed to be rising and we were just over 2,000 deaths away from Sir Patrick Vallance's benchmark for 'success', less than 20,000 as a total. There were of course still no care home deaths being included in the total numbers – there was certainly no success here.

Many studies were now being carried across several countries to ascertain how many people might have already contracted the virus and therefore have potentially built up antibodies. If a large number of people had these antibodies, it could then create a level of herd immunity to fight any future virus outbreaks. This was a theory that had allegedly been expounded by UK scientists at the start of the pandemic but was subsequently criticised. Findings in Wuhan, California and France, as examples, revealed that only a small proportion of people had actually tested positive for the virus, raising concerns that the easing of Lockdowns may be too premature. Chief Scientific Adviser Sir Patrick Vallance thought that only 5 per cent of UK citizens may have had Covid-19. Either the Covid-19 was not as virulent as expected or there was more misery to come and it would get worse before it got better. Maybe the 'antibody census' being planned for 300,000 people over the next year, might reveal how many have actually had the virus.

~

TODAY'S DAILY TIP: With bins being emptied with less frequency and more rubbish being produced due to Lockdown, our various waste bins have been filling up quicker and in some cases overflowing. If safety allows, space can be created in your bins by getting an appropriate ladder, climbing in the bin and trampling down surplus rubbish. You would be amazed at how much room you end up with. (PHYSICAL)

Day 30, Wednesday 22nd April: A stab at life after Lockdown

The Lockdown weather over nearly five weeks had been simply glorious apart from a couple of days, and today was no different. Once again Alex and I completed a morning 5K run, without any hitches, and knocking a couple of minutes off of the previous days' time. I was probably now becoming more and more convinced that Alex could actually complete his challenge as long as I continued to support him. A strenuous day of pool, cricket and puzzle followed.

"A lovely picture of all three children"

The World Health Organisation (WHO) tended to appear on our TV screens when they had something significant that they thought was worthy of mention. To that end a spokesman from the WHO announced: '....the virus will be with us for a long time...' and the only way to exit Lockdown, was to 'find every case' and 'trace and quarantine every contact', something the UK had set out to do in the early stages of the pandemic. Health Secretary Hancock was on hand with a timely announcement: 'Our goal (now) is to get to a point where we can test, track and trace everybody who needs it.' It was almost as if he had a hotline to the WHO as he planned to communicate his 'contact tracing strategy; if only we had been able continue 'track and trace' at the very start of the pandemic, maybe we would have been as effective as Germany were in fighting the virus.

As far as social distancing was concerned, Chief Medical Adviser Professor Chris Witty gave us even more 'good news', stating that it would be in place at least until the end of the year. Cases and hospitalisations might have been on the wane, but experts were keen to bring everyone back to a sense of reality and not allow complacency to settle in.

With the virus and social distancing here to stay, what might life look like for us after Lockdown? Would people be poorer or just not spending in the way they did before? Would there still be the nervousness and fear to venture outside or, heaven forbid, travel around the country for some sort of summer break – or even abroad if the airline industry was back up and running? Would everyone be paranoid about cleanliness and hygiene, washing our hands 20 times in a day for fear of still catching the virus? Would other shopping experiences mirror that of a trip to the supermarket with queuing, restrictions on numbers and regular hand sanitising? Would we still be able to venture freely into our favourite church, pub, restaurant, cinema, theatre, and nightclub or wherever else we had liked to go? Would Coronation Street be back on our screens for three nights of the week? Whatever the things were that we might be able to do, depended on keeping the 'R' value being below one, and ideally at 0.6.

Any attempts to restore our lives to a semblance of normality would depend on the continued positive progress of developing a vaccine. News that the first trials of Sarah Gilbert's Oxford University vaccine (Recombinant vector vaccine) were to start on humans forthwith, brought some much-needed hope. Health Secretary Hancock decided to pledge even more money (£42.5 million) to this project as well as the vaccine development taking place at Imperial College, London (RNA vaccine). This was still only the next stage of a potentially lengthy process which could go well into next year.

The armed forces were becoming more and more involved in the distribution of PPE, as they sought to get on top of an issue that had caused the government one of its biggest 'Covid-19' headaches. Initial findings suggested that PPE had been poorly distributed by NHS supply chains in the early stages of the crisis, meaning that there was an over-supply in some trusts and subsequent stockpiling, leaving other trusts with serious shortages.

The government also had to answer questions on why so many British businesses had their offers of aid to help manufacture PPE turned down. 8,331 companies had originally offered their assistance which was whittled down to 159 potential manufacturers, but it was taking far too long for items that were needed urgently to be produced. Also, the government had supposedly chosen not to take part in an EU scheme to purchase PPE and ventilators at the start of the crisis, based on a 'political decision'. Was this because they were trying to re-enforce that we were leaving the EU and we could fend for ourselves? Or was it because they, inadvertently or otherwise, twice missed the tender process? Whatever happened, there were clearly missed opportunities to have been better planned and resourced on the PPE and ventilator front.

As the Covid-19 situation seemed to be improving in hospitals, the pressure was mounting and the list was growing to treat patients with other medical conditions, most notably those with cancer. Concerns over a European 'cancer epidemic' were rife and leading light Professor Karol Sikora, Chief Medical Officer of Rutherford Cancer Centres, was once again troubled at the lack of cancer diagnosis and treatment. The attempts to overcome the Covid-19 pandemic was at the expense of 60,000 cancer patients. Cancer Research UK thought there may have been up 2,000 undiagnosed cases of cancer each week, notwithstanding the many other potential mental, cardiac, liver, lung and other medical issues. With spare capacity now in ICU and the Nightingale hospitals being under-utilised, surely it was time to free up beds to get so many other aspects of the NHS back up and running again.

Prime Minister's question time (PMQ) was back in the House of Commons after an enforced break, but there were big differences to the last time MPs had met in such circumstances. Most notably, there was no Prime Minister, just the 'stand-in'

Dominic Raab. He was joined for his first appearance at PMQ by another making their debut, Sir Keir Starmer, leader of the opposition, whose predecessor sat quietly on the back benches. There were only 30 MPs allowed to attend in person, all distanced very safely at six feet apart using hard board and 'crime scene' masking tape. For those not in attendance, there was a virtual aspect now to PMQ, with eight strategically placed screens for MPs to 'Zoom in'- not everyone perfected their connections and one MP was accidentally heard castigating a colleague using the 'f' word, causing both mirth and shock in equal measures. Everyone's hair appeared longer or bushier than usual as a result of our hairdressers' and barbers' temporary lay-off; and it was a decidedly shorter affair than usual without so much of the habitual cross-party abuse and heckling, with the two debutants both performing solidly, if not, with restraint. I am sure many MPs were not entirely happy with the new set-up, but it was certainly a mildly comical affair.

One opinion that was gathering pace particularly amongst the more senior Tory MPs was that the Lockdown was going to prove to be even more damaging to the economy than many had initially thought, especially with the government's 'safety first' approach to the virus when it came to the nation's health. I am convinced more and more that this approach by Boris Johnson was as much to do with him contracting Covid-19 himself and his subsequent suffering, as anything else. It proved also that it was pretty straightforward to enforce Lockdown, but not so easy to ease restrictions, with the incredibly fine balancing act between health and prosperity.

As much as there was some mild optimism around certain parts of the world that we could have been over the worst of the pandemic, it was not going to be an easy ride out of Lockdown: Lombardy, the most affected part of Italy, was still reporting more new cases than other regions, partly due to its aged population; a large consignment of defective face masks meant that more than 1,000 Spanish medical workers had had to go into unexpected isolation; France was experiencing its fourth night of rioting by disaffected youths and threatening to bring the army in to restore order; Germany was forced to cancel the world's biggest beer festival, Oktoberfest, for the first time since 1946 which was due to take place in Bavaria, Germany's most affected region; American nurses were protesting outside the White House about a lack of PPE, a familiar story to the UK; and Greece was experiencing a problem that would increasingly hit the shores of Southern England, migrants, many of whom were carrying the virus.

While daily death rates were coming down in Europe, the US had a total of 2,437 deaths in one day, bringing their total to 46,149. This was now by far the highest of any country in the world and President Trump was coming under increasing pressure with fear of an even more deadly second wave.

~

TODAY'S DAILY TIP: Exercising regularly can help improve our sleep patterns, and although not for everyone, if one does one's exercise in the morning or earlier in the day our ability to sleep can be that much better. (PHYSICAL)

Day 31, Thursday 23rd April: More testing and PPE misery, and someone called Cummings

Alex and I decided to take a rest from the running for the day, which was probably a wise move in light of the previous two days' exertions. Rest days were going to be an important part of the build-up to the 10K challenge scheduled for 13th May and I was mindful that Alex's head might be ruling his heart as he started to gain confidence from attainments thus far.

"We did love a game of 'Scattergories'"

After another relaxing day of puzzle, pool and cricket, as well as our weekly 'Clap for our Carers and the NHS' we settled down to play one of our favourite Lockdown 'board' games, 'Scattergories', which can be played individually or in couples. Each player or couple is presented with 12 categories on a card and based on what letter (of the alphabet) comes up on the dice, you have three minutes to name something from each category that begins with the nominated letter. The idea is not to write down the same thing on any category as any other player or couple, otherwise you do not score, and the player or couple with the most points wins. Owing mainly to the competitive nature of any game we play as a family, we tend to have some pretty colourful debates about some of the answers that each of us comes up with and today was no different.

The misery surrounding PPE shortages continued apace, this time for care home and home care workers, GP's and hospice staff, leading to criticism that they were being treated by the government as second class citizens, with the perception that the government were doing everything to make sure the needs of the NHS were prioritised. Meanwhile the delayed consignment of gowns, due to arrive from Turkey a few days earlier, was eventually picked up by the RAF, but was missing several thousands of gowns.

23,560 tests were carried out the day before, which represented only a small increase on previous days, although testing capacity was now at 51,000. In order to have any chance of reaching his self-imposed target of 100,000 tests per day by the end of the month, Health Secretary Hancock ramped up testing by offering thousands of key workers and their families the opportunity to book tests on-line with a 72 hour turnaround. With a significant increase in the number of drive-through and mobile pop-up testing centres and home-testing kits potentially available from the following week, there appeared to be plenty of capacity.

Analysts tracking traffic movements in England, announced that there had been a steady increase in cars and lorries on our roads in the previous week, indicating that there were a few more companies opening their doors again for business, particularly in manufacturing and those in supplying services. This was not breaking any Lockdown rules as the only businesses that were told to close originally were those in non-essential retailing, hospitality and health and fitness. As long as work premises had the necessary Covid-19-secure safety procedures and social distancing in place to protect their employees, it was fine to be open for business.

Unlike in England, Scotland's First Minister, Nicola Sturgeon, produced her 26 page document outlining her exit strategy from Lockdown, piling more pressure on Boris Johnson to reveal what his plans were. Arlene Foster, Northern Ireland's First Minister, was claiming that her country would be out of Lockdown quicker than expected. The Welsh First Minister, Mark Drakeford, had his own three-phase 'reverse traffic light' plan, scheduled to begin from 7th May. We might be the

United Kingdom, but it was becoming increasingly apparent that the four nations were not exactly taking an aligned approach.

Dominic Cummings, the Prime Minister's senior cohort, was one of several government officials and advisors who had contracted the virus around the time of the outset of Boris Johnson's illness. It was initially thought that he was isolating with mild symptoms when the symptoms were supposedly so severe that he nearly collapsed and went to hospital, with great difficulty breathing. His wife was also very ill with Covid-19, as they both struggled to look after their son. This story would re-emerge in dramatic fashion at the end of May, when Mr Cummings was accused of flouting the Lockdown rules he helped conceive, by controversially travelling to the North-East to seek childcare assistance from his parents and sister.

As the economy was reportedly collapsing at record pace with more than a quarter of the workforce temporarily laid off, there were 616 new deaths in the UK, bringing the total to 18,738, although the death toll was still trending downwards. It was also very concerning to learn of more detailed data indicating that black people were dying of the virus at twice the rate of whites, particularly if they were of Caribbean heritage. There was more pressure on the government to speed up the review into whether the black and minority ethnic (BAME) backgrounds were at greater risk of the virus than those from other backgrounds, particularly with the high number of BAME deaths in NHS hospitals and care homes. Talking about the shocking new data, Chief Medical Officer, Professor Chris Witty, said 'These figures are really startling..............(it is) absolutely critical that we find out which groups are most at risk so that we can help to protect them.'

~

TODAY'S DAILY TIP: With the number of people confined to their homes during Lockdown, consumption of our utilities (gas, water and electricity), would have probably been at an all-time high. These are costs that we all have to incur but we can control them better by being more aware of what energy we are wasting, whether it is leaving gas burning unnecessarily, taps running for longer than they need to be or lights being left on when rooms are not occupied. (SOCIAL / EMOTIONAL)

Day 32, Friday 24th April: Boris on the bounce back

"The Otter pub in Otterbourne served us well on Friday evenings in Lockdown with their excellent takeaway service"

We always looked forward to a Lockdown Friday as it bizarrely felt like the beginning of the weekend despite some of the monotony associated with this rather strange time in our lives. Weekdays tended to have more of a mundane feel to them, particularly with the recent daily routine of chores, run, puzzle, pool and cricket. Another lovely day ensured Alex and I had invigorating morning run, this time raising our previous longest distance by 500 metres, as we completed a fairly straightforward 5.5K. This set us up nicely for our Friday fish and chip takeaway supper with a couple of real ales from the Otter pub, followed by another really enjoyable Zoom quiz night.

After a period of convalescence at Chequers, Boris Johnson said that he would be returning to work in number 10 Downing Street, 'raring to go' after the weekend, but by no means at full fitness and still under instruction to take it easy. It would not be the easiest of returns to his desk, with a split cabinet on how and when to ease Lockdown restrictions and with calls for him and his cabinet to stop 'hiding behind the science' and to start taking courageous and timely decisions. There would be some of the hardest decisions that Boris would have to make in his life, let alone his political career, less than three weeks since he nearly lost his life and with some MPs raising concerns that his ordeal may have left him 'tentative' and 'quite frightened.

With a continuation of the amazing spring weather, many of the British public were taking full advantage of their entitlement of one period of exercise per day, and I am sure there may have been some that had a second or even a third, particularly those with dogs or young children. Home Secretary Priti Patel was becoming increasingly more aware of some Lockdown complacency and issued warnings for us to comply with all the Lockdown rules. The police were praying for rain and threatening more severe enforcement, which included closing more parks. I did feel this was quite short-sighted, especially where access to parks was so important for those living in high rise apartments with young children or in poorer communities.

So, with Boris back in office on Monday, hopefully with renewed focus and perspective, how ultimately was Britain going to beat this deadly Covid-19 disease? I think we were starting to get a picture that a mixture of anti-viral drugs, contract tracing and herd immunity would all play their part, but realistically the only thing that would give us a permanent solution would be a safe and effective vaccine that would be produced for the whole world. In the meantime, 'Tomorrow's World' might be looking strangely different for a while yet.

Bill Gates, the £75 billion pioneer who created Microsoft and second richest man in the world, was on what appeared to be his own personal and singlehanded crusade to find a way to stop the virus's spread. Mr Gates who is reported to be an expert on vaccines, testing and treatments, having already done much work in fighting polio, malaria and HIV, was allegedly determined to do everything in his powers to find a vaccine for Covid-19 and was reportedly already in collusion with Sarah Gilbert about producing her Oxford vaccine. I think it is very easy to be cynical about someone so wealthy who has such an interest in fighting Covid-19 and who has clearly made a fortune from his business ventures over years. He might be seeing this as another massive money-making opportunity for his own personal gain, but his apparent deep desire to get the world back up and running, may actually have been genuine; conspiracy theorists may beg to differ!

Captain Tom Moore's stock rose another level as he added the number one spot in the charts to his incredible fundraising achievements. His rendition of 'You'll Never Walk Alone' supporting Michael Ball and the NHS Voices of Care Choir, initially sold 82,000 copies and he unsurprisingly became the oldest individual to be number one in the UK singles chart. 'What wonderful news to receive today....my grand-children can't believe I am a chart-topper', he joyfully exclaimed.

President Trump had us all in stitches by supposedly suggesting that an injection of bleach would help treat those who had Covid-19. Whether tongue-in-check or not, he seemed quite convinced of bleach's credentials: 'I see the disinfectant that knocks it (the virus) out in a minute, one minute........So you're going to have to use medical doctors but it sounds interesting to me', he enthused. Meanwhile the USA reached the grimmest of all statistics thus far with a further 2,084 added to their death toll, meaning they were the first country to reach 50,000 deaths, at 50,952. Rather than being seen as a strong supportive leader, President Trump seemed to be frustrated by being reportedly isolated in the White House, rarely attending task force meetings; if he did attend, he would be ill-prepared – maybe, on the other hand, he was elsewhere dealing with other matters.

A further 684 deaths were reported in the UK bringing the total numbers of deaths to 19,905, dangerously close to Sir Patrick Vallance's threshold and yardstick for a 'successful' handling of the pandemic. The daily death toll still appeared high but the average over a week indicated that the trend really was heading in the right direction and that things had plateaued after the peak had been reached.

~

TODAY'S DAILY TIP: As we are on our phones and emails more and more these days, the threat of 'scammers' and 'phishers' is never too far away from us. These are shady people or organisations who are after our personal information to create new identities with fake addresses or email data. It is important to remember that desperate people will do desperate things in the criminal world. (SOCIAL / EMOTIONAL)

Day 33, Saturday 25th April: A word for the over-70s

Just like Fridays in Lockdown were the start of the weekend, Saturdays WERE the weekend, with a heavy emphasis on having fun, and this Saturday was no different. It always helps when the sun 'has its hat on' and it probably aided Susie and me in getting Holly and Alex up out of their deep slumber for what was the most lovely early morning dog walk through the woods, with the bluebells looking their absolute best. That was followed by another hearty breakfast of 'eggy' bread and baked beans on the patio and a read of the paper – a perfect start to the day.

"Tizzy misbehaving"

During Lockdown, my family developed a healthy obsession with not only trying to do their 10,000 steps per day, but also trying to outdo each other. Needless to say, Holly needed little convincing to join Alex and me for another Saturday run, something she again embraced with great zeal. From Alex's perspective, he had put the hard yards in during the week, and a steady 1.5K jog just kept things ticking over as part of the preparation for the big event three weeks hence.

Much like many in this great country of ours, we are blessed in our neighbourhood with a great community of kind, caring and genuine people. We are all different, with different jobs and careers and at different stages in life, but what Lockdown did was probably brought some of us closer together. With it being such a glorious day, we arranged via social media a carefully distanced social gathering outside the front of our houses, with our deck chairs strategically placed three metres apart. This was something we had seen working very effectively on Thursdays' weekly 'Clap for NHS and Carers' evenings between different communities around the country, which strangely we always did in our back gardens. It was simply great catching up with everyone over a beer or glass of Pimms and just seeing that everyone was okay and in good spirits.

After this really uplifting gathering, and as it was such a lovely evening, we migrated to the back garden for one of our steak, chicken and sausage barbecues with a nice glass of red. The evening continued with another Zoom quiz night, this time with our 'Bournemouth family', the Goodrums and the Sabets. It was so good to see them all again, particularly with Amelia's passing still so raw. Despite this, everyone was in good spirits and it was probably one of many enjoyable quizzes we did in Lockdown. All in all, it was a great Saturday, full of positivity and fun, doing things human beings do naturally, socialising, albeit from afar!

Travellers from other parts of the world were still being allowed to enter into the UK unchecked for Covid-19 but there was finally talk of a scheme to quarantine for 14 days anyone entering the UK, the expected timeframe by which someone could potentially catch the virus and endure the symptoms. There did not appear to be a great deal of urgency to introduce this scheme as the government claimed that 'all (so-called) evidence suggests it (international travel) is only a tiny proportion of the cause of the coronavirus outbreak'. Why this scheme was not introduced in the early stages of Lockdown, particularly as it was later revealed that Spain and Italy were two of the main sources of the virus, remains to me an unanswered question. It was now almost a case of 'shutting the door after the horse had bolted'.

At the outset of Lockdown, the Prime Minister contacted those with serious health conditions to ask them to shield for three months. Additionally, those in the over-70s age group were asked to do the same. As talk of an easing of restrictions became commonplace, there was increased anger amongst the over-70s about rumours that they would be asked to shield for a further four months.

If my father-in-law and aunt were anything to go by, although they completely understood why Lockdown was imposed in the first place, now to be 'told what to do' rather than making their own choice, suggested that the government was giving no consideration for some of the other implications of the crisis, such as mental health and loneliness. This is a generation that fought for our freedom and survived a World War; surely those who were fit and able should be allowed to calculate their own risks and the risks to those around them, and make their own decisions.

Just as the over-70's might be asked to self-isolate for a further four months, so those under-50, who were not affected by the virus, would be encouraged to get back to work as soon as was possible. Statistics now revealed that there was much less chance of someone under-50 dying of Covid-19. In fact there was barely any risk of someone dying who was under-29, but the biggest challenge for the government would be convincing these people that it was safe to return to work after all the fear that had been instilled into the nation. As one member of the cabinet said, getting people back to work would be 'delicate and dangerous'.

As if life was not challenging enough, with a deadly virus wreaking havoc all around the world and changing our way of life, reports of a 1.2-mile-wide asteroid heading uncontrollably towards earth was enough to exhaust everyone's nervous energy. This was the usual media scaremongering that arises when there is anything that is mildly threatening to our planet, but I suppose this giant rock was only 3,908,791 miles away from earth!

Unfortunately, but inevitably, the UK reached the milestone that no-one would have ever imagined would have been passed on March 5th, when the first death from Covid-19 was reported in the UK. There were now a heart-wrenching 20,319 deaths, as Sir Patrick Vallance's hopeful prediction of less than 20,000 deaths was surpassed with another 813 added to the daily death toll.

Every one of those deaths will in turn have impacted many thousands of family members and friends and so many will have perished alone without that crucial loving and physical comfort in the last few moments of their lives. Spare a thought for all those medical staff who had to act as those family members and then had to portray to them those last dying moments – simply awful. Every story is tragic in its own and locally we heard of twin sisters, both nurses who had died of Covid-19 within days of each other; their family recalled that the pair had always planned to 'go out (of the world) together'.

~

TODAY'S DAILY TIP: Those of us lucky enough to have been able to get out and about to exercise or just to take a stroll, every now and again, why not take a break from your usual routine and try going somewhere you have never been. You might find you have an unknown beauty spot on your doorstep. (PHYSICAL)

Day 34, Sunday 26th April: Virtual 'Wizard of Oz'

After a particularly enjoyable and active Saturday, Sunday was a much quieter affair. Alex and I again decided to do a shorter run, which ended up being 2.6K. The significance of this was that today should have been London Marathon Day, another event that was so frustratingly cancelled due to the virus. So, we felt we were doing our bit to honour the 26-mile road race (by doing 2.6K) normally run through the streets of the UK's capital city. How all those struggling charities could have done with the extra money that would have been raised as a result of the London Marathon, which would now potentially be run on 4th October.

"Domestic amateur dramatics with The Wizard of Oz"

From an early age, Holly had always loved drama, musical theatre and dance, and duly joined a local amateur performing arts group when she was 13. Not only did she improve her technical skills and ability over the years, but she has also performed in many shows and starred in a number of lead roles in local venues and theatres. As a result, Susie, Alex and I have seen many of her shows that we would not otherwise have known about or been interested in, had she not been involved. As a thespian and performer, she has built up many amazing friendship groups, most of which still exist and it forms a big part of her personal and social life; she happens to be incredibly talented too!

This particular Sunday afternoon, Holly thought she would introduce her directing skills to her family, as some of her work colleagues had challenged her to produce a short re-enactment of a virtual musical theatre production of her choice. After much debate and subsequent coercion, it was decided – not by me, I hasten to add - that the 'Wizard of Oz' would be the choice, and then it was about who was going to be playing what part, but without the benefit of any auditions. The roles were cast as follows: Dorothy – Holly; Straw man – Susie; Tin man – Alex; Tizzy – Toto; and the dubious honour of the Lion – Yours truly!

What followed was frankly farcical and absurd with a mad dash for costumes and a learning of lines. Alex and I ended up with the two most ridiculous outfits: Alex was dressed in Holly's silver hot-pants and head-to-toe in tin foil with a colander on his head; I donned a ridiculous brown curly wig, a mixture of Susie's shaggy and fur coats, Holly's winter mittens and my costume was finished off with lines of black shoe polish as whiskers. I can only describe it as domestic bullying of the highest order and Lockdown insanity! Once I had adopted an 'if you can't beat them, join them' mind-set, I wholeheartedly immersed myself in the 'project' and we produced what I thought was actually quite a decent end-product. It certainly had us in absolute stitches and proved what can be done with a bit of innovative spirit and positive mentality. I was none too pleased though when it appeared on social media!

In the evening, Susie cooked one of her amazing Sunday roast dinners, strangely our first one in Lockdown: roast chicken, Yorkshire puddings (yes, Yorkshire puddings with roast chicken!), crispy well-done roast potatoes, broccoli, carrots, 'pigs-in-blankets', stuffing and lashings of gravy – and of course smooth and creamy bread sauce; Lockdown was really not that bad!

With all the talk of finding a safe and effective vaccine, First Secretary of State and outgoing 'stand-in' Prime Minister, Dominic Raab, was urging extreme caution about the availability of a vaccine much before the end of 2020. His sentiments were echoed by one former Chief Medical Officer, who said that we needed to be 'realistic' about the likelihood of a vaccine as we have not had that much success with finding vaccines for coronaviruses. A common cold is a form of coronavirus and we have never found a vaccine for this, rather we have learned to live with it, interestingly without having face masks imposed on us. England's Chief Medical Officer, Chris Witty, was even less optimistic, saying the chances of finding an effective vaccine were 'incredibly small'. Sarah Gilbert, the professor of vaccinology, who had just started human trials of her Oxford vaccine, conversely stated that she was 'very optimistic it's going to work'! I am not sure any of us were convinced one way or another. What was for sure, was that until a vaccine was in production, this new strain of coronavirus was here to stay, and we would need to continue to adapt our lives accordingly.

With cases of the virus in hospitals and the daily death rate dropping, there appeared to be every indication that the infamous 'R' or reproduction number, that shows the number of people we will infect on average if we have the virus, was heading below one. Those working in care homes, however, may have been mildly cynical about how things might be improving based on the 'R', as their crisis deepened. I was always intrigued as to how this 'R' number was worked out and how many people in a community it might be based upon. As much as the government was being 'guided by the science', I think many in the UK felt they were being 'blinded by the science'!

Health Secretary Hancock was furiously trying to ramp up testing to achieve his 100,000 tests per day by 30th April. These tests could be a mixture of antigen tests (a swab test to see whether one has the virus) or antibody tests (a finger prick test to see whether one has had the virus). On Saturday 25th April 'only' 29,058 tests were carried out; how in heaven's name was that number going to increase to 100,000 in the space of four days, notwithstanding Boris Johnson's original target of 250,000 tests per day?

Now I am sure it was a monumental task to set up everything related to testing from scratch and get it functioning effectively in such a relative short space of time, but the whole management of the process has been pretty fraught from the start. Then for the Health Secretary to make perceived unrealistic targets that the public and media seemed to 'hang their hats on', just seemed ill-thought-out. For Dominic Raab to claim on the following day that the government was on track to achieve their target, was either naïve or misplaced; or were they just taking the public for fools?

I am not a great fan of shopping at the best of times, but on hearing some of the sketchy plans for when shops were likely to re-open I was definitely going to be deterred even more. It was already abundantly clear from a trip to the supermarket, in my case Waitrose, that something synonymous with life in Britain would become the main part of the shopping experience, queuing. If you are lucky enough to get in the shop and work out the one-way system, it is people, not trolleys, which you are trying to avoid to keep your distance. For those of us like me, who like to have an in-store coffee to take away the pain of shopping, these facilities as well as the toilets, were likely still to be closed. For all those people who might want to try clothes on, the changing rooms would be remaining firmly shut. If Lockdown had increased demand for on-line shopping, it seemed it would probably 'go through the roof' post-Lockdown.

The numbers of deaths in the UK grew by a further 413 to a total of 20,732, which appeared much lower than recent totals and almost lulled us into a false sense of security that we were heading beneath the plateau. In fact, this was evidence of the weekend lag which always seemed to show that the figures were lower, only for those early the following week to be a lot higher. The overall trend of daily deaths, however, was definitely coming down, and that was one of the key criteria for the Lockdown to be eased. In Italy and France, dates for the start of an end to Lockdown had been set provisionally at May 4th and 11th respectively; with the UK supposedly 12 days behind Italy, we were starting to get an idea of our timeline.

Fears were growing in the US that it was about to enter its deepest recession for 80 years with unemployment predicted to be at 15 per cent or 27 million in the second and third quarters. President Trump will have been concerned by these figures, not to mention having the highest death toll in the world at nearly 55,000. His whole response to the virus had seemed erratic throughout, at times as if he did not care about his reputation and almost that he had his mind on other things. There appeared to be a lack of inspirational leadership to bring a seemingly disjointed America together.

As we were about to enter the fifth week of Lockdown, Prime Minister Boris Johnson returned to Downing Street to take back the reins that he had reluctantly relinquished after becoming so unwell just two weeks previously. His in-tray was fuller than it had been since he took on premiership and the country yearned for some much-needed leadership and strong direction; he was now about to take on one of the biggest challenges of his political career.

~

TODAY'S DAILY TIP: With an indifferent weather forecast for the rest of the week, it was important to get as much done outside as possible before the rain came; maybe a good time to undertake the cleaning of the cars or some other necessary yet mundane outdoor task – or not as the case may be! (PHYSICAL)

Day 35, Monday 27th April: Boris is back at the helm

"Sisters 'working from home"

There was every indication that the weather was on a turn for the worst as cloudy skies greeted the new week. That did not deter Alex and me as we embarked on another morning 5K run. The fact that he achieved this pretty effortlessly in his best time was an important indicator that his body was now adjusting well to endurance running. As long as we were taking water breaks at the right times, this was helping to control the pains in his stomach caused by the backflow of blood as it worked its way through his conduit. Things were progressing nicely with just over two weeks to go until the big run.

One of my least favourite chores is cleaning the car and this was something I had avoided throughout the period of Lockdown, thus far. I never really see any point in cleaning cars because as quickly as you clean them, they get dirty again. That said, that was a very poor excuse for not having cleaned my car since January, when I had so much more time on my hands. I had every good intention of cleaning my car today and then my 'monkey mind' started telling me that it was pointless because it was going to rain tomorrow – I am embarrassed to admit, the car did not get a clean!

I do not often let my 'monkey mind' take over my day but sometimes it wins me over. The 'monkey mind' is a term used to describe a confused, unsettled or restless mind and can mean that one's brain becomes distracted from getting productive things done in one's life, like cleaning the car; the challenge is to get that 'monkey mind' shut down.

As if he had never been away, Boris Johnson properly resumed his premiership for the first time in a month. He appeared spritely and it was only when he opened his mouth and spoke at his 9.10am address to the nation in front of 10, Downing Street, that one noticed a huskiness to his voice. But he certainly looked much better than the day he came out of hospital a week earlier. Despite concerns for his health, one colleague said about him: 'He's in properly good nick'.

After thanking the British public for the 'sheer grit and guts' that we had shown during Lockdown, he stressed: 'We have so nearly succeeded. Keep going!' With his fluffy mop of recently washed but unkempt hair moving slightly in the light wind, he implored us to keep going, apologised for his 'lengthy' absence and thanked Dominic Raab for doing '......a terrific job'. Mr Raab did a decent if unenterprising 'holding' job as the Prime Minister's stand-in but, despite his efficiency, he lacked Boris's charisma and the authority to make more things happen.

Boris continued his fighting talk, saying boldly yet cautiously that 'we have begun to wrestle it (the virus) to the floor – the moment of opportunity but also the moment of maximum risk'. He concluded with a sympathetic word for those in business, particularly in my industry, hospitality, imploring us to keep going, and we will be 'stronger than ever before'. There is no doubt that we needed Boris back and his words of encouragement were welcome but what everyone really wanted to know was, how and when Lockdown was going to be eased – he assured us that a plan for the 'second phase' of the battle against the virus would come in the next few days, with 'maximum transparency', almost suggesting he had not been transparent before!

One of Prime Minister Johnson's main tasks on his return to work was to address the increasingly worrying situation in care homes. It was slightly embarrassing for the government that Chief Scientific Advisor, Sir Patrick Vallance, had suggested that the risk of the virus to care homes 'was flagged up very early on'. With an estimated 7,500 deaths now in care homes, Boris would surely be facing interrogation as to why there had been and still were such delays in the provision of PPE and in the testing of frontline care workers.

One of the things I really missed during Lockdown was the opportunity to go out for a meal in a pub or restaurant. After initially finishing work in London in January, I had several pleasant breakfasts, lunches and dinners locally but with the country firmly stuck in Lockdown, it appeared that the hospitality industry, with its 45,000 hotels and 76,000 pubs and restaurants, would be one of the last to re-open. Once it was back up and running, the two-metre social distancing rules would surely cause restrictions to numbers allowed in premises and there would be some high costs associated with implementing new safety and distancing measures. With revenues seriously down and many employees furloughed, prospects were gloomy and there were some very worried business owners who would need to make some incredibly tough decisions.

The number of patients in the UK being treated for Covid-19 in the 1,257 NHS hospitals had fallen from 18,667 to 15,051 in the past week. Where most hospitals' resources were pretty much being taken up treating Covid-19, this was at the expenses of treatments for many other illnesses. There is no doubt from many of the agonising tales from Covid-19 patients who were seriously ill and survived to tell their story, that it is a very unpleasant and terrifying disease. That said, it was probably now time for the government to redress the balance and start to re-focus on other health issues either for ongoing and routine healthcare, including a backlog of an alleged two million operations, or illnesses caused as a consequence of Covid-19. As it was, there had already been an estimated 10,000 deaths not related to Covid-19 because patients had not been able to access the healthcare system or had paradoxically been too fearful of going to A&E in case they may catch the virus. It was not just the treatments for other illnesses that was affected, but also over 2,000 research projects had been halted for new diseases, cancer and diabetes, amongst others.

Health Secretary Hancock, rarely out of the news these days, announced that it was their intention to free up more hospitals as 'Covid-19-free zones', initially for cancer and mental health treatment. In turn the 10 UK Nightingale hospitals, that had originally been built to cope with the peak if the NHS became overrun, would start to be used solely for treating Covid-19 patients. This was a great plan in theory but there were clearly some practical challenges – and it needed first to be signed-off.

The death toll for the previous day was the lowest it had been during the month of April, at 360, but like Sunday's statistics, there would have been a delay in the reporting of some deaths due the weekend lag. There was some slightly welcome news for families of those NHS and social care workers who died on duty on the frontline, with a promise of £60,000 government compensation per family, but no amount of money was ever going to replace the loss of a loved one.

Thoughts in Spain turned to the summer with the hope of thousands of tired and frustrated Brits descending upon Hispanic beaches and resorts for their annual dose of sun, sea and Sangria. Despite Spain being one of the hardest hit by the virus in Europe, many regions were desperate to open their doors to tourists as tourism represents 12 per cent of their economy. Prime Minister, Pedro Sanchez, preached caution and nothing was going to happen unless the airline industry was back up and running. These were the first signs that this was going to be no ordinary summer.

~

TODAY'S DAILY TIP: Building up a strong core is great for ones all round body strength. Some exercises that one could try are: the 30-day 'Abs' challenge, an app. that comprises of four different exercises for the core muscles; the 30-day 'plank' challenge, again that can be downloaded as an app.; wall-sitting for four repetitions of 30 seconds. The body will quickly become more toned and one could even develop a great six-pack! (PHYSICAL)

Day 36, Tuesday 28th April: Mourning in the rain

"Waiting for the long-awaited rain to relent"

And the rain came pouring down, and goodness me, did it rain! To be fair we had endured five weeks of truly incredible springtime weather, interspersed with only one and a bit days of rain. Clear deep blue skies and unseasonably high temperatures had ensured that Lockdown could be enjoyed by many in the fresh air of their gardens or out on exercise, and the air was not so polluted because of an absence of air travel and less traffic on the roads. The much-needed rain would be great for the garden and just give us a chance to do more things indoors for a couple of days.

On the running challenge front, it was time to ramp up the distance slightly. Undeterred by the rain, Alex and I set off on a different route and completed 6K for the first time. With still two weeks before the run, it was important not to push Alex too far and small daily increases in the distance would hopefully be the key to success, at the same time improving a little on our times. What was very welcome after the run in the rain, was a lovely hot bath – at 1.00pm in the afternoon!

With the rain teaming down outside, I took the opportunity to make some headway with my 3000-piece jigsaw puzzle, which I had started on April 7th and which had played second fiddle to the outdoor activities of running, pool, garden cricket and hedge-cutting! A late-afternoon showing of the very average – in my opinion - film

'American Woman', re-affirmed why I am not a film-buff and coupled with the wet weather, made it a rather strange day all round.

During the evening, we again connected with our 'Bournemouth family' with an on-line game of 'Scattergories'. These things are always done better face-to face but in the present circumstances it was the next best thing. Zoom may not have been everyone's 'cup of tea' but it sure was a necessity in these difficult and unprecedented times.

At 11.00am, a one minute's silence was held across a very wet Great Britain to commemorate all the frontline medical and key workers that had so tragically perished in the line of duty. I watched on television as images of their colleagues mourning their losses were shared from up and down the country. It was a truly sad and heartrending moment to reflect on the damage that this disease had done to so many, in such a short space of time. It was poignant also for the fact that deaths in care homes were still very much on the rise, with a concern that the death toll could be higher than it had been in hospitals.

As Boris Johnson got well and truly back into the swing of things, it was revealed that one of the main reasons he suffered so badly from Covid-19 was because he had been carrying so much excess weight. As scientists and medics were learning more about the virus from the many cases both in the UK and in other parts of Europe, it was becoming more widely appreciated that obesity significantly decreased ones chances of surviving Covid-19. Whilst not being critical in any way of those overweight, interestingly slimmer characters such as Health Secretary Hancock and Professor Chris Witty recovered much quicker from the disease, with less severe symptoms.

The Prime Minister had no time nor inclination at this stage to dwell on his recent illness. Instead, and amongst many other important matters, he was working on one of the most complicated aspects of the crisis, a post-Lockdown plan that encompassed getting children back to school. That would then enable their parents to go back to work, which would in turn hopefully kick-start all aspects of the economy including retail, travel, leisure, hospitality and entertainment. This was going to be some undertaking and it would require something that was supposedly quite alien to Boris, a plan with minute detail!

Health Secretary Hancock made another of his 'dangerous' pledges. This time around contact tracing, a means of controlling the virus in the longer term, which he claimed he would have up and running in three weeks or 18th May, for a national launch subsequent to a week of trials. The key to its success was going to be testing, which had only reached 43,563 the previous day despite a potential capacity for 75,000 tests – there were two days for the government to reach its magic 100,000 per day target.

In essence, contact tracing would work via an app., which would be downloaded onto a smart phone and tell the user if he or she had come into contact with someone who has been infected by the virus and therefore has Covid-19. If the user then develops symptoms, these should be reported on the app, and he or she would then isolate for up to 14 days, subject to a test. 18,000 people were to be trained as contact tracers to ensure the process could be adhered to and that those who had been near a confirmed case remained in isolation. To issue this promise when the testing target seemed nowhere near being reached, was brave to say the least. Although the contact tracing process sounded great in theory, a lot of things need to go right in practice for it to work effectively and sustainably, in just three weeks.

First Minister of Scotland Nicola Sturgeon was the first leader in the British government to make a decision on face coverings, advising that they should be worn on public transport and in some shops. The aim in asking people to wear them was to slow the transmission of the virus, particularly in enclosed areas, describing it 'as a precautionary measure'. The scientists continued to be vague on the effectiveness of face masks as the WHO themselves were not sure of their efficacy. Because the government were 'guided by the science', they were not sure either! Health Secretary Hancock described the evidence from the scientists as 'weak', so for England, no decision was made. At last someone was starting to talk about forethought and the need to stockpile face masks as and when face coverings might become mandatory in England.

Devastating news was coming out of the travel industry with reports that British Airways (BA), who some might say were the pioneers of modern day commercial air travel, were about to make 12,000 redundancies, which was more than a quarter of their workforce. With so many planes still grounded and no immediate prospect of this changing, BA bosses, IAG, felt they were left with no alternative but to start a consultation process with potentially affected employees to try to balance the books. Losses for BA in the first quarter were expected to reach £1.8 billion as flying was decimated around the globe. With 22,000 of their employees on the furlough scheme, which was meant to be running only until the end of June, and even though there was talk of there being an extension, IAG wanted to act now – this of course did not go down at all well with many people. It was not just the airline companies being affected as travel companies were now having to refund thousands of disgruntled punters who were going to miss out on this year's summer holidays. Was this now the start of a collapse of an industry that had connected the world so well, but in doing so had inadvertently spread a deadly virus from continent to continent?

Italy and Spain's respective daily death tolls were 382 and 301 and totals were 27,359 and 23,822, illustrating that the situation in Europe was improving. Plans continued afoot to ease Lockdown restrictions in these countries during May, with a big emphasis on testing, social distancing and mask-wearing. In Germany, where the virus has been very well controlled, resulting in 6,177 deaths so far, there were reports of a surge in cases leading Chancellor Angela Merkel to consider whether to ease Lockdown or not.

One country that could claim it got on top of the virus early and suppressed its ability to spread was New Zealand. Their total death toll only just got into double figures during the pandemic, which was probably down to a very strict Lockdown imposed by Prime Minister, Jacinda Ardern from 26th March. Although with only five million residents and much less overcrowding than more populous countries, they were always going to be at more of an advantage. In fact, there are five times more sheep in the country than people, so it certainly would have been a greater problem, if sheep could have caught Covid-19!

In the UK, a further 586 deaths were reported, bringing the total to 21,678 and grim reports that, during the previous week, the highest number of total deaths (22,351) had been recorded for any week in Britain since records began in 1993. The virus had clearly had a massive impact on these numbers, but more bad news was about to come when care home deaths were finally included in the daily death toll.

~

TODAY'S DAILY TIP: I have been blessed with reasonably good health over the years, and I appear to have found my own daily formula for a healthy life: a banana for potassium and vitamins B and C, cranberry juice for a healthy heart, age-related damage and urinary tract infections, and cod liver oil for omega-3 fatty acids, vitamins A&D and joint pain. Everyone will have their own methods, but this routine has certainly helped my health over the years. (PHYSICAL)

Day 37, Wednesday 29th April: Welcome, Baby Wilfred

"Boris may have baby Wilfred but we have little Tizzy"

It was another cool and wet day in Hampshire something we were not used to, going by the previous five weeks. Another 5.5K kept Alex and me on track for our 10K challenge, although I was starting to feel the effects of some continuous road running manifested by a recurrence of my chronic lower back pain. Despite this, nothing was going to stop me helping Alex achieve his goal particularly as we had got this far in our build-up.

Interactions with anyone other than the family or the neighbours, were rare these days. There was always a chance of seeing someone we knew at the petrol station or the supermarket, but generally we were thankful for our 'phones and how technology had developed so much over the years. Because of the continuing egg shortage I took a trip again to my tried and trusted 'egg supplier', the local Nisa grocery store, and it was great to bump into our club cricket captain, Ben, at a distance. It was ironic as our cricket season was meant to start a week later and we would have been ramping up our net practice in readiness for another exciting new league season. This would be one of the many things that sadly would not take place this summer.

Prime Minister Boris Johnson's story of his previous twelve months could have been an epic tale in its own right: what with gaining the leadership of the conservative party from Teresa May in July 2019, and then winning the election with a large majority in December 2019, followed by 'Getting Brexit Done' at the end of January 2020, then having to send the UK into Lockdown in March, and dramatically becoming very seriously ill himself with the virus at the beginning of April.........what else could possibly happen?!

On the same day that Captain Tom Moore was appointed an honorary colonel, for his amazing fundraising of over £29 million for the NHS Charities Together, Boris Johnson's fiancé Carrie Symonds, gave birth to a healthy baby boy, Wilfred. The pregnancy had been fraught with so much stress whilst both parents succumbed to the virus and particularly when Boris became so unwell. Thankfully all was fine and Boris was now a proud father again. He now joined David Cameron and Tony Blair who had fathered new-borns at 10, Downing Street, whilst in prime ministerial office.

The police were bracing themselves for an increase in crime once Lockdown was eased and there were also concerns of a summer of discontent and violence fuelled by unemployment, boredom and complacency in the social distancing rules. Gang crime had reduced considerably due to Lockdown and some reports suggested that some gang members were more fearful of the effects of Covid-19 than they were of being fatally stabbed by a knife. More immediately, the police were having to deal with thousands of calls from the public, calling to complain about........ the public!! I think a large proportion of the population were being completely compliant when it came to observing the 'STAY AT HOME' and social distancing messages, but if individual or groups were still flouting the rules certain members of the public were not averse to contacting the police, even if it was their neighbours. It must be a tough call to snitch on your neighbours, particularly if they are acquaintances or even close friends, but I can only assume that some of these neighbours maybe did not get on in the first place.

I expect there were times when the police wished that the government had adopted the same approach to social distancing that they had in Sweden, where Swedes were advised to distance themselves from each other rather than compelled to do so. They were in essence trusted to observe the rules around social distancing while the government focused their energies on protecting the elderly in nursing and care homes. No Lockdown was ever imposed and the death toll thus far was significantly lower than most countries at 2,586.

There were so many sectors that were now being seriously impacted by closure due to Covid-19. One of these sectors that may well have been forgotten in all the media hype was the heritage 'industry', synonymous with our museums and historical sites. Despite lottery funding, they still rely so heavily on visitor footfall for their weekly and monthly revenues and being closed was causing serious concerns for their long-term future. Over 80 per cent of organisations were already braced for a very difficult few months ahead, some concerned already for their long-term prospects and viability.

More widely, financial analysts and economists were predicting that the deepest of global recessions was on the way. The American (the world's largest) and German (Europe's largest) economies were shrinking rapidly by the day, driven by sharp falls in consumer spending and business closures. France in fact was already on the brink of recession. Global mass unemployment was also now a depressing reality with a reported 30 million job losses in the US alone. As the airline industry was reeling from BA's shock declaration the previous day, about a large number of potential job losses, Boeing followed suit by announcing that they were going to axe 16,000 people. The effects of Covid-19 on the global economy were really starting to cut deep.

There was a sudden and dramatic 17 per cent increase in the daily death toll in the UK of 4,410, bringing the total to 26,097, alarmingly now the second highest in Europe and third highest in the world. Up until 28th April, only the number of deaths in hospitals were being declared to the public on a daily basis. The government had been under increasing pressure to include all Covid-19 related deaths, but now the figure included deaths recorded in care homes and the community; of the extra 4,410 deaths, 3,811 were not from hospitals. Some scientists claimed that the death rate in the UK due to Covid-19 was comparable with that of Ebola, in Africa. Ironically Remdesivir that was used to treat Ebola was still being muted as a potential treatment to slow the impact of Covid-19.

I was always touched by reports of any deaths, but it was very sad to hear of another young teenage boy dying of Covid-19, one of seven child and teenage deaths that had been reported thus far. With reportedly no underlying health conditions, this must have been absolutely heart-breaking for the parents and family. There was also another very sad local story where a couple, who had been married for 63 years, died on the same day in Southampton General Hospital. On hearing of the death of his wife, her husband refused to wear a mask and tragically met his end also.

As the UK was hopefully moving towards an easing of lockdown it was crucially important that we were looking at other countries to learn any lessons. This was unlike we had done, it seemed, in the lead-up to and during the inception of the virus.

~

TODAY'S DAILY TIP: One of my main inspirations in both my personal and professional life is a gentleman by the name of Stephen Covey, mentioned previously in the book, a best-selling author and keynote speaker. He wrote an excellent book called 'Seven habits for highly successful people', which is well worth a read. Towards the end of the book, he refers to the '4 dimensions' that we should try to live our lives by which cover our physical, mental, social and emotional and spiritual well-being. (SPIRITUAL)

Day 38, Thursday 30th April: Happy 100th, Captain Tom the Legend!

I had been working on my 3000-piece jigsaw puzzle for over three weeks now and it certainly proved to be one of the more difficult jigsaw challenges that I have undertaken. It was high time though that I put the hard yards in to complete the wretched thing, in no small part due to the fact that it was taking up the whole of the dining-room table. I therefore rose earlier than usual to get on with it, but also so that I could watch the fly-past of a Hurricane and a Spitfire on the TV to honour the Second World War veteran, Captain Tom Moore's 100th birthday. He was also on the receiving end of over 140,000 birthday cards as well as a cherished one from the Queen.

"About to raise a glass of champers to Captain Tom"

Captain Tom's inspirational walk of 100 laps of his garden had now raised an absolutely incredible £32 million for NHS Charities Together; not bad for someone who initially only intended to raise £1,000. He offered his usual uplifting call to the nation, insisting that 'eventually we'll win', referring to the 'battle' against Covid-19. I imagine his experiences as a soldier in India and Burma and those of his military colleagues in other parts of world during the war, were hugely different to ours in this so-called 'war' that we were supposedly fighting. Although I understand the notion to make comparisons between the two, I would say that they are two markedly different situations, both unfortunately incurring large loss of life.

Another day of rain, in fact some really rather heavy showers, restricted our daily run to a brisk 2K. This then allowed me to potter around the house doing a few much-needed jobs like replacing the light bulbs, sorting out a few more cupboards and doing some more of the puzzle, which was now becoming a great source of frustration to me. Of course, Thursday would not have been Thursday without the weekly 'Clap for our Carers and NHS workers', which was still bringing communities out in force for mutual appreciation of what our frontline medical staff were doing all around the country.

It was still very strange getting used to life without any live sport. Not only should we have been looking at the build-up to a summer of sport, but the English Premier League and lower league seasons remained unfinished and in a state of limbo. All sorts of scenarios were being discussed including making the season completely null and void, which was not going down very well with Liverpool supporters, worried about whether they would earn their first top flight league title in 30 years. Whatever was going happen, one thing we did now know was that any football would have to be played without fans in attendance, behind closed doors, potentially at least until Christmas – a hammer blow to all those used to going to watch their teams week in, week out.

Boris Johnson made his first live appearance at the daily 5pm press briefing since his return to work from his Covid-19 illness on the Monday. He confirmed what we probably knew already, which was that the virus was now finally past its peak. As a result, during the following week, he was going to produce his 'comprehensive plan' as to how he was going to navigate the nation out of Lockdown. Still sounding breathless, probably as a result of his illness, he claimed that due to the government's interventions and the work of the NHS, that hundreds of thousands of lives had been saved, and he was at pains to say: 'We will not risk a second spike in infections'. Boris was very much on the 'spin offensive', whether it was trying to convince us that there would be not just 100,000 tests per day but 250,000, or that Lockdown had been imposed at just the right time. He also was resolute that economic recovery would not be achieved through austerity but through a quick 'bounce back'. Good old Boris – ever the optimist or was this a theme in the government, that he was just taking us for fools?

Talking of testing, miraculously 81,611 tests were carried the previous day, a sudden jump of 50 per cent on the day before the 100,000 per day target was meant to be achieved. Ironically in Germany, testing was at over 300,000 per day, and that was still short of capacity. Meanwhile scientists in South Korea were starting to believe that someone who had already had Covid-19 could not actually be re-infected. This is exactly what UK scientists hoped that antibody tests would prove.

674 more deaths were reported in the UK bringing the total to 26,771. In America, the death toll increased by another 1,923, more in one day than any European country had had as a daily figure, bringing their total to a horrific 62,418. Even more significantly, more people had died to Covid-19 than had been killed in the Vietnam War and things were not about to improve anytime soon.

~

TODAY'S DAILY TIP: When replacing faulty light bulbs around the house as a precaution use a rubber glove to avoid depositing a grease residue from ones hand onto the new light bulbs, which could reduce their longevity and effectiveness. (PHYSICAL)

Day 39, Friday 1st May: That testing target

"Zoom quiz with the girls and their funny hats"

On a much nicer day than of late it was time to ramp up our running distance slightly, with under two weeks to go now until Alex embarked on his 10K challenge. This time we took a route with more hills, and with more road-running and less cross-country. As we climbed the first steep hill, I saw the first signs that Alex was really struggling with his breathing and the pain that he had endured in his stomach when we first started these runs came back with a vengeance. That did not deter Alex and despite a number of water stops, we continued, notching up the longest run yet at 6.5K.

After the run, Alex's recovery was much slower than his previous exertions and I once again feared that doing a 10K might just be beyond his limits. Of course, Alex has always been a resolute and determined young man, and in his eyes this was just a minor setback that he would overcome. Being parents of a 'heart child' always come with the dilemma that we have always wanted Alex to live his life as normally as possible but knowing that he has endured an awful lot of suffering for someone so young and therefore he does has limitations. I guess it makes it even more special and rewarding when he does stretch what we feel are his boundaries and achieves the things he does. As much as I was going to continue to support him wholeheartedly, the doubts had crept back, and I genuinely thought that we may have reached the 'end of the road'.

Because of my inner concerns about Alex after today's run I was a little down for the rest of the day so it was good that we had our usual Friday evening routine of an 'Otter' takeaway and quiz night, followed by my first dabbling with Ricky

Gervais's new venture 'After Life'. Ricky Gervais has been one of my favourite comic actors ever since I saw him in the 'fly-on-the –wall' sitcom documentaries, 'The Office' and 'Extras'. I know he is not everyone's 'cup of tea', but his dry subtle wit can be very mirthful, and it was evident again in 'After Life'.

So we had finally reached the end of April and the '$64,000 question' was whether Health Secretary Hancock had managed to meet his target of 100,000 tests in one day, even though only 29,000 tests were being done per day the week before. Of course he did, and some – a total of 122,347 were recorded as a jubilant Mr Hancock smugly announced: 'We have met our goal'. In fairness to Mr Hancock, by setting a testing target (excuse the pun!), it clearly did have the 'galvanising effect on everybody involved' to increase testing and testing capacity. But to claim that the mailing out of nearly 40,000 home testing kits should actually count as completed tests to ensure they got to their target in time, could be perceived as slightly manipulative and 'massaging' the figures. It became even more suspicious when testing in the ensuing days dropped back below 100,000 per day for a whole week! Mr Hancock's attention now moved to trialling his contact tracing app on, of all places, the Isle of Wight, a location with many mature residents, many of whom would not even know the meaning of the word 'app', let alone have a mobile smart phone.

It had been an eventful week for the Prime Minister since he returned to 10, Downing Street as he eased himself back into the 'driving seat', after spending two weeks convalescing at Chequers. We saw him briefly and publicly on Monday morning as he returned to work before he got down to business again with his cabinet colleagues focusing on the continued PPE shortages and trying to achieve the testing target by the end of the week, amongst other things. On the Wednesday he became a father again, before briefing the nation on Thursday and revealing some of his plans for the next stage of the 'battle' against Covid-19. But it was this next stage that would once again prove that to close down the nation was a little more straightforward than re-starting everything again, and whatever he did, he just simply could not please everyone.

More and more pressure was being put on the airline industry as would-be tourists were reluctantly cancelling their summer holiday plans, meaning the grounding of even more aeroplanes. Even though summer flights could be made available, it seemed that a lack of consumer confidence suggested that many people would rather just stay in the UK this summer. So bleak was the outlook that Ryanair was the next airline company to announce that 3,000 jobs would be lost, almost a sixth of their workforce and mainly pilots and cabin crew. The cost of refunds was also growing although many were disgruntled at how long some refunds were taking – and this situation would only worsen across the industry.

Fears were also growing about the state of the housing market, with a worst-case scenario prediction of a fall in house prices for over 30 per cent over the next two to three years. In realistic terms that would take a property worth £225,000 now to just under £160,000, and thus reduce an owner-occupier's wealth and equity by around £65,000. On the plus side, it might make things easier for first-time buyers or the younger generations to get on the property ladder. But only, of course, if they were in gainful employment, and this potentially deep recession was promising mass unemployment, especially for many younger people – it just seemed like a vicious circle.

A further 739 more deaths in hospitals, care homes and the wider community, were recorded in the UK, bringing the total to 27,510, amidst claims by the Office of National Statistics (ONS) that twice as many people were dying of Covid-19 from deprived areas than in more affluent areas. One of the main reasons for this was that people living in these areas were in poorly paid key worker roles that meant that they could not work from home, and therefore were exposed more to the virus. We were slowly becoming more aware that obesity, ethnicity and demographics were key factors as to whether or not one contracted this virus.

~

TODAY'S DAILY TIP: With the talk about the possibility of having to wear face masks on public transport and in shops increasing as we move towards an easing of Lockdown, it was a good to invest some time in making one's own face masks. One could make them out of sewn fabric, old T-shirts or even paper. One thing is for sure, they could soon be in very high demand not just with the numbers required, but also because they will be disposed of in high quantities as the advice is not to re-use them. (SOCIAL / EMOTIONAL)

Day 40. Saturday 2nd May: The big Re-Match

Alex took a much-needed break from running for the weekend after his tremendous efforts the day before. Instead we started an eventful and exciting day with one of our long family morning walks with little Tizzy, that we had done most weekends during Lockdown. These walks generated so much fun and laughter, with Holly and Alex dishing out the banter. The usual source of great amusement was sticking goose grass on each other's backs without the victim knowing it, something we used to do in our childhoods. It seemed just as funny now as then, especially when we managed to get home and a victim still had goose grass clinging to their clothing.

"Alex with his girlfriend Charlotte; the two families embarked on a couple of epic zoom quizzes"

I was now so close to completing the very tough 3000-piece jigsaw puzzle that had consumed me for nearly four weeks and I was fiercely determined to get it finished by lunchtime. I probably only had 50 pieces to input but it seemed to take an age to find their correct positions, eventually at just before 1.00pm, the puzzle was finally completed – or at least I thought it was! Two pieces were missing and I had a fairly good idea where they had ended up – in little Tizzy's tummy! Only a seasoned jigsaw-maker would appreciate how unbelievably annoying it is to do your hardest ever puzzle and then find that it was missing two pieces. It would take me a couple of days to get over it.

I went from one challenge to another as Alex and I completed our two-day marathon pool tournament, with Alex upsetting the odds with a shock 10-6 victory, the first time he had ever beaten me in a such a pool challenge. But the really big contest was looming large, with the Zoom quiz night re-match between the Stones and the Inds, and our chance to avenge our very painful defeat three weeks earlier.

Much planning had gone into this next quiz challenge, and it was our turn to choose the six categories. The key was to include a category or two that Stones might find a little more challenging and which we might find a bit more straightforward when answering their questions. So the categories we chose were: 1) Pop music 2) Football 3) 'Where in the world?' 4) General knowledge, and then the two 'jokers in the pack', we hoped: 5) Food and drink 6) 'Songs from the shows'. After some final preparations and fine-tuning over one of our lovely steak and sausage barbecues, we were ready to go into 'battle'.

Round one was one of our 'jokers', food and drink, but the Stones were on fire and took a narrow lead; round two was pop music and again the Stones prevailed, taking a three-point lead into the next round; round three was football and Alex 'pulled out all the stops' to win this round by three points, evening up the contest at the halfway point – you could have cut the tension with a knife; into round 4, and the general knowledge round, which the Inds just nicked by one point, so one point in it, with two rounds left; round 5 and maybe the 'coup de grâce' for the Inds with their second 'joker' category, 'songs from the shows', which Susie and Holly absolutely bossed, winning it by three points and taking a four-point lead into the final round; and finally round six, and the 'where in the world' category – a one point win for the Inds meant an overall and very nerve-wracking five point win for the Inds to draw the contest level at one win each. The Stones were magnanimous in defeat, but like us three weeks earlier, were intent on revenge; the next chapter in this epic rivalry would have to wait until June.

A very enjoyable day and evening ended with a couple of late-night episodes of the highly-acclaimed yet slightly risqué sitcom 'Friday Night Dinner', something everybody except Susie and I seemed to have watched. There is no doubt the star of this particular show was Jim, the rather eccentric next-door neighbour of a family called the Goodmans, and famed for his catchphrase, '.......something smells nice...'. I have to say for me, it was Martin Goodman, the father, who 'topped the bill' and who I found absolutely hysterical at times.

We were again hearing how very seriously ill Boris Johnson had become whilst in hospital with Covid-19. Such was the severity of his illness, particularly at the point he may have needed to be intubated, that contingencies were being made in case he lost his life. At one point, Boris thought to himself, that with no medicine or apparent cure: 'How am I going to get out of this?' In an emotional and candid newspaper interview, he admitted to 'feeling pretty groggy' and 'pretty rough', and 'in denial' as to how ill he was becoming. It must have been pretty frightening for him but also for the many, many others in the same situation and many that ended up dying alone without their families and friends around them.

As much as the medical profession were focused on the fight against Covid-19, many doctors were becoming even more concerned about the disruption to the treatment and care of those with non-Covid-19 illnesses, ailments and conditions, some which were as life-threatening as the effects of Covid-19. With A&E attendance still way down on the normal levels, there were real concerns that people were just suffering in silence as their conditions worsened. One leading medic claimed: 'Many ill patients are not getting the care they so desperately need now and are risking their conditions getting worse and with some, maybe dying as a result'. The government had a tough balancing act which needed to be addressed quickly.

One thing doctors may also have become increasingly concerned with, was the amount of alcohol that nation appeared to be consuming, maybe as a means of seeking solace from some of the anxieties of Lockdown. A drop in champagne sales and an increase in beer and cider sales across Britain, may have indicated that people certainly had a lot less to celebrate. That said, Prosecco seems to have become the 'new champagne' in this country. It was evident from the various Zoom quizzes that we did that the 'gin craze' was still very much in evidence. Many would have used alcohol to enhance these virtual social occasions and experiences as an important replacement for socialising in pubs and bars. Sadly though, excessive alcohol intake will have been the cause of many tragic and very unpleasant accidents or incidents, which may well have changed lives forever, in the way that Covid-19 has.

Deaths in UK rose by another 621, to a total of 28,131. Cases and hospitalisations might have been falling but the death toll was still depressingly high. Every time we listened to the daily briefing we just yearned for the time when the death toll was in single figures, if not none at all.

~

TODAY'S DAILY TIP: When you set yourself a task, particularly one that is likely to take a long time to complete, there may be a tendency to give in and not see it through to the end. I have had a couple of these tasks in Lockdown, so it is important to stay focused and resilient, to ensure their successful completion. (MENTAL)

Day 41, Sunday 3rd May: Family reunions on Zoom

A lot of what I did in Lockdown related to tidying and sorting with moments of cleaning almost tantamount to classic spring-cleaning, and of course it was exactly the right time of the year for doing this. After a busy Saturday and our usual long Sunday walk with Tizzy, it was now time to give the house a really good tidy-up and clean from top to bottom, not that Holly and Alex were going to contribute much!

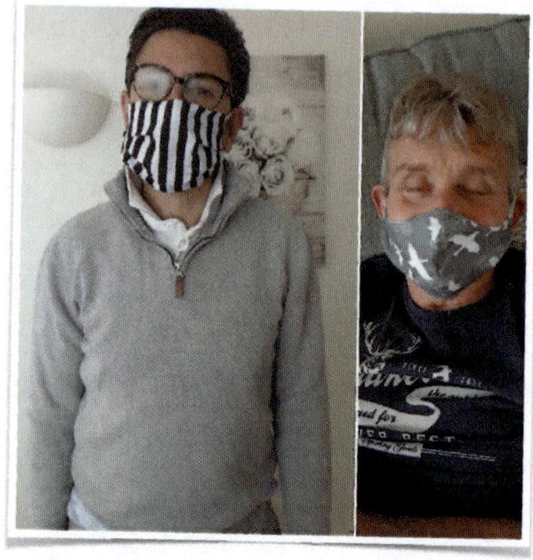

"Masks, modelled by brother-in-law Mark and my goodself, eventually became compulsory on public transport and in enclosed spaces"

Zoom had been so good for so many people during Lockdown, whether for business or pleasure reasons. We had used it predominantly for quizzes and to catch up with Susie's side of the family in Bournemouth. What we had not yet done up until this point was to have a virtual catch-up with my side of the family; that was until today. After a number of technical hitches and the usual 'you're on mute' issue, we finally saw altogether on one screen: my mother and father, Jack and Elizabeth, my sister and her husband, Rebecca and John, and one of their sons, Peter, all in Tonbridge; my brother and his wife, Hugh and Jo and their children, Ben and Amber, in southwest London; my sister, Katharine, in southeast London; and my niece and her boyfriend, Victoria and Alex, in Devon. It was fantastic to see everyone on the one screen and for us all to connect after so long. I know it absolutely made my mother and father's day, and I think they were stunned that such a connection with everyone could be established in such a way – the wonders of technology!

With the likelihood increasing that we would have to utilise face coverings in some way shape or form in the coming weeks, Susie took it upon herself to make a couple of them for each of the family. She had some old black and white striped fabric and created some rather wonderful elasticated face masks. Some might have thought they were Juventus Football Club (FC) or Newcastle United masks. Maybe the red and white stripes of Southampton FC might have been more in order! It was another example of how supremely talented my wife, Susie, is. Not only is she an incredible wife, mother and much-loved family relative, she (amongst many things) is incredibly well organised, keeps a great home, has sharp eyes for design and detail and is an exceptional cook especially her cakes and cookies. She does it all with a smile on her face and an infectious and endearing wit. I am truly lucky to have her as my partner and it has been an amazing 28 years of marriage thus far.

I did find it rather disappointing that we were still not able to partake in outdoor 'summer' sports such as tennis, golf and cricket. If, as the scientists seemed to believe, the virus was less contagious in the open air and possibly not so virulent in a warmer climate, why could we not at least play golf, a sport that is for the most part played a safe distance away? I imagine the 2.9 million anglers in the UK who go coarse, game and sea fishing, were even more baffled, as there surely cannot be a more isolated sport or pastime.

We had now come to the end of our sixth week in Lockdown, which seemed to have gone strangely quickly. Although one day appeared to merge seamlessly into another, so far in our family, we always found that we had something to do, whether it be work (for Susie and Holly), a chore or a form of fun and relaxation. In fact, some of the chores even became quite enjoyable, my favourite being the emptying of the dishwasher. It was apparent from the government's daily press conference, chaired by Cabinet Office Minister Michael Gove, that Boris Johnson's so-called 'comprehensive plan' to ease the Lockdown might be quite low key and we might not actually see the plan until a week's time. Our new found lifestyles could well be continuing for a good while yet.

For those who had been on the government's furlough scheme and with talk of an easing of the restrictions, the thought of going back to work would have been very much on many people's minds. If working from home was not an option there will have been concerns about the safety of their working environment. For some, the big concern will have been the journey to and from work on public transport. Throughout Lockdown many stoic key workers will have been using public transport and have found trains and buses to be almost empty. This must have been incredibly surreal for those who remember the days of overcrowding in stations and on platforms and long bus queues. With estimates that trains, in particular, would continue to run at reduced capacities, Transport Secretary Grant Shapps further tried to reassure would-be passengers that working hours could be staggered and one-way systems could be created for commuters. Those working more locally were being encouraged to cycle and utilise a scheme whereby you could buy a bike through your employer.

Amazingly, nearly seven weeks into Lockdown, there was a still large number of airline passengers that were reportedly flying into the UK from abroad on a daily basis who were neither having their temperatures taken nor being asked to isolate. Mr Shapps again alluded to the fact that the government were now looking into the possibility of imposing quarantine on flyers and introducing temperature scanners at airports, but there was still no great urgency to get anything implemented. The whole thing just seemed very strange, where so many other countries had already imposed their own tight restrictions around air travel several weeks previously.

In many countries across Europe deaths in care and nursing homes accounted for a large proportion of all deaths from Covid-19. Research from the London School of Economics suggested that there could have been between 42 per cent and 57 per cent of deaths in these areas across countries such as Italy, Spain and France. The figure was less in Germany as it was claimed that they had stricter regulations around discharging patients from hospitals back into care homes as well as quicker response times, better testing and more PPE. The knowledge that had now been gained as result of some very harsh lessons learned needed to be used to prevent a situation like this recurring, particularly in the UK.

The daily death toll in the UK, rose by another 315 and now totalled 28,446 which was only 438 behind Italy's total of 28,884. Britain was now on course to have the highest death toll of any nation in Europe and despite supposedly being past the peak there were likely to be many more deaths to come. The North-West had now become the UK's worst-hit region with 2,191 people in hospital. London's hospitalisations were now at last on the decline at 2,033, which had fallen by a quarter in a week.

As the death toll in the US continued to rise exponentially reaching 68,173, the Italian government was trying to get back on its feet easing its people back outdoors. This was greeted with a mixture of fear and apprehension of contracting the virus again and relief at being able to do some normal things once more. With Italy 12 days or so ahead of the UK in their virus timeline it was another good indicator of what might be in store for us in a fortnight's time. Prime Minister Guiseppe Conte told the nation: 'We must maintain social distancing, maximum hygiene levels and masks' adding: 'I implore you, do not lower your guard'; a sign of things to come and maybe that 'new normal' that everyone was talking about.

~

TODAY'S DAILY TIP: With a new week ahead of us why not plan the meals that you are going to have each day, and maybe to add a little bit variety, choose different foods of the world. Grab a map of the world, close your eyes and put a pin in it, then choose dishes from the countries that the pin ends up in. To top things off, get a little blackboard so everyone can see what the daily offering is and hope that you have a good cook in the kitchen! (SOCIAL / EMOTIONAL)

Day 42, Monday 4th May: Test, track and trace

"The fitbit was a key element to the 10K challenge"

On a lovely Monday morning - that normally would have been a Bank Holiday but for the 75th anniversary celebrations for 'Victory in Europe' (VE) Day the next Friday - and after a couple of days rest and re-focus, Alex got his running shoes and 'fitbit' back on and hit the road again. We tackled the same hilly route that he had struggled with on Friday, knowing that we would have to encounter several steep hills during the 10K on 13th May. During today's run it was great to see my good friend and ex-Saints footballer and philanthropist, Nicky Banger, who was out doing his daily bike ride and he offered us words of encouragement in his inimitable style as we passed him by. Alex completed today's 5K without any difficulty at all and once again my faith in him was restored. So far we had only done a maximum of 6.5K on any single run; we had just over a week to ramp things up to a level higher and hope that Alex would not have another setback.

For most of the afternoon Alex and I renewed our garden cricket rivalry. Like we had done with pool a couple of days before we played out a marathon contest, which unfortunately he also won 10-6. Whatever sport Alex and I play there is always really fierce level competition, but now he was defeating me in resounding fashion at pool and cricket, and outsprinting me during stages of our daily runs. I began to think that my days as a sporting icon, were numbered.

Today was one of those days when I had to pop out for some essential shopping as we were running very low on some of the items that unfortunately had not arrived as part of our on-line weekly shop. I also had to get some comestibles for my aunt as well as posting a parcel for her to her daughter and my cousin, in Switzerland. Now, I had not been to a post-office in months and when I saw the massive queue outside I nearly turned around and went home. Knowing how important the parcel was though, I joined the queue. Once I got inside, said queue snaked endlessly up and down three aisles. What made things worse was a gentleman disputing the price of his postage, which made it an unnecessarily lengthy process. I could only assume that this was a sign of things to come and an example of the 'new' shopping experience!

Reports of a return of some live sports to our screens was very welcome news after nearly two months without it. Dates had been pencilled in for horse-racing and golf events, and it was being muted that there was a strong appetite amongst the clubs somehow to get the Premier League season finished. The last top-flight game took place controversially on 11th March at Anfield, home of Liverpool FC. The team that stood to lose the most if the Premier League season was indeed going to be declared null and void.

Health Secretary Hancock was still 'dining out' on his '100,000 per day' testing success that he had achieved by the end of April. The fact that each day since then was between 15,000 and 25,000 tests short of 100,000, was neither here nor there – except Boris Johnson was now going to extend the testing target to 200,000 per day by the end of May! Undeterred, Mr Hancock embarked on his next project, telling us that we would all have to download his new test and trace smartphone app which would in turn help the nation back to work, as well as giving us a mechanism to help control the spread of the virus.

The trial on the Isle of Wight had commenced with some residents the evening before and would be available to all of the 140,000 population - about 40,000 of these were senior citizens - by Thursday, or at least to those who had smartphones with downloadable apps, though there were still concerns about the system's ability to provide 'privacy and security' for the public. All things considered and as long as the testing increased sustainably and testing capacity was maintained, this test and trace app was going to be the way to control the virus and prevent a second wave, whilst we awaited a vaccine. Much like it had been successful in South Korea – it sounded great in theory but had Hancock 'bitten off more than he could chew'?

The government had now produced draft guidelines for workers to ensure their safe return to a number of different types of workplaces, but ministers stressed that the safety of employees was very firmly in the hands of the employers. The guidelines included hand-sanitising, working at a safe distance where possible and one-way flow systems in corridors. As far as possible, there should be limited contact between employees and working from home should still be encouraged.

The argument regarding whether over-70s should be kept in Lockdown once the restrictions were eased rumbled on, as they were the most 'at risk' age group of contracting the virus. Health Secretary Hancock came to the rescue, insisting that there was and would be no 'blanket ban' on over-70s as long as they followed social distancing rules. He offered reassurances and said that, '........the suggestion that the clinically vulnerable include people aged 70 or older regardless of their medical conditions, is wrong'; my aunt would hopefully be a lot happier now!

As Lockdown was relaxed in Italy for the first time in eight weeks and since 10th March, 4.4 million Italians eased their way back to work. Meetings with loved ones were also now permitted, parks re-opened for exercise, cafes re-opened for takeaways and travel was now allowed within your own region. Non-essential shops would be allowed to re-open from 18th May and bars and restaurants from 1st June, but schools would not re-open until September. In Spain, they would start to lift their restrictions further from 11th May, but in careful stages. In

Germany, however, there were serious concerns that youngsters and young adults had been spreading the virus in large numbers during Lockdown, as there appeared to be 'lesser adherence' to social distancing rules. In many cases these young people were asymptomatic, unaware of that they might have been spreading the virus.

The daily death toll brought about a further 288 new deaths in the UK, bringing the total to 28,734. Although it was one of the lower daily death tolls than of late, particularly in hospitals, and notwithstanding the weekend lag, deaths in care homes were still worryingly on the increase. What was also on the increase was the death toll in America, which had regularly been at between 1,000 and 2,000 per day, and was predicted in a leaked government report to be as high as 3,000 by the end of June. With nearly 70,000 deaths in total in the US, and if these forecasts were true, the final death toll could be in the hundreds of thousands. Where Lockdowns had controlled the virus in Europe, America's and President Trump's disjointed approach had things on a course that was spiralling out of control.

~

TODAY'S DAILY TIP: With the new found time that some people may have on their hands it might be a good time to learn a new language or two for the next time you go to visit your favourite foreign countries. There are many apps and means by which one can learn, in fact my daughter has been learning Spanish on an app called 'Duolingo'. It may be just a few basic words, but it is a start and it can be very rewarding. (SPIRITUAL)

Day 43, Tuesday 5th May: Tension in the household

Alex and I were back on our usual route through the woods for the start of today's 6K run. The majority of this route would represent the second part of our imminent 10K challenge. I have to say it was probably the most enjoyable and rewarding run that either of us had done since we started this epic challenge. I think because we had been forced to push ourselves more during the hilly road runs, it was starting to pay dividends in improving our general levels of fitness. Alex's recovery was as good as it had been after any of our runs.

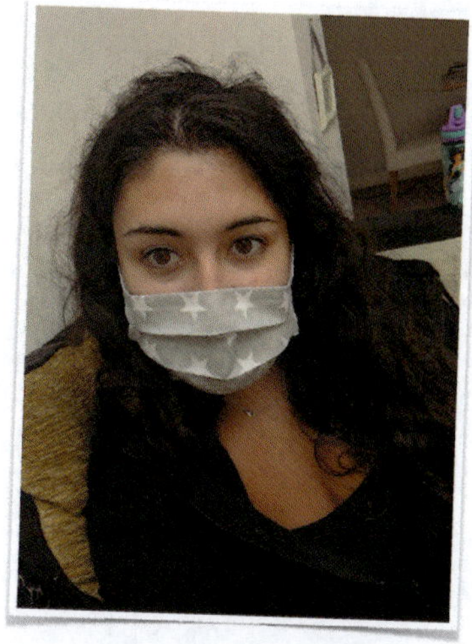

"Holly gets in on the mask act"

Whilst Alex and I were building up to our run on 13th May, Holly was working 'her socks off' from home. She had been working relentlessly throughout the six weeks of Lockdown and I had been very conscious of the need to give her the space to perform her role as effectively as possible. At times I sensed she was fraught, particularly in the past few days, made worse for her I am sure because she did not have the direct hands on support of senior colleagues to help her through some very challenging situations. Holly and I are probably quite similar in character and it was therefore only a matter of time before the 'lid came off the pressure cooker'. As is often the case with these things, it was the pettiest thing that set us off, but the underlying argument was that I was trying to do things in my house which was effectively doubling up as Holly's place of work. There was a 'wild' difference of opinion for about three or four minutes and then the proverbial 'storm blew over'. What was impressive was that it had taken us 43 days to get to this point and it was all over very quickly – I think my peace offering of a packet of 'Jelly Babies' probably helped too. I am sure we were not the only household in the UK to have the odd family disagreement as these were of course unprecedented times.

I was delighted to hear that part of Boris Johnson's proposed Lockdown exit strategy was to increase the amount of outdoor exercise that we could all do. It was becoming increasingly apparent that many in the population appreciated greatly the opportunity to run, walk or cycle once a day and the positive impact it was having on people's mental and physical well-being. With the open air, warm weather and social distancing, surely people were less likely to catch the virus outside anyway. I would wait with bated breath for Boris's official announcement at the end of the week to see whether more chances to exercise would stretch as far as being able to play golf and cricket.

Much of the planning for the easing of Lockdown restrictions would have been discussed initially by the scientists at the Scientific Advisory Group for Emergencies (SAGE) meetings that took place throughout the pandemic – and if we did not know it already, the government were 'guided by the science'! In a shocking revelation, the scientist and SAGE member who had recommended Lockdown to the government, Professor Neil Ferguson, resigned dramatically from his government advisory role over illicit liaisons with a married lover, which had broken social distancing rules. Professor Ferguson had changed the government's whole approach to the virus after predicting that half a million people may die if a herd immunity strategy was followed, prompting the sudden change in advice to Boris Johnson to go into Lockdown. Although he would offer advice from afar, there was no doubt he was going to be a loss to the government's frontline advisory team, but he simply could not preach social distancing and then not practice it himself.

SAGE meanwhile, were aware that some of their decision-making may have been perceived as lacking transparency, so they made available some of the advice that they offered to the government. It is plain to see how difficult some of the decision-making was and how wary they were of public sentiment, particularly in enforcing Lockdown. But ultimately SAGE was only an advisory body, and it was the government that would always have the final decision – 'guided by the science'!

It was now widely regarded that one of the main sources of coronavirus to the UK, before the crisis kicked in, was the many thousands of people arriving back in the February half-term from Italy after skiing holidays and Spain after finding a bit of winter sun; these were two of the countries in Europe that were most ravaged by the virus. Very few of these people were then forced into quarantine or any form of isolation, meaning they were major vectors for the rapid spread of the virus throughout the UK during the latter part of February and beginning of March. Many of these people would have been children or young adults who may not have shown symptoms, passing the virus on unknowingly to older family members or their friends. The only people in that time that were forced to quarantine were those who had been on three plane loads from Wuhan in China, initially the alleged source of the virus, and those on the 'Diamond Princess' cruise ship that was stricken by the virus off of the Japanese coast. When it came to the part Europe played in the UK contracting the virus it appears that we were really caught off our guard.

Chancellor of the Exchequer Rishi Sunak had been very busy over the previous weeks ensuring that all the various government policies and hand-outs to employees and businesses, including the furlough scheme, were being implemented as this was always go to be the initial measure as to how successful they were. The Chancellor and his various teams deserve an awful lot of praise for the relative speed in which many people received their money, when one thinks of the numbers of people up and down the country that were affected. The problem is schemes such as furlough cannot last forever and there were already rumours circulating that Mr Sunak was planning to wind down the scheme at the end of June because the £10 billion cost per month was not sustainable. It was after all a similar amount to that which the government was spending on the NHS on a monthly basis. He was concerned, as one government source said, that: 'People are addicted to the scheme...................and we have to get them back to work'. One of the main ways to get people back to work was to re-open schools, freeing parents from the burden of childcare. The problem was that re-opening all schools simultaneously was going to present, as Mr Raab said, '.......... a real risk of a second wave'. At this stage it was thought a staged re-opening of only certain year groups, might be the most sensible course of action.

There was more heartache in the airline industry with an announcement that Virgin Atlantic was to cut over 3,000 jobs, one third of their workforce, and quit Gatwick Airport as a result of the impact of the pandemic. Virgin joined British Airways and Ryanair who had also reported that there would be major losses. Locally to me, the Southampton community, amongst others, was still reeling from the collapse of FlyBe earlier in the year. Aviation was in complete turmoil and there seemed no end in sight to the misery.

Another depressing milestone was reached in the UK with an increase in the daily death toll of a further 693 deaths, which now meant that the UK was the worst-hit nation in Europe with a total of 29,427 deaths and the 2nd highest in the world, only to the US who were now at 71,148 total deaths. Notwithstanding the fact that some countries may work out their numbers of deaths differently, this was, as Foreign Secretary Dominic Raab described in the daily press briefing, a 'massive tragedy'. If one also factors in excess deaths – deaths from other causes that are attributable to the overall pandemic – we could have been looking at a number close to 55,000; this was indeed a bleak day.

~

TODAY'S DAILY TIP: There is so much that we can learn about in the world of wine. Globally there are so many fantastic white, red and rose wines, as well as a plethora of sparkling wines and champagne. Instead of just quaffing wine why learn of its origins, grape varieties and why one year might be better than another. (SPIRITUAL)

Day 44, Wednesday 6th May: 8K done with a week to go

"I took up sketching in Lockdown; a nice picture of Tizzy!"

With one week to go until Alex's brave 10K challenge, we decided to increase the distance to one that was thus far unchartered territory, 8K. This would be a real measure as to how close Alex was, both physically and mentally, to being in a position to complete this tough undertaking. Thankfully, it was another lovely day and usually when the weather conditions were favourable it bode well for a good run. Not only did we complete 8K, but we did it in one hour and 10 minutes. More importantly, and despite some tough moments, in relative terms Alex breezed through the run. The question was, would we actually do a 10K before next week or take the risk by not doing one and preserve our energy with a couple of shorter runs leading up to the big day? This really was going to be the big call. In the meantime, I needed to focus on my pool performances as I could not allow Alex to defeat me again, especially in such a convincing manner. That afternoon, I sought revenge and another marathon pool challenge commenced.

The shopping habits of some in the UK appeared to be changing in Lockdown, with a continued demand for egg cups, teapots and coffee grinders. People were having more time in the mornings to eat a leisurely breakfast rather than having to rush out of the house first thing for breakfast and coffee on the run. This of course did nothing to improve the egg shortages that had been a regular source of my Lockdown frustration. Board games, jigsaw puzzles, hair dye, elastic (for homemade face masks), baking products and alcohol, were amongst other things that experienced a hike in demand in Lockdown. Some households though were struggling to make ends meet, barely able to put food on the table for their hungry young families; depravation and poverty were beginning to hit the nation hard, with many people now relying on food parcels and the generosity of kind benefactors.

The Nightingale Hospital at London Excel, built to manage the potential high demand for intensive care beds during the height of the pandemic, was stood down for the time being with barely 40 beds having been occupied at any one time and bearing in mind that we were supposedly past the peak. It would however be kept on standby in case of resurgence in hospitalisations. The other nine Nightingale hospitals dotted around the UK had also been used sparingly, though for the time being they would remain on standby. There is no doubt that the incredibly fast erection of these field hospitals helped greatly with our preparedness for the peak; either the virus was not as serious as had been anticipated or the NHS hospitals deserve even more credit for how they treated their Covid-19 patients, many of whom recovered before need to go to ICU.

Private hospitals were also deployed by the government as virus-free centres and to try to keep other aspects of healthcare going. Reportedly up to 8,000 beds had been bought by the NHS at huge cost to the taxpayer. The problem was, staff and equipment were being used elsewhere to treat Covid-19 patients, and although some cancer, cardiac and other treatments were being carried out, it was not enough to address the fast-growing backlog of cases; many of these beds in private hospitals lay empty suggesting that alot of public money might have been wasted.

Job losses in the US, the country with the world's largest death toll by far, reached a record 20 million for the month of April and a total of 33 million, as the world's largest economy was nearly at a standstill. With a halt on consumer spending and the closure of bars, restaurants, hotels and shops in Lockdown, the American economy 'sunk to its knees'. We already knew that Europe was heading down a similar path towards their deepest recession since the Great Depression between 1929 and 1933, after the stock market crash in October 1929. The economies of Spain and Italy had retracted by 10 per cent and the largest European economy in Germany, by nearly 7 per cent. The Bank of England, who stood to lose a whopping £80 billion due to Covid-19, was predicting the worst recession in Britain for 300 years with up to 2 million job losses. Recovery would likely be very slow and might be seriously hindered further by our good old friend, Brexit, especially if trading relations with the EU remained uncertain.

On a slightly brighter note, the German tourism commissioner indicated that there may be a chance for German tourists to venture across borders to lap up a bit of summer sun in European coastal resorts. With a dearth of beaches in Germany and a choice of only the North Sea or Baltic Sea, Germans are frequent travellers to the Continent's coasts. With tourism being the lifeblood of countries like Spain, Greece and Cyprus, the German government were looking at 'corona travel corridors' to allow for safe travel between countries, although Chancellor Angela Merkel was keen not to get people's hopes up. More immediately, Germans were excited about the imminent opening of bars and restaurants and a resumption of the German Football Bundesliga season, albeit behind closed doors, which could be the template for the possible return of the Premier League.

The UK's death toll reached yet another grim milestone with a further 649 deaths, which took the total past the 30,000 mark, to 30,076. Theories were being expounded as to why the UK was now the nation which had the highest death toll in Europe, and was second only to America. Was it because of our dense population, or levels of obesity, or the high median age of Covid-19 patients, or were our borders open to too many for too long, or did we not test enough, or were we simply counting and recording deaths differently to our global counterparts? I suspect it may have been a combination of all of these things, some factors accounting for more than others. One thing is for sure, that the government was slow to react to the initial danger signs of the virus and the advice from the scientists. And as for care homes' crisis, which Boris Johnson 'bitterly regretted', some poor errors of judgement were made.

New research confirmed what was thought, that there was a double risk of hospitalisations for patients who were obese, which may well have touched a nerve with Boris Johnson. Meanwhile he was preoccupied with fending off Sir Keir Starmer, the new Leader of the Labour party, who was challenging the Prime Minister in PMQs, for the first time. After wishing Boris well with the birth of baby Wilfred, Sir Keir took him to task on his handling of the crisis, which Boris had claimed was thus far a 'success'. You can imagine that went down like a 'lead balloon' and the 'gloves came off'! Boris appeared to sidestep a number of the challenges from Sir Keir, and using a subtle deflection tactic, announced that he intended on easing some social-distancing restrictions from Monday – would this at last be an end to the 'STAY AT HOME' message and the start of a return to normality?

~

TODAY'S DAILY TIP: With all the uncertainty around, our mood can be impacted causing worry and anxiety, why not take up something that is proven to improve one's mood and do 45 minutes of drawing. Once one is relaxed the negative thoughts and pessimism are replaced by positive thoughts and optimism; all one needs is paper, pencil and something to draw. (MENTAL)

Day 45, Thursday 7th May: Hair today, gone tomorrow

"The hair got longer and longer in Lockdown"

So, the decision was made – we were NOT going to do a 10K before the official run on Wednesday 13th May. Instead Alex decided he wanted to take it easy with some shorter runs over the next few days and get plenty of rest. It was unlikely that fitness levels would drop before Wednesday and it would make sure that neither of us experienced any unwanted and last-minute injuries, which might compromise the challenge. Alex's thoughts turned towards his fund-raising and after a brief and relaxed 2.5K on another beautiful spring morning, he set about creating his 'Just Giving' page with any donations going to Wessex Heartbeat. A target of £1,000.00 seemed stretching yet achievable, in light of Alex's compelling life story. Within hours of launching the page he had raised £300.00, which included the £20.00 that our neighbour Sue had given Alex to inspire him to fundraise in the first place.

The nation's hair had been growing longer by the day, or at least the hair of those who had not succumbed to a domestic shearing. There were some horror stories, with associated photos or video footage on social media, of people who had allowed their family members to tamper with their locks, causing potential relationship-ending strife. Thus far and with an ever-lengthening mop of hair, I had managed to avoid Susie's scissors despite her frequently offering to use them on me. That was until today when I just could not endure the cranial discomfort any longer. At 12.45pm, out came the 'shears', but these were no ordinary human hair trimmers – it was only a pair of dog clippers that were used on our beloved Sully, our first dog! To be fair to Susie she did a great job, to such an extent that Alex, who is very particular about his hair, had no hesitation in jumping into the 'barber's' chair next.

As I continued to improve my pool performances I was starting to win more and more frames against Alex and put him firmly 'back in his box'. Pool was such a godsend during Lockdown and the more we played, the more strangely addictive it became. With it being in a covered area outside, we could still play on in the rare occasions that it rained.

The usual 'Clap for our Carers and the NHS' took place for the seventh time at its usual 8.00pm slot. There were reports of 'clapping fatigue' with suggestions that this very uplifting ritual had done its time., But in our 'neck of the woods' the mood was still as impassioned and the clapping as rapturous as it had been the first time that we did it on Thursday 26th March.

Another good day came to an end apart from the fact that just as we rested our weary heads on our pillows and our eyes were weighing heavy with tiredness, little Tizzy decided to empty the contents of her stomach on the carpet. To be fair she was still very small, so it was not so much the quantity of what 'came up' but the content: mainly green tennis ball 'hair' and bits of bark and string. For those who have a puppy, I believe this is all part of the learning to know what is edible and digestible and what is not; Tizzy seemed to do this learning all in one day, but was 'right as rain' in the morning!

Any hope of coming completely out of Lockdown after the weekend was understandably dashed with reports that the UK would keep some restrictions in place until June as there were still nearly 6,000 cases of coronavirus being recorded per day; this could have been more like 16,000 with testing still not matching capacity. Also, the death toll, particularly in care homes, was still far too high. We were after all supposed to be nearly two weeks behind Italy and they were only just starting to ease their restrictions.

Some things would be eased, most notably and as I had hoped, more periods of exercise would be permitted, churches would be allowed to open for prayer and garden centres would be able to satisfy the demand for outdoor pursuits which had grown in Lockdown as many people were spending more time tending to their gardens. Most disappointingly, there would still be no mixing people from more than one household, which meant that many families would still not be able to connect face-to-face with each other; good old Zoom would be required for a good few weeks yet. Further details of what would and would not be allowed for the coming weeks would be outlined in a 'roadmap' at 7.00pm on Sunday but with an emphasis on 'maximum caution'.

With Boris's imminent announcement on Sunday about allowing more exercise and outdoor activity, and with a lovely sunny VE Day bank holiday weekend around the corner, the government and police were fearful that the public may interpret this as a 'free pass' to go to beaches and beauty spots. One police commissioner said: 'Everything I'm hearing is that the public think the dam is being opened and the door is open on Monday. Police officers have to manage that expectation'. The police were resigned to having once again to be the 'villains of the pandemic' as Britons planned their VE Day celebrations.

As testing had been ramped up and more samples were being produced, it put extra pressure on laboratories to get test results back to patients. Unfortunately, due to the demand, the 48-hour target was regularly not being met and it was taking up to 10 days for some tests to come back. As it was, only 69,463 tests were carried out the previous day, over 30,000 tests away from the Health Secretary Hancock's 100,000 per day target, which had miraculously been achieved on the final day of April, but not since then.

About the testing targets and delays in getting test results, one public health official said: 'It is all very well having a target but if it is not part of a wider strategy then it can actually be a distraction from what you really need to be doing. It is all very well saying you've got these tests but if they can't be processed in a timely way then you're storing up problems for yourself'. I wonder whether testing would continue to be a 'hot potato' in the ensuing weeks and months.

In Mr Hancock's new project, 30 per cent of residents on the Isle of Wight had now downloaded the track and trace app. This was in essence just over 40,000 people, which, if correct, was a pretty good effort for the first five days and was possibly made up of all the young adults who actually possessed smartphones with downloadable apps and knew how to use them. In other news, PPE was still a source of great frustration for frontline medical workers in all sectors, not just the lack of it, but the quality. Those surgical gowns from Turkey that we waited so long for were deemed unsuitable for NHS use and faulty masks were being delivered to hospitals. Poor Health Secretary Hancock – everything he was involved in was subject to criticism and he was as much on the frontline as his exhausted and frustrated NHS and care worker colleagues.

539 new deaths were reported from the previous day bringing the total to 30,615. Of these, 27,432 were in England, 1,703 in Scotland, 1,062 in Wales and 418 in Northern Ireland. There had been a total of 206,715 cases of Covid-19 since the start of the pandemic, which meant that nearly 15 per cent of those who tested positive had sadly died of the disease. In Italy, this figure was slightly less at 14 percent, but in the US it was surprisingly at 6 per cent, suggesting that more testing had been done in America.

On the eve of the 75th anniversary celebrations for VE Day, it was interesting to observe the parallels of the Covid-19 crisis to the Second World War: both have resulted in significant loss of life, although one would hope that we would not reach the 450,000 death toll incurred during the war; both are likely to have taken the country into deep financial difficulty with significant job losses and personal hardship, as after the war this persisted well into the 1950's. This is not, of course, saying that this crisis will not persist, but we are a bit better equipped now and we have not, as yet anyway, been subject to measures such as rationing. Despite everything, there will always be that British 'stiff upper lip' and resilience, supported by (sometimes blind) optimism, that somehow sees us survive whatever is thrown at us; bring on those VE Day celebrations!

~

TODAY'S DAILY TIP: Inspired by Izzy, our next-door neighbour, for her two young boys, it was suggested that creating a quarantine time capsule for your children or even your spouse, might be a good way to look back at Lockdown. The 'capsule' could comprise of a box of artefacts and literature or a book of dialogue and pictures related to Lockdown, which will hopefully evoke lots of positive memories in years to come when we look back at these unprecedented times. (SPIRITUAL)

Day 46, Friday 8th May (VE Day): Celebrating our freedom in Lockdown

As the money rolled into Alex's 'Just Giving' page through people's amazing generosity, he took a complete rest from running today. Instead, as it was pretty much a weekend day being a Bank Holiday, we did one of our long and invigorating family walks to the Quarry and Bluebell Woods. It is certainly the first Friday Bank Holiday, apart from Good Friday, I can remember that actually replaced an early May Bank Holiday Monday. Despite Lockdown, it did feel a little bit like the start of another Easter weekend as we basked in glorious vernal sunshine.

"Yet another family walk in the sunshine"

After our walk, I continued with a stroll up the road to get some essential items for my aunt and a VE Day souvenir newspaper. Along the way I passed by a myriad of houses and gardens adorned with bunting, balloons and memorabilia, in fact, on the pavement outside one house there was an old gramophone playing classic war-time songs. One got a real sense of the pride of the nation when seeing how people were commemorating such an historic day. It almost brought a tear to the eye as one remembered the sacrifices that so many brave souls made for our future.

On my return from the shop I dropped off my aunt's shopping and checked on her wellbeing. It was just such a shame we could not celebrate the day properly with her, particularly as she was all on her own without her three daughters and very probably remembering her many happy years of marriage to her husband and my late Uncle John. It brought back memories of my youth when my mother and father used to host my aunt and uncle and other extended family to celebrate special occasions like the Queen's Silver Jubilee in 1977 and Charles and Diana's wedding in 1981. This was already a special day that was evocative for many reasons.

The television channels did a great job in covering the VE Day celebrations despite the lack of visitors to London. So many of those traditional London events had succumbed to the virus including 'Trooping of the Colour' and the Queen's Buckingham Palace Garden Parties. London was like a ghost town without the many thousands of tourists visiting the historical landmarks, theatres, hotels, bars and restaurants. It was a far cry from the images that we saw on TV from 75 years ago, when crowds in their thousands thronged the streets of the capital celebrating 'wildly' in unbridled joy.

After watching the Red Arrows' flypast and Churchill's famous speech with some of Susie's lovely homemade cakes, we migrated outside to raise a glass or two to the memory of VE Day with the neighbours from afar. We did not quite get to singing: 'We'll meet again.......', but I am sure there were many good-spirited 'distanced' street parties and sing-alongs up and down the country. Hopefully people were able to forget about Covid-19 and the state of the world for a day at least. The usual Friday visit to the Otter pub ensued for a fish and chip takeaway and a pint of local ale, which seemed so appropriate on the most British of days.

After our other Friday evening ritual, a Zoom quiz, which we amazingly came second in, we watched the Queen's 9.00pm VE Day broadcast when she gave us a rousing message saying: 'Never give up'. She continued: 'It may seem hard that we cannot mark this anniversary as we would wish. Instead we remember from our homes and our doorsteps. But our streets are not empty; they are filled with love and the care that we have for each other'. Once again our monarch, who herself had served in the Auxiliary Territorial Service (ATS) during the war, had captured the imagination of her nation and proved again that she knows the right words to say at the right time.

The main symptoms of Covid-19 that we were always asked to observe were a new and persistent cough and high temperature. Although it was not diagnosed initially and not confirmed until mid-May, loss of taste and smell became a very tangible sign of the disease. Now we were advised of other symptoms to look out for, which included a headache, sore throat, fatigue, muscle pain, diarrhoea and stomach pains. The problem was now that if anyone experienced some or all of these symptoms the first thought was that one had Covid-19, when in fact it may have been flu or some of the other common illnesses that we were used to. This of course would lead to more anxiety amongst an already nervous population, particularly if they were then unable to get a test.

Talking of checking symptoms, this was something that had not been observed at UK airports throughout the pandemic, as thousands of potentially infected passengers were continuing to pass through our airport terminals. There were no temperature checks or calls for travellers to go into isolation if displaying symptoms or even to just go into quarantine anyway as they may have been asymptomatic. Now at last, there was real speculation circling that all arrivals into Britain would be quarantined for 14 days – but not to start until early in June!! I can understand that the infection rate had reduced but we were constantly being told that the virus was still very much circulating around us, in fact there were still over 15,000 daily infections, so why not introduce the ruling sooner? Anyway, one industry that would certainly not benefit from this ruling would be the airlines, potentially causing more heartache and wrecking any possible summer holiday season.

The number of deaths rose by another 626, which tragically included the youngest death from Covid-19 at aged six weeks old, a baby that also had an underlying health condition. The daily death toll still seemed an awfully high number when we were supposed to be over the worst. Even though cases and hospitalisations were still coming down, unfortunately a lower death toll would be the last concrete measure to reduce, particularly where many people were ill for several weeks before they could just not withstand the disease any longer, and subsequently perished. The total number of deaths in the UK was now 31,241, second only to the US at 77,851, and above Italy which was now at 30,201.

~

TODAY'S DAILY TIP: Challenging ourselves to do things that we do not think we are able to do is a mental challenge in itself. When Alex undertook to do his 10K, the initial hurdle to get over was the psychological one. So why not push yourself to try something beyond what you think are your limits are, maybe to a level you have not ever achieved before. There might be pain along the way but the sense of satisfaction on reaching your achievement will be tangible will be so rewarding and fulfilling. (MENTAL)

Day 47, Saturday 9th May: Not a normal cricket Saturday

After our habitual long family morning walk and having adopted the 'rest and shorter run' strategy to the build-up his 10K challenge, we were back out on the roads again for relaxed 2.8K just to keep things ticking over during the weekend. As we drew closer to the run we were becoming more conscious of what we were eating, so poached eggs and baked beans were in order for breakfast, as we strove to boost our protein levels. With plenty of rest and relaxation also required, we spent most of the day enjoying the sunshine, reading, playing cards and pool. Being a Saturday though, we were not half missing watching live sport on the TV, particularly when it should have been the penultimate game of the football season.

"Oakmount cricket club has been a great source of enjoyment and camaraderie over the past five years"

One other thing that we were really missing was playing cricket with our friends at Oakmount cricket club. Today should have been the start of our new league season and after avoiding relegation the previous campaign and with Alex back to full fitness, we were thoroughly looking forward to another progressive season. Despite being played in the open air, unfortunately team cricket was perceived as being too social to play at present and the ball was regarded as a vector for the virus to spread from person to person.

Whether or not we would get any cricket in at all this season was very much in question. So to mark what should have been our first gathering Zoom came to the fore again and we had a really good catch-up with everyone, virtually. It was great to see everyone again, although some hairstyles were a little longer and different to how we had remembered!

After the Zoom call and a couple of beers, it was back to the protein enhancement with a nice steak barbecue on a stunning early May evening. The 'last-minute' preparations were very much underway as the countdown to Wednesday had started.

There were a further 345 deaths in the UK bringing the total to a sobering 31,586, and after a weekend of joyous celebrations, which the whole country needed, thoughts turned to what the Prime Minister, Boris Johnson might say in his update the following day. There had been plenty of speculation but also confusion about what Boris might already have inferred, with a headline in one newspaper: 'Hurrah! Lockdown freedom beckons', and another claiming that it would be: 'Happy Monday'. Yet, this was followed with Boris apparently urging 'maximum caution' – so what were we to expect? The country was at a crossroads once again, where clarity in the message, strong leadership, trust in the people and above all, honesty and integrity were required. As we 'sailed further into unknown waters' we needed a captain to steer us who was fully in charge at the helm.

~

TODAY'S DAILY TIP: After VE Day on 8th May came 'Victory in Japan' (VJ) Day on 15th August, which marked the official end of the Second World War. This might have been a further opportunity to celebrate like we did yesterday especially where Lockdown might have been relaxed that little bit more. (SPIRITUAL)

Day 48, Sunday 10th May: Is there an end in sight?

An incredible £1,120 had already been raised for Wessex Heartbeat in under a week, since Alex launched his 'Just Giving' page. If he needed any motivation for Wednesday, people's generosity in what were harsher times financially for some with the ongoing crisis, provided the perfect tonic. With the expected announcement that we could do more amounts of exercise per day, and like the previous day, we embarked on the family morning weekend walk, followed by the longest run that Alex and I were going to do before the 10K, a tough and hilly 6K. This was achieved in just 49 minutes, the fastest time yet that we had attained for this distance and further illustrated that Alex's fitness levels were in a pretty good place especially with how good his recovery was afterwards. I was now cautiously optimistic that Alex could see this challenge through, although there was as always, a slight doubt in the back of the mind.

It was a typical lazy Sunday for the rest of the day topped off with one of Susie's amazing roast dinners, again with plenty protein to build up our strength for the week ahead. Physically, the fitness was good, we were drinking plenty of water and eating decent amounts of protein and carbohydrate. A couple of good nights' sleep would ensure that we were mentally prepared and well rested; it was drawing closer by the day.

"One of Susie's mouth watering roast dinners"

As expected, Prime Minister Boris Johnson appeared on our screens at 7.00pm to give us some idea of what the next few weeks might bring as we yearned to get our lives back to some sort of vague normality. For Boris it was 'the shape of a plan', 'a sense of the way ahead' and the 'first sketch of a roadmap' but it probably lacked the clarity that we yearned for and as Sir Keir Starmer, leader of the opposition said: '..............it raised more questions than answers'. This was more a broad message for the people of the nation, and he reassured us that a more detailed plan would follow on Monday in the House of Commons

So was there anything tangible that Boris could tell us that might give us some hope that things were changing for the better, apart from encouraging people to go back to work if it was safe to do so from Monday morning? Indeed there was:

1) From Wednesday, and as long as it was in family groups, unlimited exercise and outdoor activity, including golf (get in there!!), tennis and fishing, could be taken. This meant also that people could now travel to parks and beaches to sunbathe and swim, something that had up until been a 'crime' serious enough to warrant a fine. As expected also, garden centres could re-open and one would be entitled to meet one person from another household, as long as those individuals were two metres apart. Alex and his girlfriend, Charlotte, were understandably 'over the moon', as were Holly and the new mystery man of her life, John Amor (not Amour!). The government's message was definitely no longer to: 'STAY AT HOME'.

2) From early June primary schools would open up again, but only for years R, one and six. Also, more non-essential shops would be allowed to re-open their doors.

3) At some point in July, some other non-essential shops and hospitality businesses (cafes & restaurants but potentially NOT pubs) would be able to resume trading. Churches and cinemas might also be able to re-open their doors to worshippers and film-buffs respectively with strict distancing rules. But sadly, for all those who needed their flowing locks to be trimmed, not hairdressers. With regards to secondary schools, years 10 and 12 with exams scheduled for next year, might be asked to return to their studies.

Boris also introduced us to his five-level 'traffic light' measure. Level five (red) effectively meant that the infection was still rife in our communities and the magic 'R' number was above one, as well the health service being push its capacity. Whilst level one (green) meant that the virus has effectively disappeared into the ether with a vaccine in place to eliminate the risk of another pandemic and ultimately people being allowed to gather safely in crowds again. Levels two to four (orange / amber / yellow) were something in between. It was now widely accepted by the government that the country was now at level three, which meant that the virus was being contained and the 'R' number was just below one, which was probably achieved because we had been in Lockdown.

The message had indeed changed from: '**STAY AT HOME**, **PROTECT THE NHS** and **SAVE LIVES**' to: '**STAY ALERT** (I am not sure even to this day what this actually meant), **CONTROL THE VIRUS** (I am not really sure what this really meant either) and **SAVE LIVES** (I completely understood what this meant, but not so sure how it linked to the first two). In my humble opinion, the initial Lockdown slogan definitely had more clarity and less ambiguity then this one.

Once again we became aware of the differences of opinion that the leaders of the other countries in the UK had as the First Ministers in Scotland, Wales and Northern Ireland forcibly suggested that their message to their people was still very much: 'STAY AT HOME!' The 'STAY ALERT' message was regarded as being 'vague and imprecise' and as Wales' First Minister said, '..........staying at home remains the best way (to) protect yourself and others'. This must have been very embarrassing for the Prime Minister of the UK, who was looking more like the Prime Minister of England alone.

Although there were definitely signs of an encouraging easing of restrictions, much of what Boris was now telling us was conditional on keeping the infamous 'R' rate down below one and improving testing would be key to achieving this. Those who were shielding would need to continue to do so but probably the most disappointing aspect was that wider families would still not be able to re-unite; so many grand-children and children would have been missing their grand-parents and vice-versa, and that 'door of hope' that was slightly ajar, was slammed firmly shut.

Certain members of Boris Johnson's cabinet were slightly miffed that they had not been consulted or briefed prior to Boris's announcement to the nation, which was allegedly causing strained relationships. Boris also had to fend off suggestions that he had lost faith with my 'friend', Health Secretary Hancock. There were reports that Boris had challenged Mr Hancock on the slowness of implementing the testing strategy, which did not go down well with Mr Hancock, who petulantly and allegedly responded: 'That's not fair – give me a break'. Boris denied this and stated assertively to his cabinet that Mr Hancock was doing a 'fantastic job'.

In other news: it was probably going to be confirmed in the coming days that the government's furlough scheme would be coming to an end, at the end of June; 14 day quarantine rules would be imposed on travellers coming into the UK by air in order to control infections from abroad, but this may not apply to France and would not be considered until June at the earliest; there was no further tangible advice on whether we should be wearing face masks or not, which indicated that there was still doubt over the efficacy of wearing face coverings to control the virus; and most importantly, we must continue to wash our hands on multiple occasions to the dubious strains of two verses of 'Happy Birthday'! All in all, it was quite an informative and mildly more uplifting Sunday than we had been used to lately. It was clear though that life as we knew it would take some time to return, if indeed it would ever be the same again.

Around Europe, Spain had its lowest daily death toll for seven weeks at 143, compared to 900 at its peak. Lockdown was being eased across several regions, although the populous cities of Madrid and Barcelona remained under tighter restrictions due to failing the strict epidemiological criteria. In Italy, they were hoping to open up restaurants and bars, but it was just a little too soon, while a relieved France greeted two months of Lockdown with mixed feelings. Despite a 120 million euros worth of hand-outs to 12 million workers, President Macron had been criticised for the way in which he had handled the country's crisis in the early stages with a lack of preparedness and PPE, a similar tale to another nation we know very well!

In Germany infections had risen sharply again after restrictions were eased the previous Wednesday, prompting Chancellor Merkel to talk again about re-enforcing Lockdown. The problem was, after Lockdown was eased, many Germans crowded into parks and onto streets without any thought for social distancing. In fact Lockdown had not been 'popular' there in the first place, illustrated by the number of demonstrations by radicals and extremists. Germany had often been praised for the way in which its government, scientists and medics had handled the crisis with widespread testing and a very efficient healthcare system, which had helped keep the death toll very low relative to the number of cases.

The UK's death toll rose by 269 to a total of 31,855, one of the lowest daily increases for a number of weeks. There had now been over 200 deaths amongst health workers all around the UK and there were still some very frightened frontline medical staff across all sectors. There was a surge of opinion that they should now be rewarded better financially for their great courage and the many sacrifices they had made over the past two to three months.

~

TODAY'S DAILY TIP: At the end of a run or some of form intense exercise, I like to give myself a bit of a sugar boost, so what better than a couple of Jaffa cakes to re-build those energy levels. It does of course open up the age-old debate: is a Jaffa cake a cake or a biscuit; decide for yourself! (PHYSICAL)

Day 49, Monday 11th May: A new dawn approaches

An unseasonal chill in the air greeted Monday morning and a new week, where change was afoot for the nation and hopefully a significant personal achievement was on the cards for a very courageous and determined young man. Susie returned to her workplace for the first time in five weeks, after an extended 'Easter break', to cater for the needs of key worker children, so I rose early and walked with her to the school about half an hour away, with little Tizzy in tow. One could sense a different feeling in the air after Boris Johnson's hopeful and optimistic announcement the evening before, and my mind kept drifting to when I might be able to get those golf clubs out again and blaze a glorious sliced drive down the first fairway.

"Tizzy giving every indication that she did not want a walk today"

Throughout Lockdown, doing my daily tips on Facebook and Twitter gave me some real focus to my day and hopefully I was giving those watching a bit of light entertainment and maybe some useful hints to having a more productive and fulfilling life. As we approached the 50th day of Lockdown it was time to wind down this 'process', so today's tip was the last one. Initially I had only planned to do them for three weeks, which I wrongly thought might have been the duration of Lockdown - I was pleased that I was able to dream up something mildly imaginative to share with viewers for another four weeks!

With two days to go before the 10K, Alex and I did a leisurely 4K lunchtime run in beautiful but bracing conditions. The chilly atmosphere appeared to be in the forecast for most of the week, which bode well for Wednesday. At the weekend it had been quite hot and sultry, and those really were not the conditions we wanted for our lengthy trek around the countryside and streets of Chandler's Ford later in the week. The pressure and expectation was mounting, particularly as Alex's fundraising total had now reached £1,200; there was no going back now.

Boris Johnson sought to provide more clarity and detail around his statement from the previous evening, that certain aspects of our lives could start to improve after nearly two months of confinement and limitations. It was apparent from this more detailed 50-page document of what we could and could not do, that there were slight changes in what Boris and his cabinet were saying now to what had been said the evening before, which might have been perceived as creating ambiguity or contradiction: on Sunday, we were being encouraged to go back to work on Monday (today) if it was safe to do so, yet today the message was to go back on Wednesday but avoid public transport if you could and yet we still did not really know what a safe working environment looked like; the previous evening, Boris had said we could meet one person from another household in the open air, yet in a radio interview on Monday morning, Foreign Secretary Dominic Raab confused things somewhat by saying that somebody could also meet up with both of their parents – this was quickly retracted; by Monday also, it was thought based on a 'rumour' coming out of Number 10, Downing Street, that it was not just one friend that somebody could meet, but more than one – again this was retracted.

I had never doubted that it would be far more difficult coming out of Lockdown than going into it. Shutting down our livelihoods and businesses, as clinical as it was, could be done quickly with a clear and direct accompanying message to 'STAY AT HOME', as there would be dire consequences if we did not comply. To try to reverse this message with all the challenges and complications that were to go with it, was going to be an incredibly difficult process, and I am sure everyone appreciated some of Boris's dilemmas. What was though so critical, was that his messaging and that of his cabinet colleagues and advisors was clear and consistent enough so it did not lead to further confusion. This, as often is the case, can be muddled even more by an insatiable media playing the blame game and baying for Boris's blood.

In other changes from the previous day: we went from uncertainty around the wearing of face masks to a recommendation that they should be worn in shops, on public transport and in other enclosed space – but not in Wales; the government's furlough scheme would not actually be ceasing at the end of June after all, in fact it would be continuing, albeit with reduced government subsidies; the 14 day quarantine rules on anyone coming into the UK could now come into force as soon as next week as opposed to June, which is what Boris had mentioned the day before, although it still appeared that the detail around this proposed policy was still far from being decided. One thing that had not changed overnight was opening up of golf courses on Wednesday for one to play with someone from the same household – for Alex and me, there were other priorities to be made on Wednesday and golf would have to wait a little bit longer

One other bit good news on the sporting front was, that from June, it was likely that sporting events could resume, albeit behind closed doors, and that there was a strong possibility that the Premier League and other football leagues could re-commence their season. Discussions were also ongoing with TV companies to see whether games could be screened as 'free-to-air', allowing those without Sky or BT Sports to view games at no extra cost. So many summer events had been cancelled or postponed including very high-profile events such as the Olympic Games and the European Football Championships. For there to be more than a glimmer of hope that the football could be resumed at least gave many millions of sports fans something to look forward to. Let us face it, we had had precious little to forward to up and until now, and although there might have been confusion in the messaging, we were certainly heading out of Lockdown and in the right direction

The daily death toll actually rose by a further 210, bringing the total to 32,065, which was in fact the lowest daily increase since the end of March, notwithstanding of course the delay in getting some figures due to the weekend. This may well have not been enough of a satisfactory reduction for many of the scientists and doubters that believed that Lockdown restrictions were being eased too soon and that the government was being reckless and irresponsible in their approach, especially as there was no certainty around getting a safe vaccine; oh to be the Prime Minister – you cannot do right for doing wrong!

~

TODAY'S DAILY TIP: Today was the day when the daily tips came to an end. Hopefully people could use some of the 49 suggestions to create new habits or maintain existing ones for a healthier and fuller life, whether that be physically, mentally, spiritually or socially. If there had also been a little bit of fun created along the way then I feel they have achieved their objective. (SPIRITUAL)

Day 50, Tuesday 12th May: 10K Eve

"Plenty of pasta required for the big 10K run"

As donations to Alex's 'Just Giving' page rose to nearly £1,500, the nerves and tension for me around tomorrow's 10K challenge were suddenly very tangible. We were mindful of preserving energy and avoiding any unnecessary injuries, so on another chilly yet sunny morning we eased our way through a steady 3K. In the final build-up to the run the strategy was to keep fitness levels up with shorter daily distances and plenty of rest, but thus far neither of us had as yet actually done a full 10K; would this come back to haunt us on the day?

The rest of the day was about taking our minds off of the run, so after finally re-gaining my pool title from Alex, I decided to tackle one of the infamous hedges that I had regularly trimmed during Lockdown, but that always seemed to grow as quickly as I cut it down. Whilst over-stretching at height to cut down an errant branch, I suddenly felt a painful twinge in my right shoulder. I immediately stopped what I was doing, did a few pulls and stretches and applied some ice to the 'injury'. Unfortunately the pain just worsened and having a son doing a degree in Physiotherapy meant that some sort of diagnosis could be made – it was a strong possibility that I had torn a teres minor muscle, a key muscle for shoulder rotation and mobility. We had done so much to avoid injury in the lead-up to Alex's great 10K undertaking, and then, on the eve of the run, I go and sustain an injury in a part of the body required for an effective run. At his moment of need was I going to ruin everything through my own rash stupidity?

After a nice meat and pasta tea to bolster further our protein and carbohydrate levels in readiness for the run, we each had a hot bath to relax the body and soul. Then in an attempt to get plenty of rest for the ensuing day, what followed was my worst night's sleep in Lockdown as the shoulder throbbed in pain despite a large dose of Ibuprofen. My nerves and anxiety for the following day seemed to reach new levels

As Boris Johnson had alluded to the previous day, and on the day of his 40th birthday, Chancellor of the Exchequer Rishi Sunak was the one giving out the presents, officially extending the government's wage subsidy or furlough scheme until the end of October. The scheme, which would reportedly cost the taxpayer £80 billion by the time of its ending, would in essence remain the same with any of the 7.5 million entitled employees receiving up to £2,500.00 or up to 80 per cent of their salary, but from August employers would also be responsible for making contributions. Mr Sunak was certainly concerned about the mounting cost of furloughing so many people but was convinced it was 'the right thing to do', as he told us he was 'working night and day to limit the job losses' in the long-term.

As the government continued to work on their quarantine plan for those coming into the UK, Health Secretary Hancock was forthright in responding to a question on national TV about whether 'summer was cancelled' in relation to the holiday season. He told the British nation: 'I think that's likely to be the case', although there may still be an exemption for those travelling to France. On hearing that Susie rapidly made a booking for the Channel tunnel. A summer break in August in the Loire valley with our great Welsh friends, the Griffs (real name – Griffiths) was suddenly back on the cards.

Meanwhile, Mr Hancock was apparently 'pleased with the progress' in the tracing app trial on the Isle of Wight. Although the app trial had not been running long, it was supposedly still on track to be rolled out across the nation at end of the following week, which seemed like another stretching target. The app was all part of the 'test, track and trace' strategy which was a key element to a safe release from Lockdown. Testing had been ramped up during April as the government strove to reach 100,000 tests by the end of the month, something they miraculously achieved (although no day since then) and 15,000 human tracers had allegedly been recruited; what could possibly go wrong? I once again wondered whether the decision to ditch testing and tracing in the UK at the beginning of March, right at the very start of the pandemic, would come back to haunt us?

About 450,000 people were in the midst of moving house when Lockdown started on 23rd March, so it was a great relief and a much-needed boost to the economy, when housing market was permitted to get back up and running again. As long as strict social distancing rules were observed by agents and clients alike, show homes could open. Strangely though, potential clients (be that buyers or renters) and even removal men could now come into your home, which rather made a mockery of the rules around who could meet who, and where.

As deaths in the US spiralled up to 82,555, Dr Fauci, head of the National Institute of Allergy and Infectious Diseases, issued a warning to the various states, that more deaths were inevitable if Senators tried to return people to their normal lives too soon. Like in the UK, there was the dilemma between keeping people in Lockdown to protect health, which actually might in turn be causing untold damage to the economy - something President Trump was desperate to get back up and running again. Sadly for America, they were nowhere near over the worst. A slightly amusing yet crazy aspect to America's plight was the significant increase in bleach and disinfectant poisonings in April following President Trump's assertions that there might be some benefit to injecting such products to help fight the virus!

Meanwhile, Chinese officials continued to protest their innocence that the virus had originated from a laboratory in Wuhan. President Trump, in particular, had been vocal in his criticism of China for lapses in safety whilst carrying out infection tests using the virus. Chinese scientists refuted these claims saying that their laboratories had been as safe as they could have been; this argument would of course rumble on.

In Spain, as they were coming through the worst with shops, bars and restaurants re-opening, there was a real tale of hope and valour. The country's oldest woman, aged 113, survived Covid-19 after contracting the virus back in April. In fact, she may well have been the oldest person to survive in the world, putting it down to walking regularly and not smoking. Maybe we could have heard a few more of these heart-warming stories to give everyone a bit more hope.

The daily death toll in the UK from Covid-19, recorded in hospitals and care homes, rose by a further 627, to a total of 32,692. Although this figure was still far too high and once again many more families and friends of victims were mourning the loss of loved ones, the weekly trend was coming down. Now, the figures that we were all presented with on a daily basis actually emanated from the Department of Health, but new figures produced from the Office of National Statistics (ONS) revealed today that numbers of deaths where Covid-19 was mentioned on the death certificate, were actually now 40,033, a number that also included those who died of Covid-19 at home.

One of the most tragic Covid-19-related deaths that was reported was that of a railway station ticket office worker, who was spat and coughed at in London Victoria station back in March by someone who claimed they had Covid-19. After showing serious symptoms, she was admitted to hospital during early April, and died three days later after being put on a ventilator. What was so sad was that the lady already had a lung condition but was not supplied with PPE, and she was one of many frontline public sector workers who was put in a similar position, who subsequently lost their lives. As for the assailant, the actions of this person can only be described as utterly vile.

There had been a lot debate around the number of excess deaths that might have been caused by the impact of Covid-19. With A&E departments reportedly quieter than they had been for years and GP appointments well down on the usual numbers, it was thought that many people had endured serious illnesses at home and rather than going to hospitals for fear of catching the virus, they would 'suffer in silence' and die at home. These would not be recorded as deaths from Covid-19, but excess deaths, of which some statisticians believe could be as high 60,000. One expert said: 'We have got a huge number of essentially unexplained extra deaths in homes and care homes........This rise in non-Covid-19 deaths outside the hospital is something I hope will be given really severe attention.........'

As we gradually started to adjust to Boris's new measures and to feel that going outside the boundaries of our homes was actually relatively normal again, it was time to reflect on what had happened in last seven and a bit weeks and how aspects of our lives might have changed for the foreseeable future

It would of course be a long journey back to normality, a journey that we remained on for many weeks, and still are on as I write this book. There were also incidents such as those surrounding Dominic Cummings' hugely controversial trip to Barnard Castle and subsequent 'grilling' in the gardens of number 10 Downing Street; the slightly dodgy projects that Robert Jenrick, Secretary of State for Housing, authorised; the on/off summer holiday season saga with its various short-lead quarantine dates and times; further easing of Lockdown restrictions where grandparents could finally see their grandchildren and we could return to pubs and restaurants; the return of some schooling and the Gavin Williamson examination debacles; the various local Lockdowns indicating that the virus had not left us; the uplifting and deserved knighthood of Captain Tom Moore; and most extraordinary of all, President Donald Trump contracting Covid-19 in the middle of the US election campaign. These would all play a major part in the next stage of probably the most life-changing and fast-moving crises in living memory.

Wednesday 13th May, The Big 10K Day and hope springs eternal

"Pre-10K photoshoot with our number one fan"

Another chilly and breezy yet bright morning greeted us, as we contemplated the day ahead and Alex's much anticipated 10K challenge. After a terrible night's sleep and the right shoulder still troubling me, I rose feeling desperately mentally fatigued, but knowing I had a major responsibility to help Alex achieve his goal. After one month's build-up, some gruelling training runs and persistent doubts as to whether Alex was up to it, the moment had arrived.

The morning was relaxed with a nice hearty breakfast of poached eggs, baked beans and toast. At midday, we filled our water bottles, made sure we had bananas for our energy boost half way round and I took a couple of paracetamol for the now very sore shoulder. As 12.30pm drew ever closer, I could feel butterflies in my stomach and that unbearable feeling of nervous tension, that I was trying so hard not to transmit to Alex. He certainly seemed more calm and relaxed than I did although I know he was feeling it too; I guess we both just wanted to get underway.

It was unfortunate that, for reasons of work, Susie and Holly were unable to join us for Alex's special day. In fact Holly had hoped that she would be able to be with us at the start of the run, until important work commitments took priority. We later found out that she had endured one of her most challenging professional days in Lockdown, which meant she actually had to go into the office for the first time for many weeks. I know how gutted she was not to be with her little brother,

"Halfway banana and water break"

especially where they are so close and with all that they have shared throughout his time in hospital over the years, but I knew her and Susie were very much with him in spirit.

After giving little Tizzy a big hug and exchanging 'good luck' wishes, we finally exited the house donning our Wessex Heartbeat tee-shirts and on the dot of 12.30pm pressed the 'start' buttons on our respective fitbits and 'phone stopwatches - we were at last underway. All I could think of at that moment was the immense pride I had that I was part of Alex's special challenge; it was definitely one of those 'lump in the throat' moments, which in itself created a massive boost of motivation.

Prior to starting the run, we logged on to Alex's 'Just Giving' page to see what amount he had raised thus far for Wessex Heartbeat, and with the contribution from gift aid, the fundraising had incredibly reached nearly £3,000 in just under one week. It was at that point that I thought I should try and do updates on Facebook during the run, on how Alex was getting on. As we set off, Alex expressed his gratitude for everyone's generosity, and we disappeared down the road on our pre-planned route.

One of the people who would have been amongst the proudest of Alex's undertaking was his girlfriend Charlotte, who had endured so much stress and mental pain during his time in hospital last year. During the first 2K of the run our route took us past Charlotte's house and the plan was for her and her family to cheer Alex on as we passed through. As we approached the house, slightly later than had been predicted, there was no-one to be seen – we had missed them by a split second as they thought they had missed us! Was that going to be a bad omen for the rest of the run?

The first 4K was completed without any further mishaps, but we were now about to enter a more gruelling stage leading to halfway as we encountered one of those hills that had been so challenging on the training runs. Alex had thankfully staved off the stomach pains that habitually had affected his runs, and this was a good indication that we had thus far paced things right and that his body was much more used to endurance runs. Although completing the 10K was the main objective, Alex had also set himself a target time of under one hour and 30 minutes, and we were at this stage well on schedule.

Throughout Holly's and Alex's school and college lives, they have always been surrounded by an amazing set of friends, who have possessed caring and kind characteristics that make them all a credit to their respective parents. Both sets of friends have been touched by Alex's courage in battling his cardiac issues and have supported many of our fundraising efforts and activities over the years. I know he has greatly appreciated that and found it a big source of support. You can imagine Alex's emotions when at just before halfway, two of Alex's mates – Dan and Dave – appeared on the pavement out of nowhere to cheer him on. And then at the halfway point, after he had tackled that gruesome hill, a load more of his mates – Jamie, Andy, Harvey, Sam, Harry and Josh – greeted him with cheers and shouts of encouragement, at exactly the time it was needed. I must say, looking back now, it was incredibly touching and just showed how much Alex meant to these boys.

The weather conditions were absolutely perfect for running, with intermittent amounts of warm sunshine to balance the cool breeze, and as we arrived at the

5.5K point of the run we appeared destined not only to complete the 10K, but to do it under the target time. My good friend Antony Jackson was on hand to dish out the bananas and exchange our empty water bottles for full ones, and Alex seemed to be taking everything in his stride.

The next stage of the run took us into the woods for a short spell of cross-country running, which we both always found to be the most enjoyable part of any run that we had done previously. With the fresher air that we had become so used to in Lockdown, and the peaceful surroundings, you felt at one with nature and strangely becalmed. We were almost lulled into a false sense of security as we came out of the woods and back onto the road, having completed three-quarters of the run. Although we were both being tested it had all seemed relatively straightforward so far and with only 2.5K to go, and a route we had followed many times already, surely we would breeze through this. On the time front, we suffered a little bit of a setback when Alex's Fitbit decided to malfunction, leaving Alex frustrated that there would be no record of him hopefully completing his run in a personal best time. Luckily, I still had my phone stopwatch running, which still had us potentially finishing within the target time.

It did cross my mind that the longest distance that either of us had run at any one time over the past month was 8K. In the days leading up to the run, rather than doing a couple of 10Ks we decided that we would preserve our energy, keeping up our levels of fitness with shorter runs and plenty of rest and relaxation. We were both acutely aware that we had not yet actually run a full 10K. As we approached our last 2.5K, would we come to have serious regrets about our decision and end up slowing down through a lack of stamina or some sort of injury? As my mind drifted to the finish line and with my shoulder pain now really in evidence, I was reminded of the fact that the last 1.5K of the run was not only arduous but also steadily uphill, all the way to the end. At the bottom of the hill and as we entered the uncharted territory of over 8K, it was once again great to see Alex's friends urging us on to see this thing through to a successful completion; we were so near, yet so far.

"The start of the gruelling last 2K of the run"

With 1K to go and with the end in sight came the moment I had most dreaded, as Alex started gasping for breath and his legs had become very heavy. He was visibly struggling and clearly in some sort of discomfort, and maybe this final hill was really starting to take its toll. As his mates implored him to continue, I just sensed that he was going to 'fall at the final hurdle'. Was it really worth pushing him too far and to the point that his body just could not take anymore? Would all that surgery and suffering that he had endured over the years be in vain, if he collapsed at the finish line and heaven forbid.................? How would I ever be able to forgive myself if I forced him over a 'bridge too far'?

But from somewhere, and to this day I do not know where from, Alex found an inner strength and voice inside that was clearly 'screaming' at him to continue. I was desperately trying to hold in the emotion, knowing what he was putting himself through to run those final few metres. I am sure we should never underestimate the amazing impact that the presence of his friends had on Alex's determination to succeed. As we approached the finish, two of our friends Caroline and Gill were there to capture that special moment when, against the odds, Alex finally achieved his 10K dream in a time of one hour and 23 minutes.

It is difficult to put into words the feeling of elation that I had for Alex, especially after he 'hit the wall' and came so close to not completing the challenge – it was

"The triumphant finish with the Wessex Heartbeat car"

an inspirational achievement and a true feat of courage. And how absolutely fantastic it was that not only were Alex's friends there to witness his heroic success, but also were his girlfriend, Charlotte and her sister, Olivia, as well as our friends from Wessex Heartbeat, which would benefit from Alex's fundraising – all at a distance of course. These were moments that we will both treasure forever.

With a beer and a bowl of pasta in hand, we spent the next couple of hours reflecting on what had just happened, and the realisation of Alex's attainment began to sink in. The feeling of pride and satisfaction was immensely tangible, although I was not so sure about Alex's proclamation that a full marathon was next on his 'bucket list'. As all my aches and pains came to the fore, the only thing on my mind was a nice, hot, soapy bath!

And so Alex's inspiring symbol of hope had finally come to a terrifically successful conclusion, ironically on the day that a light of optimism was shining on the nation. Certain aspects of our lives started to re-open after this period of isolation in our own homes, when we were denied so many of life's privileges.

So how did we fare in Lockdown? For some, was it a form of imprisonment, where that lovely home actually became like the confines of a prison cell? Where any minor ailment became paranoia that one had caught Covid-19? Where eagerly-awaited and structured days became riddled with idleness and sloth? Where productive working environments became muddled with Zoom meetings and conference calls from the kitchen table? Where going shopping in the supermarket became a frightening 'bun-fight' and survival of the fittest? Where precious time with the kids became torturous with endless home schooling whilst trying to work from home? Where that spouse or family member that one craved to be with all the time, became an irritating and irksome nuisance? Where grandparents not seeing their grandchildren or parents not seeing their children – and vice-versa - became almost unbearable? Where everything we heard and saw on the news and TV became more and more depressing, and impacted our outlook on the world? Where the closure of hairdressers, coffee shops, dentists, vets, re-cycling centres and the like became an impingement on our civil liberties? Where peaceful solitude became abject loneliness?

Or was it for others, a daily trip into the unknown where lives were put at risk working on the medical frontline without enough PPE and adequate testing? Where the wrath of the public had to be withstood because there were not enough toilet rolls, bottles of hand sanitiser or bags of flour on the supermarket shelves? Where one was driving lorries up and down the country at all hours god sent, trying to keep the nation going? Where looking after the children of key workers in school felt more like childcare than education?

Or was it, very fortunately for others, like it was for us, where we not only had routine to our days but fun, partaking in old pastimes and activities or finding new ones? Where emptying the dishwasher and making the bed became mildly enjoyable and somewhat therapeutic chores? Where we made maximum use of our time outside or on exercise reconnecting with everything that nature has to offer? Where we became creative and innovative in the things that we made, the meals that we cooked or songs and dance routines that we composed? Where we did things to our houses and flats, and our gardens and outdoor areas, which gave them a new dimension or added to their appeal? Where we read a new book or learned a new language? Where we did all those jobs and projects that we had never had time to do before? Where the days were so full that they were over before they had started? Where loving and cherished relationships became even stronger and inseparable bonds were made? Where some got so intimate that a 'baby boom' early next year was inevitable and new lives would be coming into the world? Where we looked out for each other and those in our communities to ensure they were not needy or completely isolated? Where we were still able, virtually, to have fun and keep in touch with other members of our family and our friends? Where we were able to save a bit money rather than spending extravagantly on seemingly unnecessary luxuries? Where we were kept safe from many of the dangers that befall us normally in ordinary and everyday life? Where we stayed reasonably fit, healthy and well, through good living, regular exercise and the odd glass of wine? And above all where, like Alex, dreams that seemed impossible were fulfilled with passion and determination?

There was of course a very serious underlying reason why the people of Great Britain were asked on March 23rd by Boris Johnson, to 'STAY AT HOME', and many families and friends of those who so sadly and tragically lost their lives too soon will be affected by those losses for many years to come. We should of course not forget those who fought to keep people alive and worked tirelessly and selflessly throughout the crisis. But I am sure there are plenty of good things that have happened to people and hopefully some really special and positive memories have been made - importantly for those too young to understand what was happening around them, as this will be their history in years to come.

The virus may have dissipated somewhat throughout the summer months, but until a vaccine can be safely introduced across the world the virus is here to stay. In fact, at the time of writing, Boris Johnson has just re-imposed tighter local restrictions with a reported surge in cases and hospitalisations and the US has just passed 200,000 deaths. There will be the sceptics and conspiracy theorists who believe the impositions placed on us are part of a wider agenda, but those who suffered with Covid-19 and survived to tell their stories, and those who lost loved ones before their time, would I am sure say that we should continue to treat Covid-19 with the utmost respect.

Therefore to stay virus-free in the future, maybe we do need to keep washing those hands and avoid handshaking, keep wearing those face coverings and avoid hugging, and to maintain our distance from others and avoid overcrowding. Above all, our government, medics and scientists must be better prepared, more trusted and wholly aligned for when the next global pandemic lands on our shores.

Whatever the future holds, we will prevail and we will overcome the adversity because that is what we Brits do, and as one former Prime Minister famously once said: 'And where there is despair, may we bring hope'.

THE END